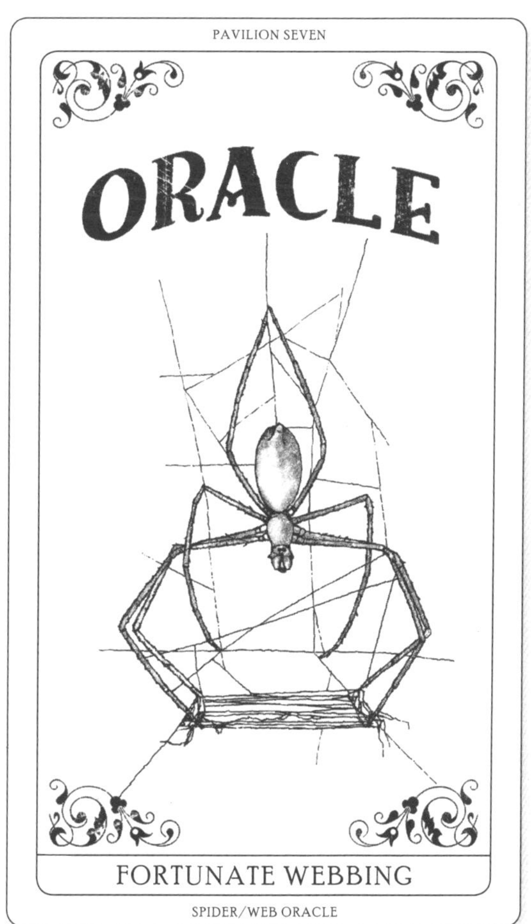
PAVILION SEVEN
ORACLE
FORTUNATE WEBBING
SPIDER/WEB ORACLE

AF478597

TOMÁS SARACENO
ARIA

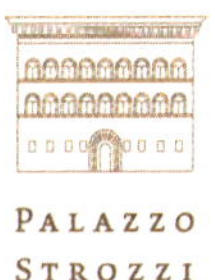

PALAZZO STROZZI

Marsilio

Tomás Saraceno: Aria
Palazzo Strozzi, Florence
22 February – 19 July 2020

Promoted and organised by

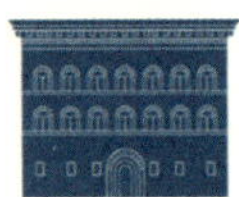

STUDIO
**TOMÁS
SARACENO**

FONDAZIONE
PALAZZO
STROZZI

Supported by

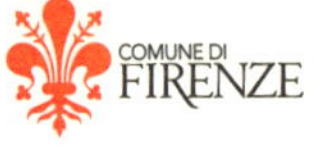
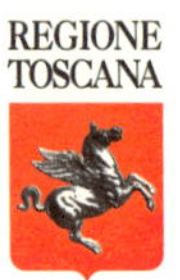
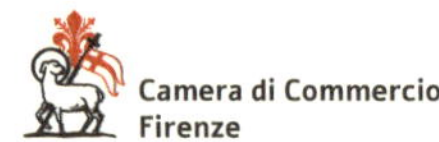
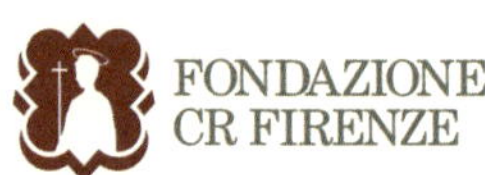

With the support of

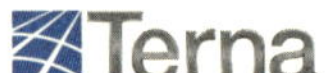

In collaboration with

MANIFATTURA
TABACCHI

With the participation of

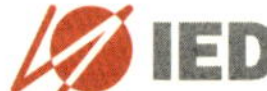

Technical Sponsors

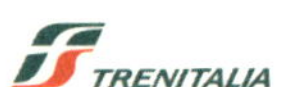
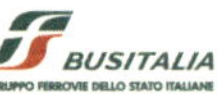
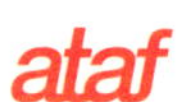
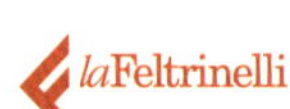
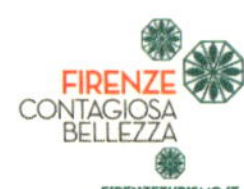
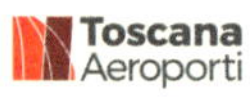
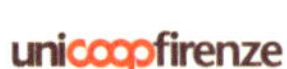

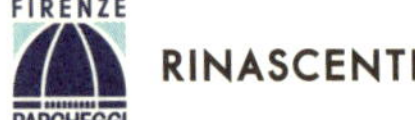
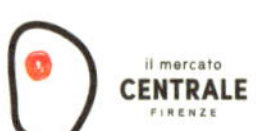

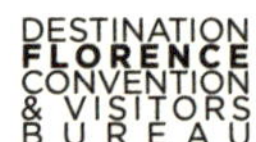

Exhibition curated by
Arturo Galansino

Exhibition layout
Studio Tomás Saraceno

Exhibition set up
Alterego
Avuelle
Atlas di Alessandro Caloia
   Lighting Designer
Carmagnini s.n.c.
Galli Allestimenti
Stampa in Stampa s.r.l.

*Expert consultant for the
installations*
Leonardo Paolini

Set up coordination
Rita Scrofani

*Exhibition graphics and
communication design*
RovaiWeber design

*Accompanying texts in the
exhibition*
Studio Tomás Saraceno

Comunication and promotion
Susanna Holm
Sigma CSC

Press office
Antonella Fiori
(National Press)
Sutton PR
(International Press)

Digital media
Ivo Riccio

*Events organisation
and membership*
Flavia Russo

Partners and Sponsors support
Martina Santoro

*Support for educational
activities*
Maria Eletta Benedetti
Marianna Di Rosa
Chiara Martini
Anna Ricciardi
Nicoletta Salvi
Azzurra Simoncini
Photographs
Giulia del Vento

Exhibition Photographer
Elzbieta Bialkowska,
   OKNO Studio

Website
Vertical Media

Technology coordination
Matteo Lotti Margotti

*Tours for individual visitors
and group*
Sigma CSC

Exhibition reservations office
Sigma CSC

Exhibition and box office staff
TML Service s.r.l.

Multichannel box office
Vivaticket s.p.a.

Audio-guide
START

Insurance
AON Artscope

Transport and set up
Arternativa s.r.l.

Head of security DM569
Ulderigo Frusi

*Head of prevention
and protection service*
Filippo Galletti

Electrical system service
Bagnoli s.r.l.

Alarm system service
Professional Security s.r.l.

Air-conditioning system service
Soc. E. Palchetti & C. s.r.l.

Cleaning service
Cooperativa Italiana Servizi

Opificio delle Pietre Dure
Marco Ciatti, *Superintendent
Department of Preventive
Conservation and Climate
Control*
Monica Galeotti, *Director*
Sandra Cassi, *Assistant
Department for the
Restoration of Mural
Paintings, Department for
the Restoration of Paintings
on Canvas and Wood,
Department for the Restoration
of Polychrome Wooden
Sculptures, Department
for the Restoration of Paper
and Parchment Documents*
Cecilia Frosinini, *Director
Department for the Restoration
of Textiles*
Riccardo Gennaioli, *Director
Department for the Restoration
of Bronzes and Antique
Weapons, Department for
the Restoration of Ceramic
and Plastic Materials*
Laura Speranza, *Director*

Condition reports
Alessandra Ramat
(*Coordination*)
Shirin Afra
Stefania Agnoletti
Sara Bassi
Francesca Bettini
Giacinto Cambini
Barbara Cattaneo
Chiara Fornari
Letizia Montalbano
Luciano Ricciardi
Andrea Santacesaria
Oriana Sartiani
Cristiana Todaro
Licia Triolo

Acknowledgements
The Fondazione Palazzo Strozzi would like to thank the countless people who contributed to the realization of this exhibit, especially Tomás Saraceno and his Studio, for designing and staging the works on display throughout Palazzo Strozzi with such care, dedication and willingness.
The installation *Thermodynamic Constellation* in the courtyard of Palazzo Strozzi is promoted and organised by the Fondazione CR Firenze, in conjunction with a broader project on environmental themes made up of several activities aimed at young visitors and schools, with the invaluable scientific collaboration of Professor Marco Bindi (Department of Agriculture, Food, Environment and Forestry - University of Florence).
Thanks to the following galleries: Pinksummer Contemporary Art, Genoa, Esther Schipper, Berlin and Tanya Bonakdar Gallery, New York/Los Angeles. Thanks also to Andrea Ferrara, Aurelio Granchietti and Malayka Picchi.
For the *Fuorimostra* program, thanks to all the people and institutes that made the secondary events in Florence and throughout the region of Tuscany possible, especially Toscana Promozione Turistica.
For the *Palazzo Strozzi alle Oblate* program and in the Florentine city library network, thanks to Tiziana Mori and to the staffs of the Biblioteca delle Oblate and of the other Biblioteche Comunali Fiorentine.

Thanks to the University of Florence, especially Chancellor Luigi Dei, for collaborating. Thanks to the Department of History, Archeology, Geography, Fine and Performing Arts (SAGAS), especially Professors Tiziana Serena and Giorgio Bacci, for collaborating in the *Art Break* project.

Thanks to Unicoop Firenze for the *Art School* and *Art Break* projects; to Wanny Di Filippo – Il Bisonte for the Exhibition Kit bag; to engineer Saverio Tozzi for his professional advice for the *Museo Aero Solar* project; Luca Carli Ballola and Michela Mei (Anna Association) for the *With Many Voices* project, dedicated to people with Alzheimer's disease and their carers; the association Autismo Firenze for the *Nuances* project, dedicated to boys and girls suffering from autism spectrum disorder. Thanks to the Fresco Parkinson Institute for the *Free Flowing* project and to Dance Well for its collaboration.

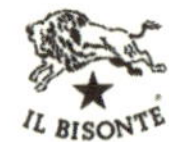

For the Palazzo Strozzi staff uniforms thanks to

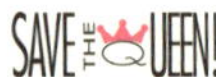

For their contribution to the lighting design thanks to

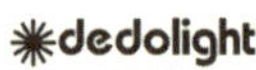

EXHIBITIONS

Exhibition Coordinator
Senior Registrar
Linda Pacifici

Registrar
Cristina Camaiti

Research and Loan Manager
Fiorella Nicosia

Images and Publications
Manuela Bersotti

Logistics
Caterina Monasta

Stage
Viktorija Carkina
Pedro Silvani
Diana Maria Vedova Arias

PROMOTION AND DEVELOPMENT

Communication and Public
Relations Coordinator
Riccardo Lami

Press Office
Lavinia Rinaldi

Marketing and sales manager
Gioia Risatti

EDUCATION

Families and Accessibility
Program
Irene Balzani

Schools and Special Projects
Alessio Bertini

Universities, Academies
and Special Projects
Martino Margheri

Stage
Anna De Bernardis
Matthias Favarato

ADMINISTRATION

Head of Administration
Luca Bartoli

Account
Simona Tecà

Secretariat and Assistant
to the Director
Silvia Michelotti

Fiscal Advice
Pietro Longari

Legal Advice
Ginevra Giovannoni
(Studio Legale Contri)

Elisa Burlamacchi

Nicola L. de Renzis Sonnino

Lorenzo Bombacci

PALAZZO STROZZI PARTNERS
COMMITTEE

Committee Secretary
Carlo Ceccarelli

Circle
Deloitte / Fondazione Deloitte
Findomestic Banca/BNL/Arval
    Gruppo BNP Paribas
iBeHuman
Palazzo Strozzi Foundation US
Rocco Forte Hotels
Salvatore Ferragamo
Silas Chou

Partners
AON
Global Blue
Guccio Gucci
Manifattura Tabacchi
Publiacqua
Terna
Toscana Aeroporti

Associazione Antiquari d'Italia
Associazione Industriali Firenze
Banor
Dedalus/Klab
Deka El.En Group
Enic Meetings & Events
Ambrogio e Giovanna Folonari
Globally
IED
Marchesi Antinori
Marchesi de' Frescobaldi
Podere Sapaio
Starhotels

Special Partners
Archea
Boston Consulting Group
RTV 38

PATRONS OF PALAZZO STROZZI

Antonella Abeti l'Hermite,
Cecilia Adorni Braccesi,
Paolo Asso, Silvia Asso
Bufalini, Riccardo Bacarelli,
Andrea Bacci, Fabio Bechelli,
Giovanni Belloni, Novella Benini,
Vincenzo Bertucci,
Gherardo Biagioni,
Giulia Biagioni, Alberto Bianchi,
Francesca Bignami, Luca Bisori,
Laura Boncompagni Ludovisi
Mazzuoli, Barbara Borghini,
Carlo Cangioli, Sigifredo di
Canossa, Fabrizio Caprotti,
Roberto Casamonti,
Mariella Casile, Massimiliano
e Donatella Cavallina Semplici,
Gastone and Maria Teresa
Chelini, Stefania Chipa,
Massimiliano Colacicchi,
Giovanni Coveri, Marco Del
Panta Ridolfi, Zelal Elbistan,
Enrico Frascione, Paolo Fresco,
Ulderigo Frusi, Vittorio Gaddi,
Valeria Gambardella,
Carlo Gentili, Lorenzo Ghetti,
Lionardo Ginori Lisci,
Ginevra Giovannoni, Claudio
and Giuseppina Girardi,
Vittoria Gondi, Divo and Anna
Maria Gronchi, Patrick Hoffer,
Roberto Lombardi,
Pietro Longari,
Gaetano Maccaferri,
Niccolò Manetti,
Antonio Marcegaglia,
Ginevra Marchi, Bona Marchi
Frescobaldi, Donato Massaro,
Camilla Morelli,
Jacopo Morelli, Enrico Morteo,
Raffaello Napoleone,
Francesca Nardi,
Carlo and Rosella Nesi,
Niccolò and Stefania Nesi,
Eleonora Nesi Frescobaldi,
Guido Nola, Bianca Orlando
Lilli, Valentina Pallavicino,
Clarice Pecori Giraldi,
Famiglia Pinzauti, Pierfrancesco
Pozzi, Erin Quiros,
Maria Vittoria Rimbotti,
Daniele Rossi, Eriberto Rosso,
Francesco Salesia,
Gianna Salvatori,
Monica Sarti, Lorenza Sebasti,
Carlo Tamburini, Silvio Zuccarini

The exhibition *Tomás Saraceno: Aria* was conceived in direct collaboration with the artist, with the aim of replicating the resounding success of Palazzo Strozzi's recent exhibitions, which have seen some of the major representatives of contemporary art such as Ai Weiwei, Bill Viola, Carsten Höller, and Marina Abramović.

Exhibiting at Palazzo Strozzi implies that an artist is willing to measure themselves against, and mediate with, not only one of the fundamental and symbolic places of the Florentine Renaissance, but also the whole breadth of culture, experiences, traditions and innovations that have marked and accompanied the history of the city, and the building, throughout the centuries.

Art and science represent a dyad that has always been closely connected in Florence; Tomás Saraceno puts forward this coupling by utilizing the building and transforming it into a space of experimentation and engrossment. In this reframing, scientific and artistic culture are no longer split into apparently distant worlds, giving way to a new way of thinking about the relationship between Man and Nature. In fact, Saraceno's artistic research permits artistic expression to interact innovatively with philosophy, biology, ecology and engineering, through a deliberate interdisciplinary approach, and to eliminate any opposition between aesthetic and scientific dimensions through fruitful integration. After all, the separation between the science of the spirit and the science of nature is, in itself, not only unsustainable but even more so in relation to visual art's expression, which has always required ongoing mediation with scientific knowledge: from geometry to anatomy, from optics to astronomy, and generally all the different sciences that study nature; it is no coincidence that in relation to painting Leonardo wrote that "it is science and the legitimate daughter of nature, because Painting is born from nature." This assimilation has its epiphany in Palazzo Strozzi, where the work is structured and positioned in such a manner that makes it possible to perceive the complex network connecting people with both the microcosm of the particles, and the macrocosm of the worlds.

I also note that the preparatory work for the exhibition has made it possible to establish a wonderful and fruitful collaboration with the Studio Tomás Saraceno, and that all who work there with enthusiasm and competence must be thanked. At the same time my thanks go to the institutions supporting the Palazzo Strozzi Foundation: the City of Florence, the Region of Tuscany, and the Chamber of Commerce; I also thank the Fondazione CR Firenze and Intesa Sanpaolo for their ongoing support of our work, as well as the Partners Committee of Palazzo Strozzi, a body that unites private individuals who annually allocate resources to our institution. A last thanks goes to all the members of the bodies of the Palazzo Strozzi Foundation—the Board of Directors, the Scientific Committee, the Director General who also curated the exhibition—as well as all the Foundation's staff, for having worked competently and passionately to make this new, demanding, original and fascinating adventure possible.

Giuseppe Morbidelli
President Fondazione Palazzo Strozzi

The issue of environmental sustainability has never been as pressing as it is today. This, by the way, is exemplified by *Time* magazine's nomination of the young Greta Thunberg as "2019 Person of the Year": the acknowledgement that the planet's health and its survival are dependent upon the behavior of all of us is in fact gaining traction, especially amongst the younger generation.

The environmental challenge lies at the core of the work of Tomás Saraceno—a surprising, utopian, visionary artist of international fame, who in his pieces erases the discord between disciplines, to facilitate a dialogue between architecture, art, science and philosophy, transforming them into visually powerful, absorbing, installations, in which the interaction with the public is indispensable. In the exhibition *Tomás Saraceno: Aria*, at Palazzo Strozzi, an original dialogue between Renaissance and modern times takes place in the inner court with the site-specific installation *Thermodynamic Constellation*, which is entirely supported by the Fondazione CR Firenze as part of several events focusing specifically on environmental sustainability.

These are grand, poetic, reflective spheres—that remain suspended thanks to the warm air contained within them, heated with solar power—which allow the artist to imagine a future world devoid of borders, and free from its dependence on fossil fuels. Art and science are no longer separate but united, helping to shape a new humanism.

Through the exhibition's title, *Aria*, Saraceno reminds us that this element is a precious, common asset that is shared with all living beings; his hope is a shift in values that sees humans no longer at the center of the world, instead finding a new balance as part of the universe. In the same way in which a spider weaves its web, the artist is inspired by his own visionary pieces, seeking new models for coexistence and social living.

The show and the installation, therefore, perfectly match the wishes behind the work of the Fondazione CR Firenze, both in the sectors of art, events and cultural heritage as well as environmental protection, which as part of its programs' objectives intends to "promote environmental awareness in youths and the community by contributing to disseminate and adopt sustainable behaviors, to inspire the community to seek new solutions for protecting the environment." These words almost sound inspired by Tomás Saraceno.

Luigi Salvadori
President Fondazione CR Firenze

Cover
Collage for *Aria*. Drawing with
Argyroneta aquatica in its
diving bell: the bubble of air in
which the spider lives, secured
underwater with threads of
silk, Oldenburg, Germany,
Berlin, 2017.
As well, *View of Florence from
San Miniato*, by Thomas Cole,
1837 and *The Arno River* by
Giuseppe Zocchi, 1744.
Courtesy the artist; Andersen's,
Copenhagen; Ruth Benzacar,
Buenos Aires; Tanya Bonakdar
Gallery, New York/Los Angeles;
Pinksummer Contemporary Art,
Genoa; Esther Schipper, Berlin.
© Studio Tomas Saraceno, 2020

Graphic Design
Enrico Bardin

Translations
Contextus Srl, Pavia (Christine
Gurthy, Daniela Innocenti,
Karen Turnbull)

Editing
Contextus Srl, Pavia (Christine
Gurthy, Valentina Vignoli)

First Italian Edition
© Marsilio Editori s.p.a.,
Venezia
February 2020

ISBN 978-88-297-0364-7
www.marsilioeditori.it

Repro
Opero srl, Verona

Print
Grafiche Veneziane srl, Venice

This book is printed on
certified paper
Fedrigoni Arena Ivory Bulk

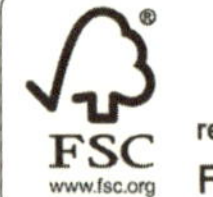

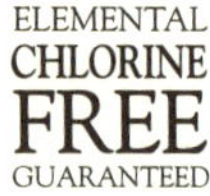

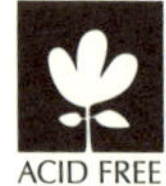

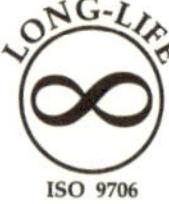

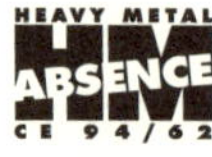

Available through
ARTBOOK / D.A.P.
75 Broad Street, Suite 630
New York, NY 10004
www.artbook.com

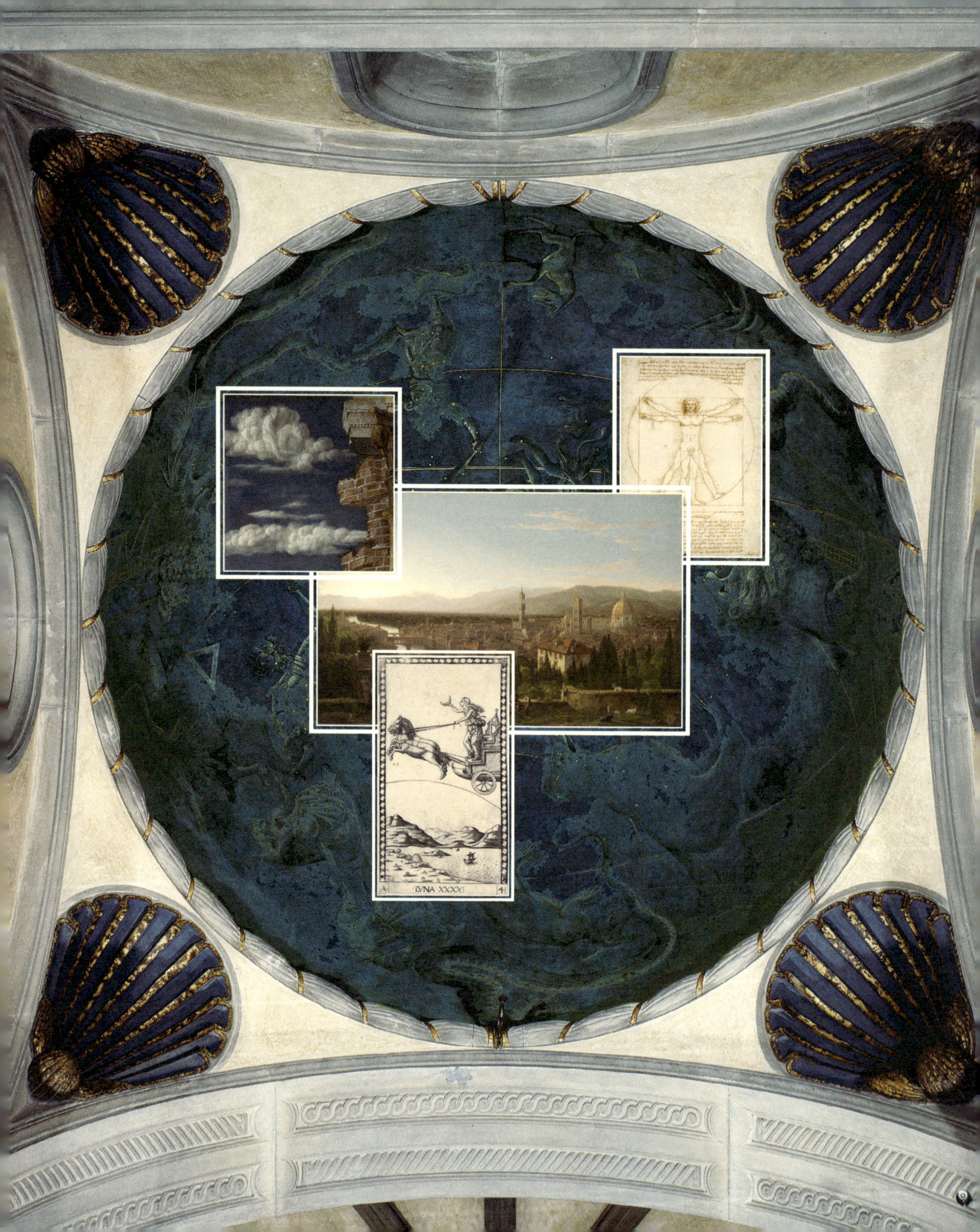

TOMÁS SARACENO: ARIA

Arturo Galansino

*I don't know if what you read in books
is true, that in ancient times a monkey
that left Rome could get to Spain by jum-
ping from tree-to-tree without
ever touching the ground.*

(Italo Calvino, *The Baron in the Trees*, 1957)

For contemporary artists, exhibiting at Palazzo Strozzi means measuring themselves against one of the Renaissance's symbols. For Palazzo Strozzi, opening a contemporary art exhibition is not merely creating an aesthetic experience; it involves assuming the responsibility of an institution intending to speak to its present times, of addressing themes that are most pressing and timely.

The art of Tomás Saraceno (b. 1973) causes us to consider the issues and challenges of our era, the Anthropocene, which have become increasingly urgent, such as pollution, climate change, sustainability and the overcoming of geographical and social barriers. At Palazzo Strozzi, his open and interconnected vision, which accesses utopian and simultaneously real worlds, is further amplified by meaning, and made unique by the contrast of a building representing humanistic culture.

This exhibition, one of the largest shows ever planned in the course of the artist's career, suggests changing the reference model through a deep and original dialogue between history and the present day: from humanity at the center of the universe, the founding thought of humanism, to humanity as part of a whole, in which to seek new harmony by eliminating all class systems and hierarchies.

FROM HUMANISM → TO AEROCENE

The humanistic symbol of the *Vitruvian Man* harmoniously inserted in the two perfect shapes of the circle (the sky), and the square (the earth), according to the golden ratio expressing the scientific laws governing the world—including the architectural proportions of Palazzo Strozzi—and formulated as the ideal of beauty, and mathematical and universal perfection, is redundant, because humanism's faith in man's rational capacity to dominate nature is where the prodromes of the Anthropocene are found.

Through the work of Tomás Saraceno, Palazzo Strozzi turns into a system that expresses the complex network that connects the microcosm of particles and dust, to the macrocosm of suns and galaxies; a cosmic jam session in which the elements comprising the universe reveal themselves as a myriad of sounds from an evolving, living orchestra. Here, every anthropocentric concept is shaken and questioned, giving voice to what is not visible and not human, i.e. to all those mysterious and imperceptible processes that dominate the cosmos and escape us, thus conjuring a new perspective towards which to steer our future.

Tomás Saraceno's approach to work is completely interdisciplinary, annulling any division between gender, hierarchy of knowledge and practices, and taking the diversity and hybridization that for centuries have marked Florentine artistic culture, to the extreme. In the same way that Saraceno's gaze reaches galaxies hundreds of thousands of light-years away, the Florentine artists of the fifteenth century carefully observed the sky with a sense of wonder. For example, the small dome in the apse of the old sacristy of San Lorenzo, designed by Filippo Brunelleschi (1377–1446) and likely frescoed in 1442 by Giuliano d'Arrigo, a.k.a. Il Pesello (1367–1446), depicts a starry sky in which the heavenly bodies are positioned with great accuracy with the assistance of astronomer Paolo dal Pozzo Toscanelli (1397–1482).

The astronomical precision is such that it allows for the determination of when the sky above the city featured those characteristics. Also in Florence, a century and a half later, Galileo Galilei (1564–1642), observing the sky armed with a telescope and an experimental scientific method, confirmed the Copernican hypothesis once and for all by invalidating the geocentric and anthropocentric vision of the universe. His watercolors from the end of 1609, depicting the moon with its changing phases and luminescence, bring to mind Saraceno's *Calendrier Lun-Air de Paris*, which indexes the air pollution at different times of the day, relative to our habits and the use of

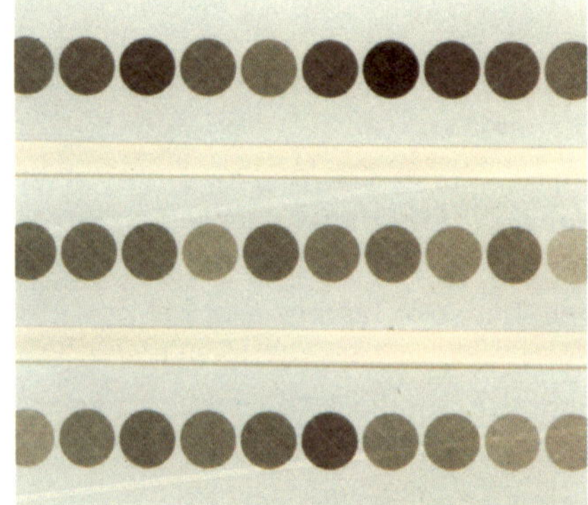

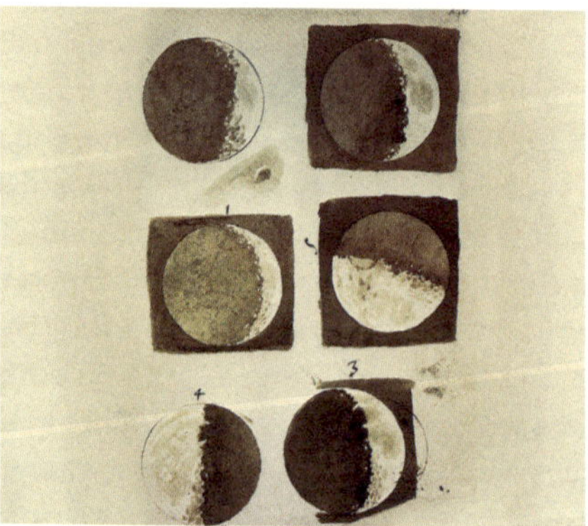

Tomás Saraceno, *Calendrier Lun-Air de Paris*, 2018

Galileo Galilei, *Moon*, 1609
Florence, Biblioteca Nazionale Centrale

fossil fuels. Galileo translated his celestial observations into fascinating and detailed representations, in which the night star does not appear as a perfect Aristotelian body, but rather, is marked by mountains and valleys, "unequal, harsh, dotted with cavities and protrusions not unlike the face of the earth."

Obviously linked to Florence and the relationship between humans and the sky, is Leonardo da Vinci's (1452–1519) flight research; his drawings of flying machines, studies of parachutes and birds, are precursors of Saraceno's Aerosolar sculptures that are lighter than air and hover and move across the sky without fossil fuels.

Certainly the best known flight experiment ever carried out in Florence is Leonardo's attempt to operate one of his flying machines, assisted by alchemist and friend Zoroastro da Peretola (1462–1520) and "filling the universe with awe."

In 2009, Tomás Saraceno caught NASA scientists off-guard with one of his flying sculptures in the Silicon Valley when, for the first time, he flew a man with just the heat of the sun . . .

The great bird will first take flight on the back of its great Swan, filling the universe with awe, filling all the manuscripts with his fame and everlasting glory to the nest where it was born.

(Leonardo da Vinci, *The Codex on the Flight of Birds*, c. 1505)

Alongside the scientific and technical components characterizing Tomás Saraceno's work, more esoteric suggestions do coexist that conjure the alogical, symbolic and unconscious elements driving our destiny. Since prehistoric times humans have used divination practices pertaining to the animal world to learn their future. The artist emulates nggám fortunetelling, a practice used by the Mambila people in Cameroon, to decode the mysterious messages of spiders through the *Arachnomancy Cards*, a deck of thirty-three divination cards for consulting the spider/web oracle.

Above all I was committed to examining the tarot cards carefully, with the eye of someone who didn't know what they were, drawing suggestions and associations from them and interpreting them according to an imaginary symbolism.

(Italo Calvino, Introduction to *The Castle of Crossed Destinies*, 1973)

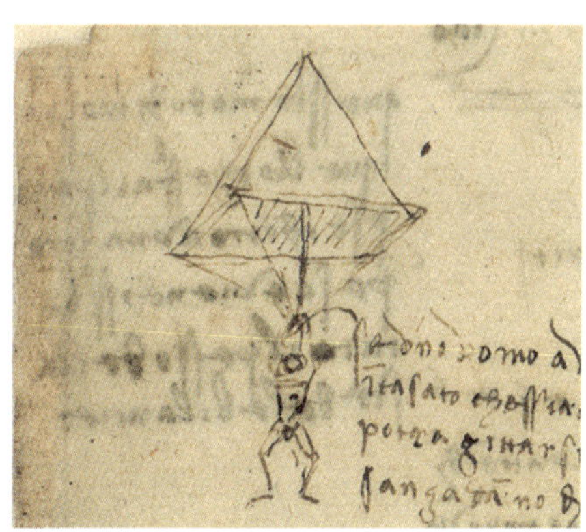

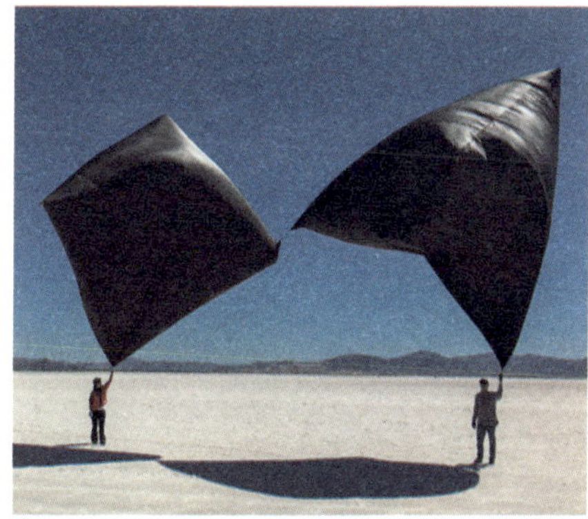

Leonardo da Vinci, *Parachute, Codex Atlanticus*, ca. 1485, Milan, Biblioteca Ambrosiana

Aerocene Launch. August 7, 2017, Salinas Grandes, Jujuy, Argentina.

As in a "palace of crossed destinies" set in a parallel universe, nine Arachnomancy cards employed as narrative tools guide visitors through the exhibition, simultaneously revealing and concealing the meaning of each of the nine installations and establishing unexpected connections between apparently remote elements. Introducing arachnomancy, the cards are inspired by the fifteenth-century tarot, a card game and repertoire of symbols popular in the courts of the time and poised between Marsilio Ficino's Neoplatonic philosophy, and Matteo Maria Boiardo's chivalric world, between the classic Renaissance imagery and the golden glow of Michelino da Besozzo or Bonifacio Bembo's late Gothic.

Afterall, the history of Palazzo Strozzi expresses Renaissance Florence's trust in the divinatory power of the stars: the palace's patron, wealthy merchant Filippo Strozzi (1428–91), placed his trust in astrologer Benedetto di Giannozzo Biliotti who, following a set of complex astrological calculations, determined that the dawn of August 6, 1489, under "the sign of the lion," was the favorable sidereal time to lay the first stone of the building designed by Giuliano da Sangallo (1445–1516).

The sign of the lion rose above the eastern horizon, which being a fixed and concrete sign, signified the building would last in perpetuity and be inhabited by great men, noble and of good health [. . .].

(*Filippo Strozzi's register of debtors and creditors, 1484–91*)

ARIA

A new card, *Aria*, lends its name and look to the exhibition and is the catalogue cover.

The title, in addition to referencing the themes and elements that are typical of the artist's work, issues a warning about respect for the planet and its critically compromised atmosphere, foreshadowing the transition from the Anthropocene to the Aerocene; a new geological era developed around this precious element the air, in which *Homo sapiens* will have finally evolved into *Homo flotantis*, learning how to live and travel by floating through the atmospfere, in an aerial nomadism free of fossil fuels and boundaries restricting thoughts and existence.

Air is the element in which we live, a platform shared with all other living beings, which marks every moment of our lives. Every breath is a complex universe containing billions of molecules flying faster than sound and colliding with one another, millions of times per second. To paraphrase

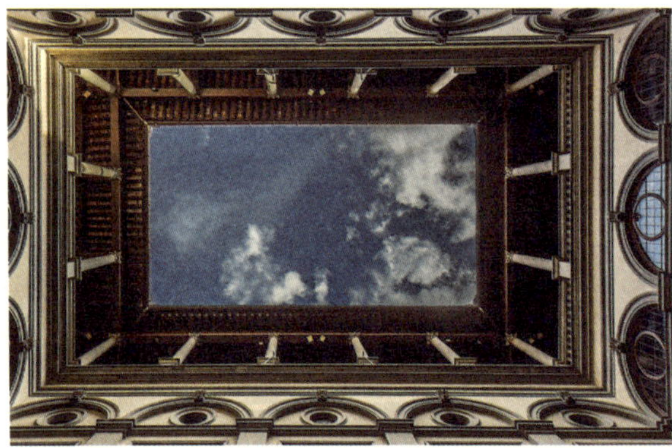

View from below from
the Palazzo Strozzi courtyard

Evangelista Torricelli (1608–47), the mathematician and physicist, Florentine by adoption and a follower of Galileo: "We swim in an ocean of air." Nowadays this ocean is also polluted by carbon dioxide and other toxic elements that compromise our right to breathe. Increasingly, political discourse centers around air; colonized, restricted by regional borders, wrecked by harmful matter and radio frequencies, and transformed into an asset for the elites. The actions and thoughts of the Aerocene Foundation circle around these issues, on the simple assumption that the air belongs to everyone, the international and interdisciplinary community seeks to develop a new set of ecological practices, to raise awareness and respect for the atmosphere, to imagine a sustainable future by using Saraceno's flying sculptures.

During the exhibition, various workshops will be organized in the area, to share these flight experiments and reclaim the air in Florence and Tuscany.

The large mirrored spheres of *Thermodynamic Constellation*, anchored and suspended in the courtyard of Palazzo Strozzi, float in the air ready to take off to faraway destinations, inviting us to move towards a new era, in tune with an atmosphere that is free of harmful emissions; the air diffuses the concert *Sounding the Air* and the dust pervading the magnified spiderweb of the *Particular Matter(s) Jam Session* rises, as we enter the sensory universe of a spider; while moving through the air we become extras in the shadow theater of the Thermodynamic Imaginary, following the course of the Aereographies balloons in the same way that the *Flying Gardens* tillandsias grow and find nourishment in the air.

Did spiders live in my house or was I living in the spiders' house?

(Tomás Saraceno)

In the *Aria* card, a spiderweb recalls what shines like distant nebulae and galaxies in the darkness of *Webs of At-tent(s)ion*, resulting from a collaboration with spiders of different species. For hundreds of thousands of years these invertebrates have woven architectures resembling the structure of the universe before our eyes: a three-dimensional spiderweb like the ruby-colored one of *How to Entangle the Universe in a Spider/Web?*, in which the galaxies are placed along strands of hot gas, and dark matter distributed along the threads of a huge cosmic spiderweb as they encroach and merge into a single large net. At the center of the image a community of *Argyroneta aquatica* use their silk to live and move

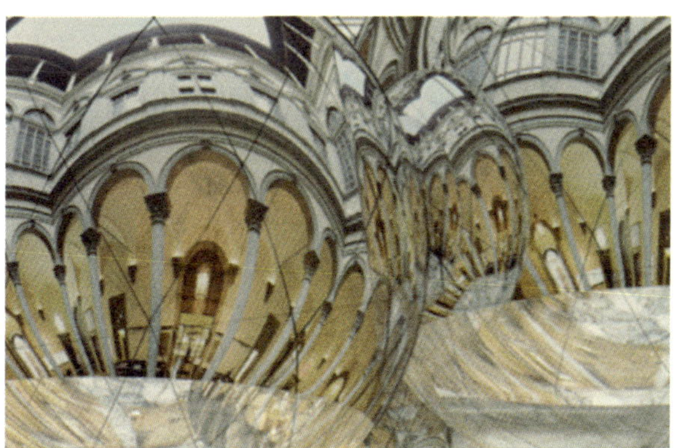

Rendering of *Thermodynamic Constellation*, Fernweh Architettura

underwater aboard an air bubble. Like the ballooning spiders—flying spiders living in colonies, which hurl long threads into the sky and take off propelled by the wind, reaching high altitudes as if attached to kites—during their evolution, these aquatic arachnids have developed incredible skills, embodying alternative futures. Below, an apocalyptic view of Florence, flooded, alludes to the recent flooding event in Venice, brought on by climate change that we keep ignoring, also recalling the Florence flood of 1966, a catastrophe that marks the history of our city and beyond.

This dystopian image likewise refers to the "Radical" architects, a movement in Florence arising in the late 1960s as a reaction to the flood, which prompted the rethinking of architecture in a mix of utopia, research and technology, personified by figures such as Frei Otto (1925–2015), Yona Friedman (b. 1923) and Richard Buckminster Fuller (1895–1983), who have become Saraceno's touchstones.

I find the comparison with Calvino fitting. I loved The Baron in the Trees [...]: a hymn to the absence of gravity, in a way.

(Tomás Saraceno)

INVISIBLE CITIES

The invisible cities are a dream that originated in the heart of uninhabitable cities.

(Italo Calvino, Introduction to *Invisible Cities*, 1972)

Saraceno's structures arise from these architects' research and incorporate modular, biological or molecular models that can be repeated endlessly as in *Connectome*, an installation inspired by the brain's neural pathways, and *Cloud City*, cities floating in the clouds, "hung by a thread," potential visions of an antithetical development to the horizontal borders created by mankind. These architectural utopias appear to be built like "a city that expands and is built by many expanding concentric cities, a spiderweb-city suspended over an abyss," as author Italo Calvino (1923–85) describes his *Invisible Cities*, whom Saraceno discovered in his youth in Italy, and which inspired him poetically.

We too, like Kublai Khan in the face of an unsustainable empire that is crushing itself, dream of "cities as light as kites, cities latticelike as lace, cities transparent like mosquito nets, cities like leaf ribs, cities like hand creases, cities like filigree," while Marco Polo recounts of Bauci, lost in the clouds and hoisted on thin stilts; of Tamara,

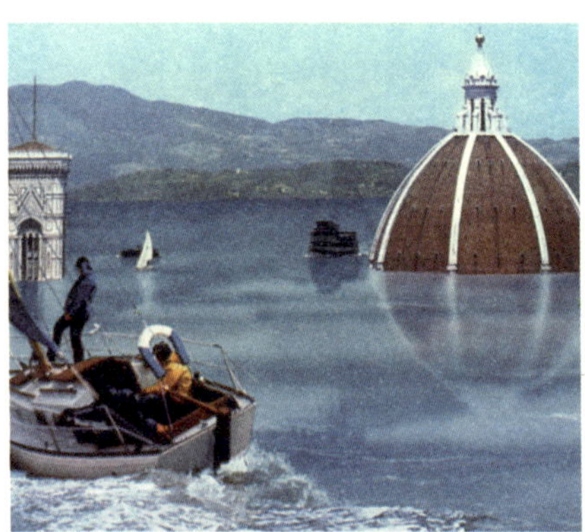

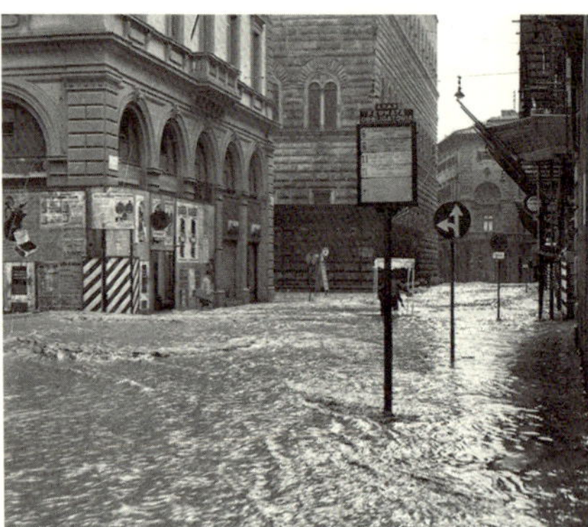

Superstudio, *Rescuing Historical Italian Landmarks*, 1972

Palazzo Strozzi during the 1966 Flood, Florence, Archivio Foto Locchi where clouds run in which known figures are recognizable; of Anastasia, suspended by kites; or Lalage, which was granted the privilege of growing in lightness by the moon . . . Unable to speak, or rendered mute by a spell, Marco could select another tarot from the deck, depicting *Aria*, a city connected to the stars, in which spiderwebs in buildings turn into segments of universes predicting radiant futures, the spiders play cosmic music and courtyards are open ports to the sky, from which to journey to the clouds floating above the domes, bell towers and hills.

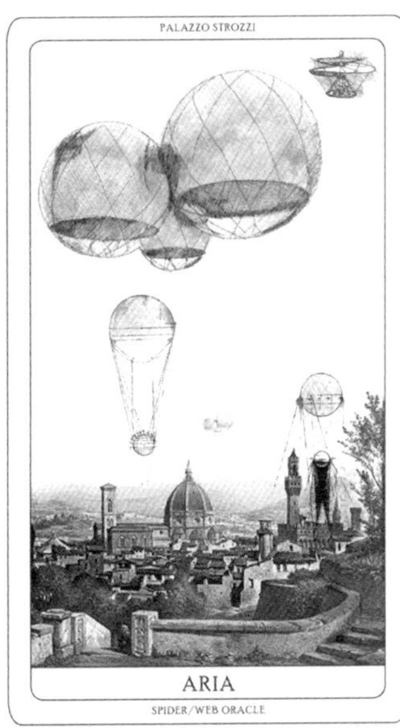

Tomás Saraceno,
Collage for *Aria*, 2019

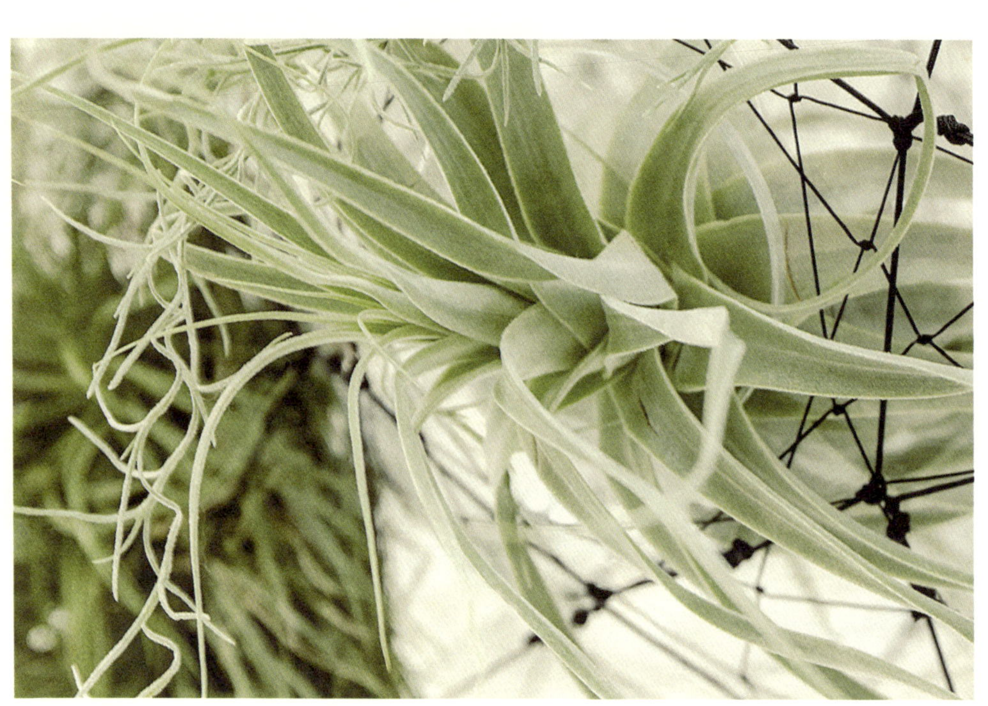

TOMÁS SARACENO'S ASTRAL ARK

Emanuele Coccia

In the summer of 1489, Marsilio Ficino—the brilliant and multidisciplinary Florentine Renaissance philosopher—informed Giovanni Pico della Mirandola, his friend and a leading figure of the time, that, on "the day you left," he had finished "a treatise on the life to be acquired from the heavens (*De vita cœlitus comparanda*)." This work would be combined with a pamphlet on healthcare for men of letters (*De curanda literatorum valetudine*) and a treatise on extending their lifespan (*Liber de vita ingeniosis producenda*), resulting in a wide-ranging book, one of the most striking in the history of thought, published under the overall title *On Life* (*De vita*).

The heavens, in their physical and astral substance—according to Ficino's thesis—not only "giv[e] life to all,"[1] but exert an action on earth: "All the earthly realities are of heavenly origin, they are immutably governed by the heavens and they are predisposed in the first place to receive influences from the heavens."[2] Just as physical reality is influenced by what the scientists at the time called the "meteors"—the sun, rain, winds—so spiritual reality is influenced by the stars "especially through the sun." Essentially, Ficino explains, "whenever a material is thus exposed to the celestials, as a glass mirror to your face and as an opposite wall to your voice, immediately it experiences something from above[,] from a most powerful agent, namely, the wonderful power and life everywhere present; and it gains power from that experience, just as from the face the mirror reproduces an image and from the voice the wall reproduces an echo."[3]

Human life is a sort of superior astral meteorology: from this perspective, human life must direct itself towards the heavens in order to achieve happiness. Morality consists "in bringing oneself closer to heaven through art, and thus becoming celestial":[4] "whoever imitates the beneficence, action, and order of the heavens, with vows, with study, with life and habits, will be, I think, like the higher beings themselves, and receive from them even more abundant gifts. Men, however, who are unlike the disposition of the heavens in their art, men who are discordant, will be secretly miserable, and will soon become publicly unhappy."[5] But because the heavens are the cause of all that happens on earth, forcing oneself to become celestial does not mean following an ascetic path: on the contrary, each person should pursue the activity that he or she is best at. "[F]or this above all else you were made by nature," Ficino wrote, addressing himself to the reader, "the activity which from tender years you do, speak, play-act, choose, dream, imitate; that activity which you try more frequently, which you perform more easily, in which you make the most progress, which you enjoy above all else, which you leave off unwillingly. That assuredly is the thing for which the heavens and the lord of your horoscope gave birth to you. Therefore they will promote your undertakings and will favor your life to the extent that you follow the auspices of the lord of your geniture."[6] Moral effort becomes something that "with the appropriate term" should be called magic: this involves "seasonably introduc[ing] the celestial into the earthly by particular lures just as the farmer interested in grafting brings the fresh graft into the old stock."[7] Taking inspiration from a saying from the *Centiloquium* attributed at that time to Ptolemy, which states that "the wise soul collaborates with the powers of heaven, just as the farmer collaborates with the nature of the earth by ploughing and clearing the ground,"[8] Ficino thus presents moral philosophy as a sort of upside-down form of farming, in which the earth must conform to the heavens rather than the other way around.

Some five and a half centuries later, Tomás Saraceno is inaugurating in Florence—in exactly the same places—an exhibition that seems to revisit and extend, but at the same time correct, Marsilio Ficino's intuition and his astral humanism. In an age that is pathologically obsessed—both for good and for evil—with geology and the earth, Saraceno has struggled to overturn points of view like those of Ficino. As a counter to the neo-Ptolemaic geocentrism of those who claim that the earth represents the final horizon for humanity's existence, the unsurpassable limit of the condition of man, Saraceno has long been mulling over Richard Buckminster Fuller's famous maxim, "We are all astronauts," even without the need to abandon this planet and leave its atmosphere. "I am sure," Buckminster Fuller wrote in his *Operating Manual for Spaceship Earth* (which is, itself, another form of radicalization of Ficino's view that the perfection of human life should be acquired from the heavens), "that you don't really sense yourself to be aboard a fantastically real spaceship—our spherical Spaceship Earth."[9] According to Buckminster Fuller, and to Saraceno, we must take back possession of ourselves and learn Copernicus' lesson—which, strangely, has not yet been heeded: if the earth turns around the sun it is chiefly because there is no difference between the sky and the earth; the entire Universe is made only of sky. Earth and sun are simultaneous metamorphoses of the same astral matter, a nebula of gas and dust. Everything in the world has a celestial and astral nature, according to different degrees and intensities: astrology holds within it all the knowledge we possess. It is not enough, therefore, to make art the site of a new alliance between disciplines that never usually communicated with each other (the plastic arts, engineering, climatology, geology, ecology): what is needed more than anything is to reform astrology. If the earth is one star among other stars, the problem will no longer be that of connecting the earth back to the heavens—as was the case in Renaissance magic—but will become the need to conciliate, associate and multiply the various parts of the heavens. This is what the *Connectome* installation does. Saraceno's art definitively breaks down every rift and hierarchy between the heavens and the earth, the geological and the astral, and builds a new topology in which the inside and the outside are only specular forms—literally the effects of mirrors that can be positioned in different ways: every planet reflects the others and every living being is an astral reflection. Precisely for this reason art becomes the discipline of astral navigation—the knowledge and technology that enable us to position ourselves in the heavens as celestial beings—as astronauts. And what must be positioned is earth itself. "Earth itself," as Saraceno often repeats, "is a balloon tethered by gravity yet moving through space almost imperceptibly."[10]

From this point of view, the *Thermodynamic Constellation* sculptures, which are presented for the first time at Palazzo Strozzi, are not so much an artefact that represents or repeats the form of the planet, but rather are the budding of Gaia, the veritable propagation of the planet. One must bear in mind that the cosmogenesis process that led to the creation of the earth is not yet finished: it is something that has repercussions even here, in each of the bodies that inhabit it and populate it. Every living being is a reproduction and a multiplication of the planet and every technical activity is simply the extension of that process. And if the earth itself is a balloon that floats in the sky, then Saraceno's installation is a perfect demonstration of the transcendental form of every earthly object. Everything is a constellation: an indefinite and unstoppable process of transformation of the astral meteorology. We are all planets that are trying to reproduce life together and take it elsewhere, give it another form. This is why the *Thermodynamic Constellations* are not just mechanical systems: they bear life (plants, fungi, bacteria, viruses) inside them, they enable them to live at various altitudes, and above all they enable them to take other forms than those they have taken to date.

Life, moreover, is never something that is rooted in a ground that would limit its travels and its existence: the true ground and foundation of all living beings is always the sky and the light that it conveys and which it is made of. This is what is demonstrated by the *Flying Gardens* installation: all the gardens are flying, spaceships in a journey that will never end. Or, to reuse the image from the *Centiloquium* maxim that Ficino used, agriculture is always and only celestial: working the land and the earth always means manipulating portions of the heavens, tilling the stars. On the other hand, Gaia is not a limited organism that continues to retreat into itself: it is the extension of a sky that never ceases to expand and that contracts only in order to be able to increase its spheres, to extend and amplify the circles of rotation and revolution.

Above all, the decision to populate these offshoots of Gaia with plants is no mere chance. Plants have literally created the world in which we live. If they are everywhere and constitute the essential anatomy of our planet, it is because they are its embryonic tissues. Through their conquest of the earth's surface and their extension throughout the whole world, plants have produced (and continue to produce) the oxygen-rich atmosphere that has made it possible for all the "higher" animals to live: the so-called "higher" animals are only able to live because they breathe the by-products and waste of plant metabolism, oxygen. Moreover, plants are immediately or indirectly responsible for the production of the planet's biomass. Not only do plants represent about 85 percent of the planet's eukaryotic biomass, but they also represent the necessary energy conditions for the existence and nourishment of all the higher animals. Indeed, by exploiting on a large scale a mechanism that was developed by cyanobacteria, plants are able to transform solar energy (the most powerful source of energy for life on earth) into living matter: organic life is simply the outcome of this ability to store solar energy in the form of chemical bonds between complex molecules, thereby transforming the sun into a living mass. And it is only through the plant variant of this process of building living matter from solar energy that life on the planet has ceased to be a mere side note—both quantitatively and qualitatively—and instead become its main characteristic, its very essence. Thanks to plants, eating signifies seeking and finding the light that the plants have breathed into Gaia's mineral body. Food is simply this trade in light that is transmitted from hand to hand, from species to species, from kingdom to kingdom, and that continues to illuminate the planet, ensuring the continuity and closeness between earth and the sun, day after day.

If the plants created the world we live in, then Gaia is a vegetable being: it is much more a garden than a zoo, and it is only because Gaia is a garden that we can live here. Every cosmological speculation must take the form of a botanical reflection. But in this garden, the plants are not (or are not only) the content or the inhabitants: they are the gardeners themselves. Like all living species, we too are the subject of gardening. We are one of their agricultural and cultural products. In other words: plants are not the landscape, they are the first landscape architects. Or, to put it in a more provocative manner, there is no landscape because everything, including the seemingly immobile living beings, is continuously shaping the face of the world. What we call landscape is the result of the action of a large number of different landscape architects. What we call garden is simply an army of gardeners. But their gardening is an astral or solar gardening: the plants are the great farmers of the heavens and of the prince of stars, the sun.

It is for this very reason that, in order to counter the speculations on the Anthropocene era—which are becoming ever closer to a form of Gnosticism in which what is at stake instead is the definition of humanity as an ontologically guilty form of life—Saraceno prefers to speak of Aerocene. Although the center of the cosmos is not in fact earth but the universe itself, the best perspective for describing our world is the one that Evangelista Torricelli expressed in a letter to Michelangelo Ricci: "We live submersed in the depths of an ocean of air":[11] everything is atmosphere, everything is a cloud, a celestial condensation of matter. Earth itself is no more than an immense spaceship or an ark, as taught in the myth of Noah, that supports us and carries us: it is an enormous kite immersed in the atmosphere of the universe.

Saraceno's work is not just a revolution in our way of conceiving and making art. It is one of the most radical speculative reflections of recent decades that, through his installations, depicts a cosmology whose consequences we have yet to measure. One of the most interesting theoretical points is the one on the vehicular nature of everything that exists. In all his works, Saraceno seems to both apply and radicalize Buckminster Fuller's insight: if the earth is a spaceship, a vehicle, then everything on this planet is also a spaceship, and it matters little whether it is called a spider's web, a sphere or a body. Everything is an astral vehicle. Everything is a Noah's Ark. Being in the world means bringing something other than oneself and being transported. It is the spaceship (or its lesser variants: the boat, car, spider's web or kite) that is the most elementary and paradigmatic form of being in the world: living means being suspended in the heavens and travelling. It means being the wind and everything that the wind carries with it. In this sense, Saraceno appears to reword an ancient tenet, according to which the body of all living beings does not define the geographic or physical belonging to a place, a space or a piece of matter: on the contrary, it is what makes movement possible, the condition of the possibility of exiting from the matter, space or place or, better still, of permanently changing them. If we have a body, it is not so as to better belong to a here and now, but so as to change place, change time, change space, change form, change matter. The body-vehicle, the body-spaceship, is the condition for the possibility of journeying, in space and in being: it makes it possible to go elsewhere, to become otherwise. It is simply a cart, a car, a plane, a boat of identity and form.

From a certain point of view, this is a brilliant reinterpretation of the Noah's Ark myth. The Old Testament in fact had made us view the entire earthly globe like an enormous vehicle, a ship that carried the living on it. But if everything in space is a vehicle, if everything is a collection of spaceships, kites and hot-air balloons in an infinite space, then the very concept of an ark that could hold all living beings collapses. In Saraceno's mind and work, the cosmos seems to become a mechanism that prevents life from concentrating in one single spot (whether that be earth or one of its places): the spaceships and the arks continue to proliferate, the sun never stops reincarnating itself in a thousand other forms of life. Each of the living beings constitutes an intensive particle of a Noah's Ark that never stops splitting apart and multiplying itself. Life is not a quality that is peculiar to certain bodies, it is merely the consequence of the vehicular nature of matter, of the planetary structure of this world. Life exists only where all the bodies are vehicles, arks, planets for each other. In this world—in our world—space can never be a pure extension and never promotes itself as a certainty. There is no space, there are only journeys. There is only life. We must learn to see an ancestral ark in every portion of matter. These arks, these stellar spaceships cross not just the geography of the cosmos, but also its history: they cross all the ostensible borders; the one that seems to separate the living from the non-living, the one that we suspect exists between matter and spirit or between individuals, species, places and epochs. They do not pre-exist the world, on the contrary, they produce it, they fabricate it, they embody it. We can never know whether every single miniscule portion of the cosmos is an individual ark because it has become so mixed up that it is no longer possible to discover its source, or whether it is a multitude of arks because they have become so tangled up with each other that they have become fused together. Because of these interminglings, they not only make the places that are furthest from earth coexist, but also the most distant and incompatible times, or forms and lives that seemingly have no kinship with each other. It is thanks to them that every being on earth bears in its body not just prehistoric elements but also other hypermodern elements. The most recent newborn, the latest living being to open its eyes—whether it is a human or a whale, a dragonfly or an oak—is made of matter that inhabited this planet before the appearance of any type of life whatsoever. Its body is older than its species or family, and yet it can change the history of the cosmos forever only in a much later moment of its true existence. Nothing that gives it life comes from the place in which it was born: its ancient atoms have travelled throughout the universe, they come from places that no longer exist and they will be destined for places that have probably not yet emerged. The Aerocene is the contraction of all these ages into a voyage that never ceases to change direction.

1. Marsilio Ficino, *De vita*, ed. Albano Biondi and Giuliano Pisani, Latin ed. and Italian trans. (Pordenone: Biblioteca dell'immagine, 1991), 357.

2. Ibid., 215.

3. Ibid., 413.

4. Ibid., 227.

5. Ibid., 387.

6. Ibid.

7. Ibid., 411.

8. Ps. Ptolemaeus, *Centiloquium* (Basileae 1550), aph. VIII.

9. Richard Buckminster Fuller, *Operating Manual for Spaceship Earth* (Zurich: Lars Müller, 2019), 56.

10. Tomás Saraceno, *Flying Plaza. Work Journal 2012–2016*, ed. Philipp Oswalt (Berlin: Spector Books, 2017), 79.

11. *Torricelli a Michelangelo Ricci, 11 giugno 1644*, in *Opere dei discepoli di Galileo. Carteggio 1642–1648*, ed. Paolo Galluzzi and Maurizio Torrini (Florence: Giunti-Barbera, 1975), 1:122.

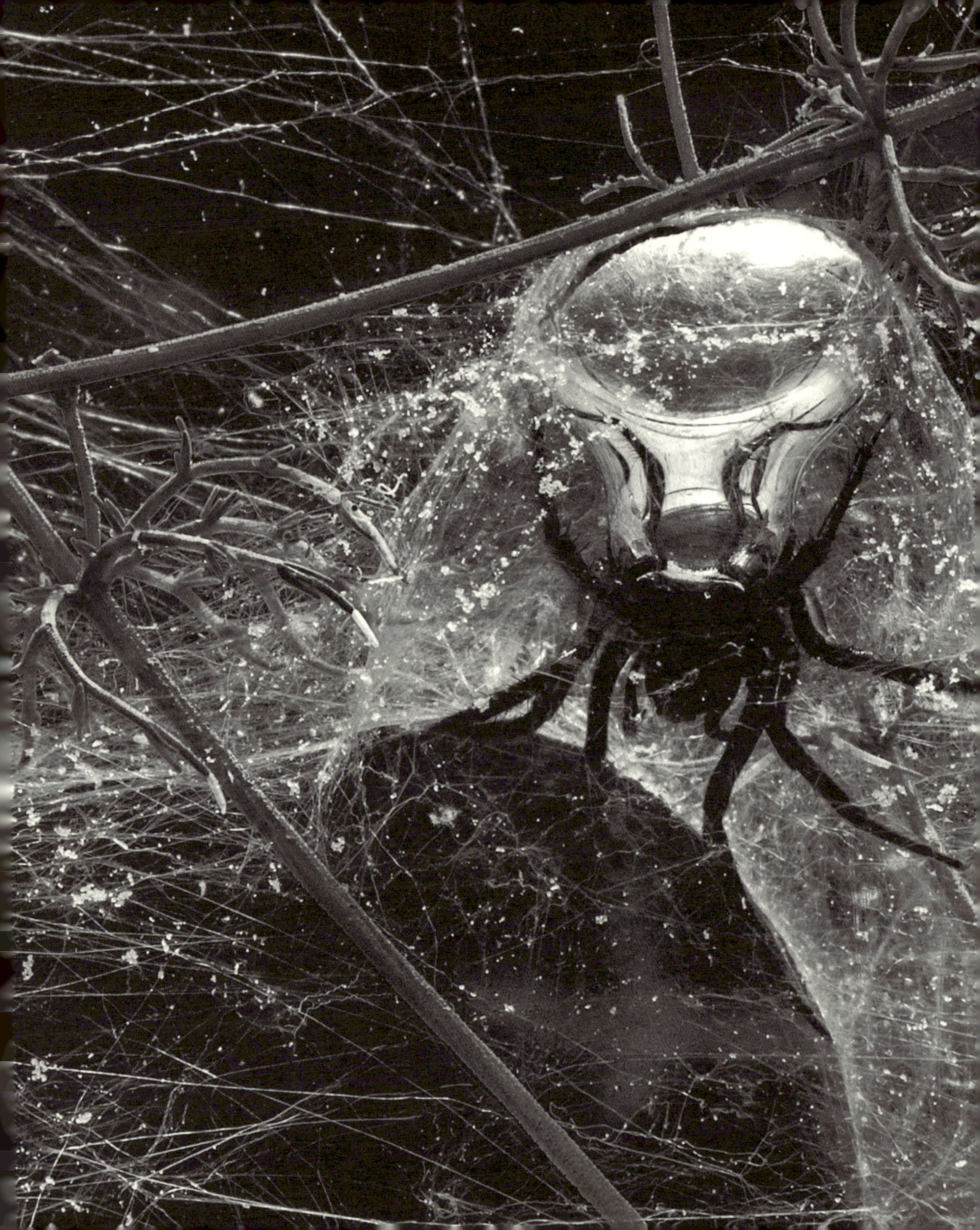

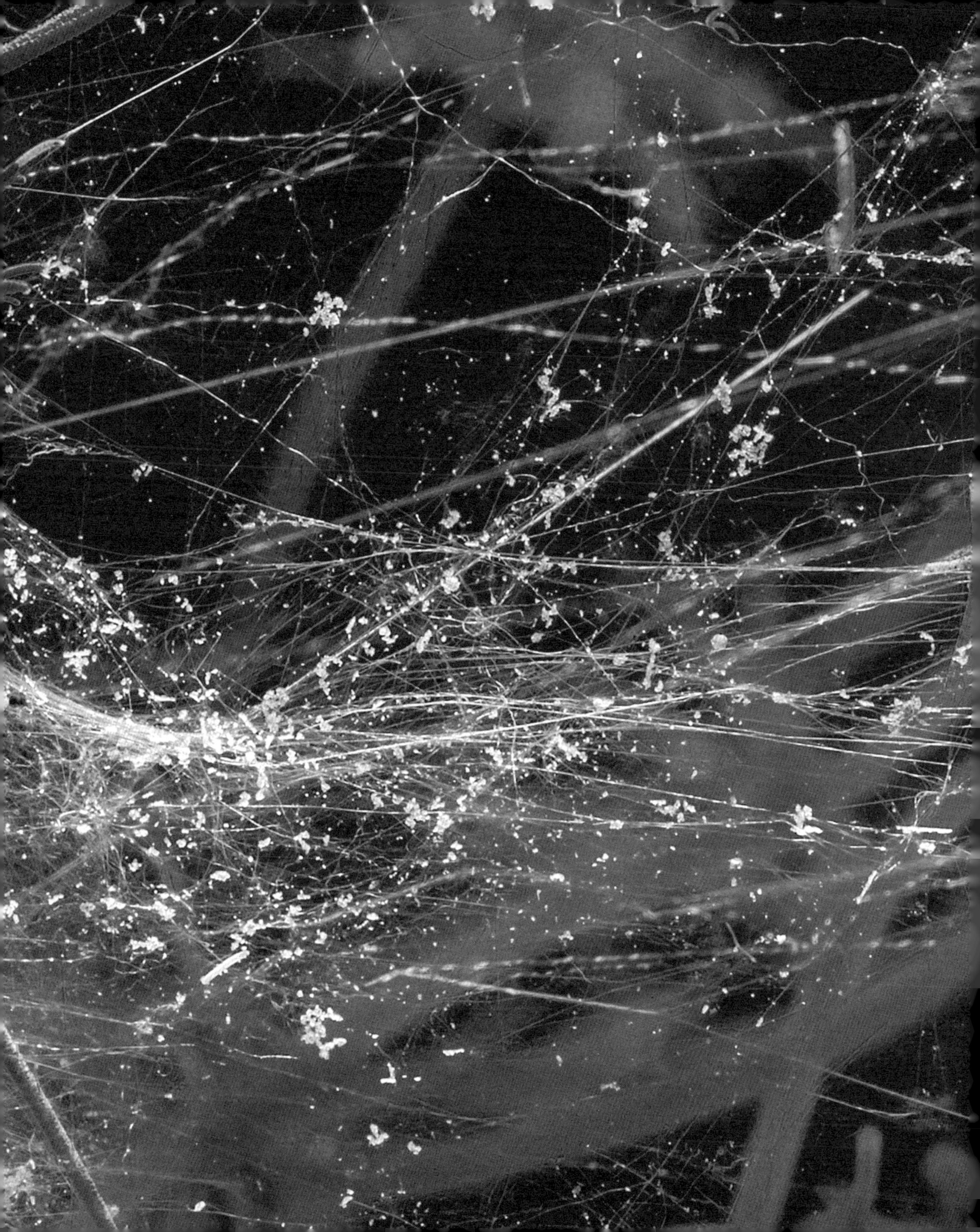

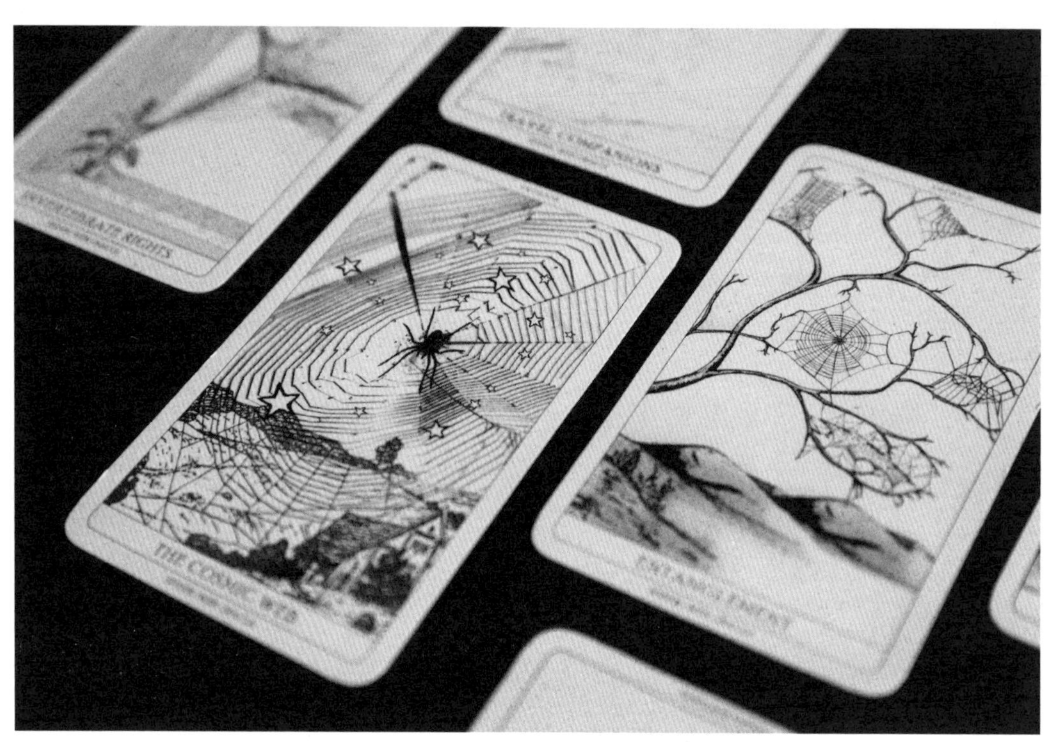

ARIA: AN INTRODUCTION

There is a theory in metaphysical cosmology that we live in not one universe but many, held together in the shape of the multiverse, in which everything that could happen does and is happening, each decision, even each moment of chance giving life to a new universe, a new timeline. *Gravitational waves resounding the cosmic web, yet to be felt. Infinite sensing of the world, lifeforms weave constellations. Close your eyes, cover your ears, I will still sense your felt vibrations.*

In an oracular reading, thirty-three futures emerge all at the same time. As you ask the spider your question, it picks your card; in another universe, it picks your card; *in another universe, it picks your card.*

Named for the vibrational melodies of our world, its sounds and songs, *Tomás Saraceno: Aria* compiles a multiverse of simultaneous futures. Organized around Saraceno's *Arachnomancy Cards*, a set of cards that act as an invitation to attune to sym(bio)poetic possibilities, it celebrates the radical interconnectedness of all things, both living and nonliving. Against the mass commodification of nature and the self-destructive cultural and economic power structures of the present, Tomás Saraceno's *Arachnomancy Cards* consult the spider/web* oracle, engaging with different forms of knowledge in an echo of spider divination methods practiced in different parts of the world. Inspired by the *nggám* collaboration of ground-dwelling spiders and their human neighbors in Cameroon, the *Arachnomancy Cards* think through the spider's oracular capabilities as a result of its sensory universe. The spider's highly developed vibrational senses allow them to attune to a symphony of biotic and abiotic tremors, knowledge that we are not able to perceive.

In the context of the current ecological crisis, named the Sixth Mass Extinction, invertebrates such as arachnids and insects are disappearing at an accelerated pace, with major consequences for the environment and ecosystems. While invertebrates make up more than 95 percent of animal species, most countries lack ethical guidelines and regulations regarding their nonhuman rights. It is imperative that we attune with nonhuman voices that join with our own in endless webs of connectivity and disconnectivity, and recognize their vibratory voices. The oracle of our present, past, and future, the spider/web connects our multidimensional universe with an ontology that extends past the living, that crosses scales—between the cosmic web, spider/webs, and connectomes; between cosmic dust and pollutive dust; between soap bubble formations and overlapping worlds that together we form.

Encounter the oracle from anywhere in the world with the *Arachnomancy App*, and participate in the collective exercise of mapping against extinction through the process of becoming sensitive to the multispecies ecologies in which we are embedded. The spider/web oracle is a messenger between perceptual worlds, transcending the reciprocal blindness between spider/webs and humans. Sense new threads of connectivity, or else face the eternal silence of extinction. By focusing less on individuals and more on reciprocal relationships, we might think beyond what means are necessary to control our environments and more on the shared formation of our quotidian. Let the spider/web guide you here.

* We do not isolate the spider from the web as the latter can be considered an extension of the spider's senses and even of its cognitive apparatus: the external world is perceived by the spider through the tensions and vibrations of its web.

COURTYARD

Lifted by the air and carried by the wind
over borders, fluid in language
in stateless movement.
If you follow their trajectories,
synchronicities emerge,
contours of possible coexistences,
in airnomadic choreographies.

Suit: Cosmic Spider/Web
Species: Linyphia triangularis
Notation: D
Plant: Brassica rapa

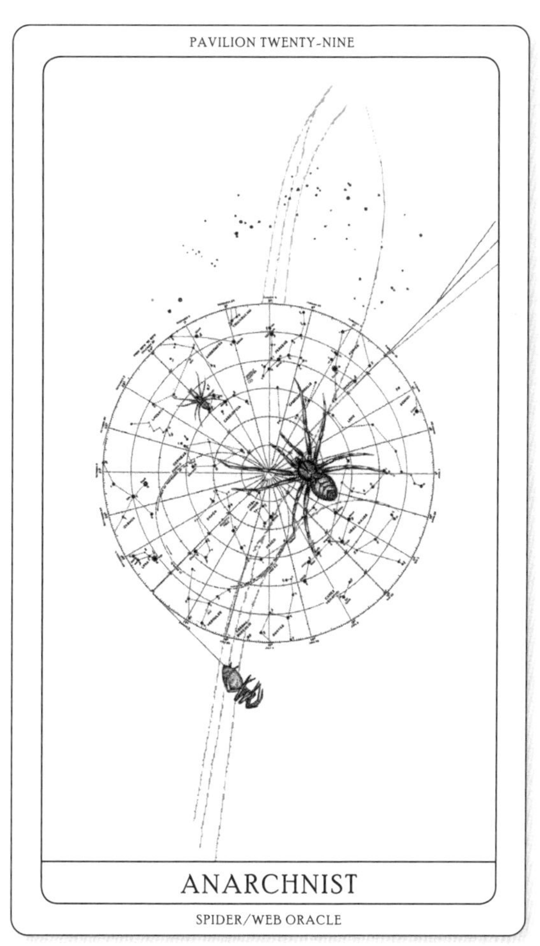

PAVILION TWENTY-NINE
ANARCHNIST
SPIDER/WEB ORACLE

Now we have had a flood of original ideas in all media, works of singular beauty as well as significant milestones in the history of inflation, but at the moment there was only this balloon, concrete particular, hanging there.

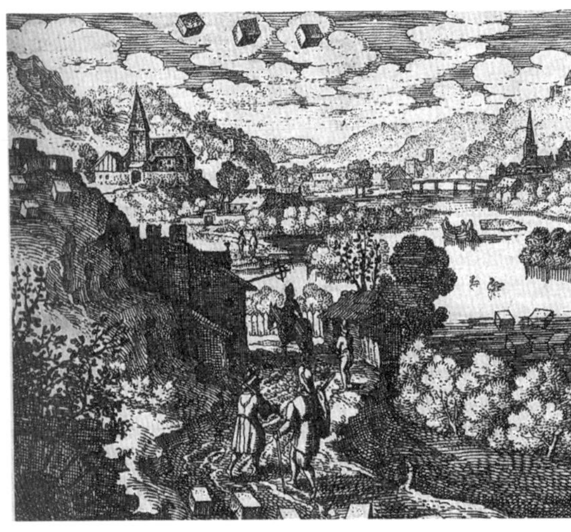

There were reactions. Some people found the balloon "interesting." As a response this seemed inadequate to the immensity of the balloon, the suddenness of its appearance over the city; on the other hand, in the absence of hysteria or other societally induced anxiety, it must be judged a calm, "mature" one. There was a certain amount of initial argumentation about the "meaning" of the balloon; this subsided, because we have learned not to insist on meanings, and they are rarely even looked for now, except in cases involving the simplest, safest phenomena. It was agreed that since the meaning of the balloon could never be known absolutely, extended discussion was pointless, or at least less purposeful than the activities of those who, for

example, hung green and blue paper lanterns from the warm gray underside, in certain streets, or seized the occasion to write messages on the surface, announcing their availability for the performance of unnatural acts, or the availability of acquaintances.[1]

Daring children jumped, especially at those points where the balloon hovered close to a building,

so that the gap between balloon and building was a matter of a few inches, or points where the balloon actually made contact, exerting an ever-so-slight pressure against the side of a building, so that balloon and building seemed a unity. The upper surface was so structured that a "landscape" was presented, small valleys as well as slight knolls, or mounds; once atop the balloon, a stroll was possible, or even a trip, from one place to another. There was pleasure in being able to run down an incline, then up the opposing slope, both gently graded, or in making a leap from one side to the other. Bouncing was possible, because of the pneumaticity of the surface, and even falling, if that was your wish.[2]

1   Or that the meaning is created from, contained within, identical to these inter/actions.

2   It was interesting to find this story after I had already installed *In Orbit* at K21 in Düsseldorf, as it's such a beautiful prediction of what I built there. Still, this passage inspires me when I think toward the future of cloud cities: that the air isn't somewhere we escape to, abandoning the surface of the earth, but somewhere we recognize as a necessary part of our biome.

That all these varied motions, as well as others, were within one's possibilities, in experiencing the "up" side of the balloon, was extremely exciting for children, accustomed to the city's flat, hard skin. But the purpose of the balloon was not to amuse children.

[...]

It has been suggested that what was admired about the balloon was finally this: that it was not limited or defined.[3]

Sometimes a bulge, blister, or sub-section would carry all the way east to the river on its own initiative, in the manner of an army's movements on a map, as seen in a headquarters remote from the fighting. Then that part would be, as it were, thrown back again, or would withdraw into new dispositions; the next morning, that part would have made another sortie, or disappeared altogether. This ability of the balloon to shift its shape, to change, was rather pleasing, especially to people whose lives were rather rigidly patterned, persons to whom change, although desired, was not available. The balloon, for the twenty-two days of its existence, offered the possibility, in its randomness, of mislocation of the self, in contradistinction to the grid of precise, rectangular pathways under our feet.

Donald Barthelme, excerpt from "The Balloon," 1968

3 "Barthelme's balloon, in other words, becomes a device for doing atmospheric things. As a lure for thinking, it becomes a strange attractor: it pulls us toward the possibility of thinking about envelopment as a process through which shapes of change emerge in the tensed space between entities and their atmospheric excess." Derek McCormack, *Atmospheric Things* (Durham and London: Duke University Press, 2018), 18.

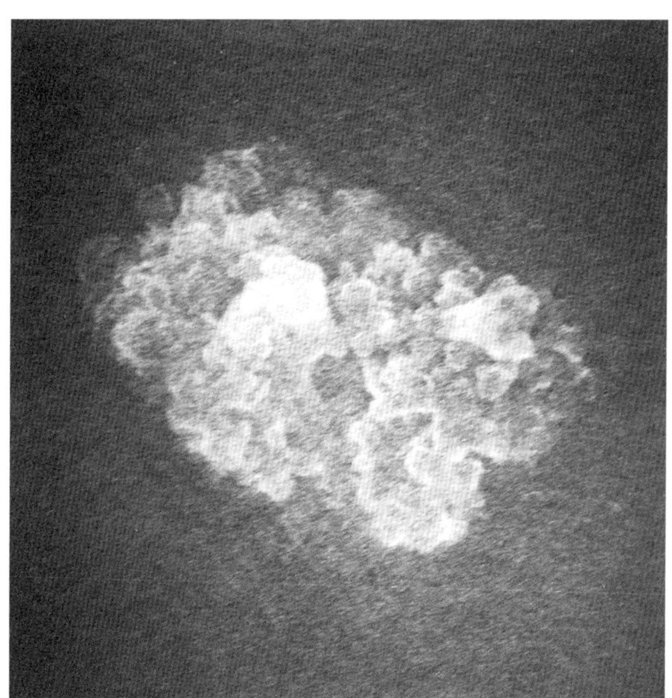

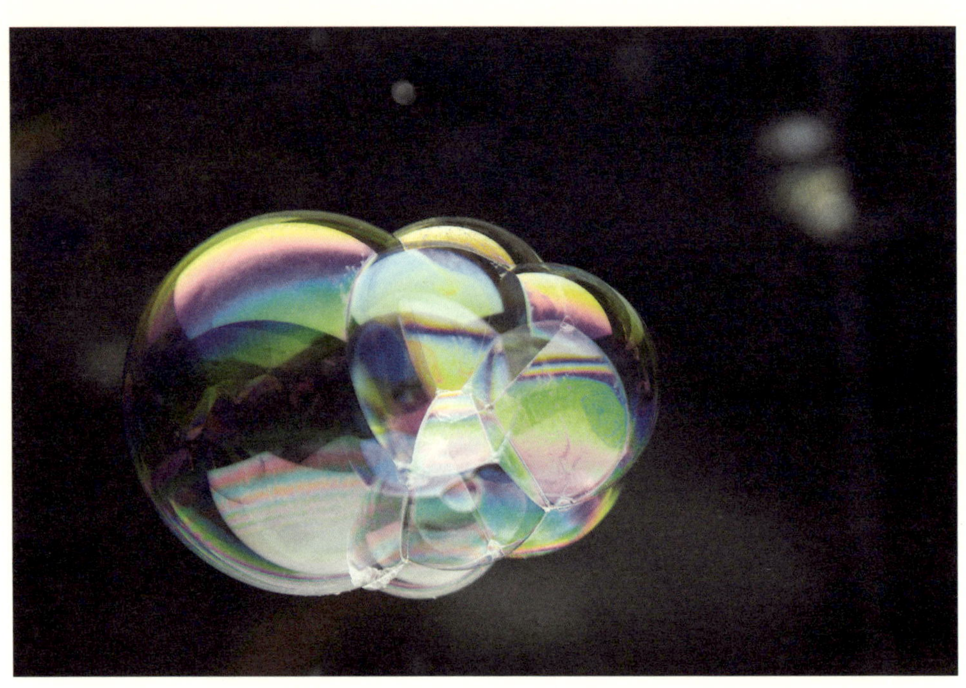

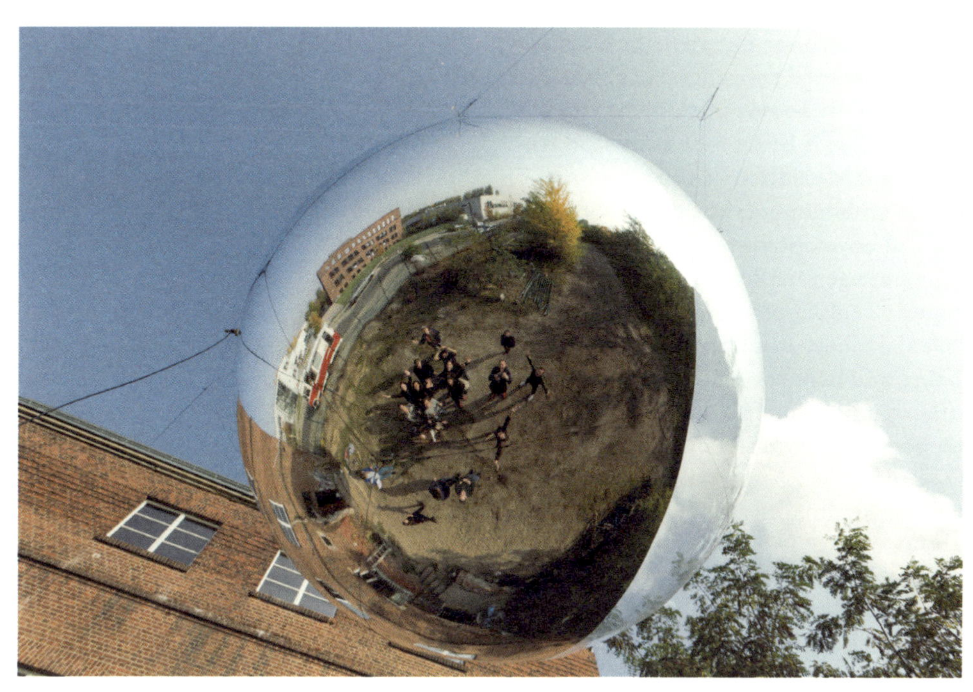

ENVELOPE – The envelope is manifold. It is a spatiotemporal surround, a surface that can be stretched, a traveling object. It suggests a degree of immersion, of nearing a limit, and of being conveyed. A theory of the envelope and of being enveloped is an account of how different senses of space-time emerge through the technical and aesthetic process of folding (Ash 2015).[1] It is an account of how envelopment involves a differentiated relation between bodies in which bodies are always more than envelopes (Irigaray 2005).[2] It is an account of a process that generates a sensed interval of difference between inside and outside: difference sensed across and through the affective capacities of skin, membrane, and fabric. This is by no means limited to envelopment in relation to the phenomenology of human embodiment, but the technical process of envelopment certainly shapes the relation between bodies and their atmospheric surrounds in distinctive ways. Indeed, this technical process is a necessary precondition for being and becoming stratospheric. Gas, whether air, helium, or hydrogen, need to be enveloped to generate buoyancy. The human body needs to be progressively more enveloped to become stratospheric.

[. . .]

The sealed envelope is a life-world of sorts (Sloterdijk 2011),[3] and the capsule is a paradigmatic example of such an envelope. The capsule can take many forms: medically, it is an envelope for the delivery of a substance to a destination in the body that would be ordinarily beyond reach without some kind of invasive procedure. Culturally and archeologically, it is a sealed, postdated container to be opened at a designated future date. Technically, it is that part of a spacecraft in which astronauts travel, usually detachable from the larger propulsion system. The capsule is the envelope of life support taken to its limits in an environment where the conditions for life fall away.

Derek McCormack, excerpt from "Stratospheric Envelopes for an Atmospheric Mode of Address," *GeoHumanities*, 2017

1. James Ash, *The Interface Envelope: Gaming, Technology, Power* (London: Bloomsbury, 2015).

2. Luce Irigaray, *An Ethics of Sexual Difference*, trans. C. Burke and G. C. Gill (London: Continuum, 2005).

3. Peter Sloterdijk, *Bubbles: Spheres*, vol. I, *Microspherology* (Los Angeles: Semiotext(e)/Foreign Agents and Cambridge, Mass.: MIT Press, 2011).

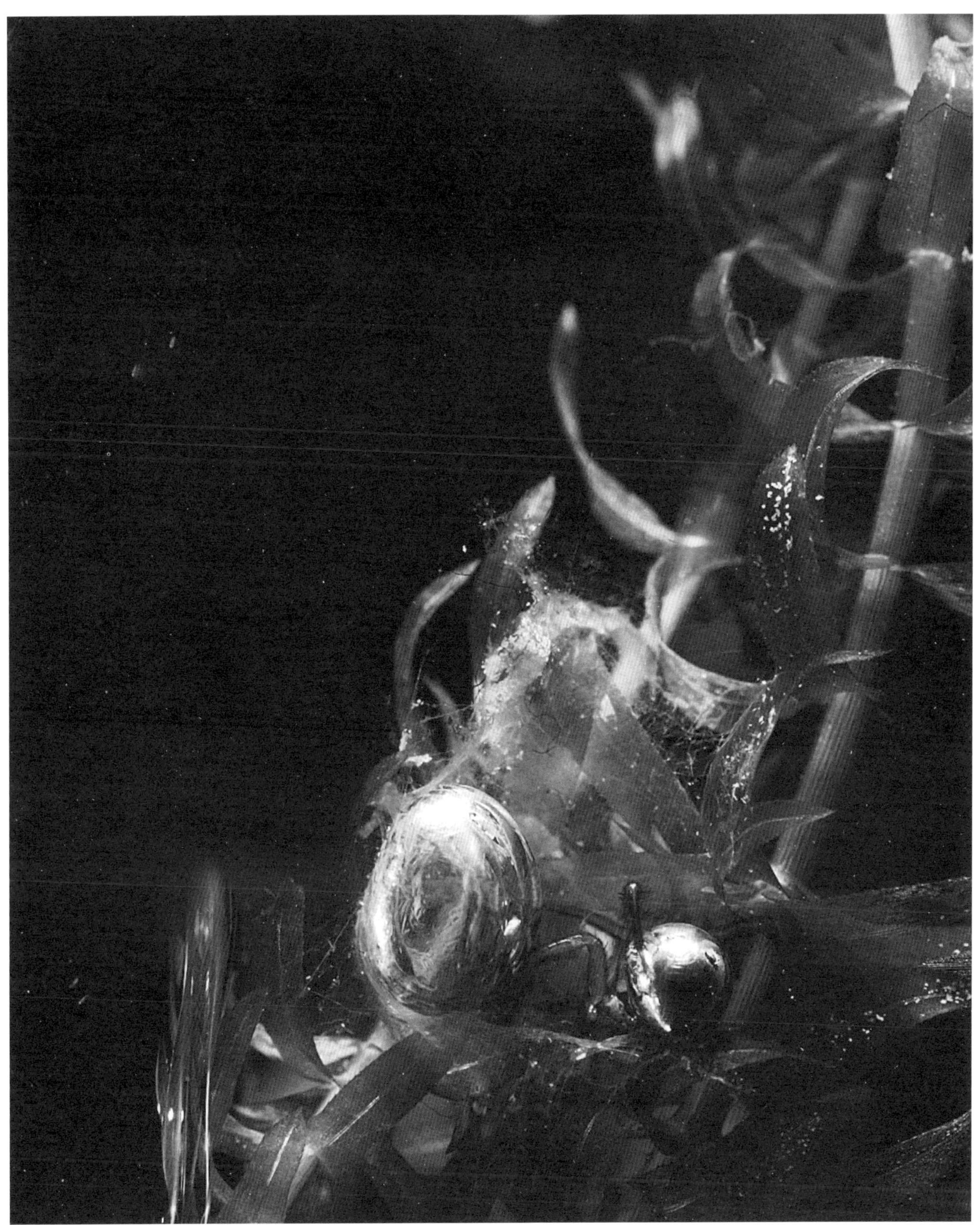

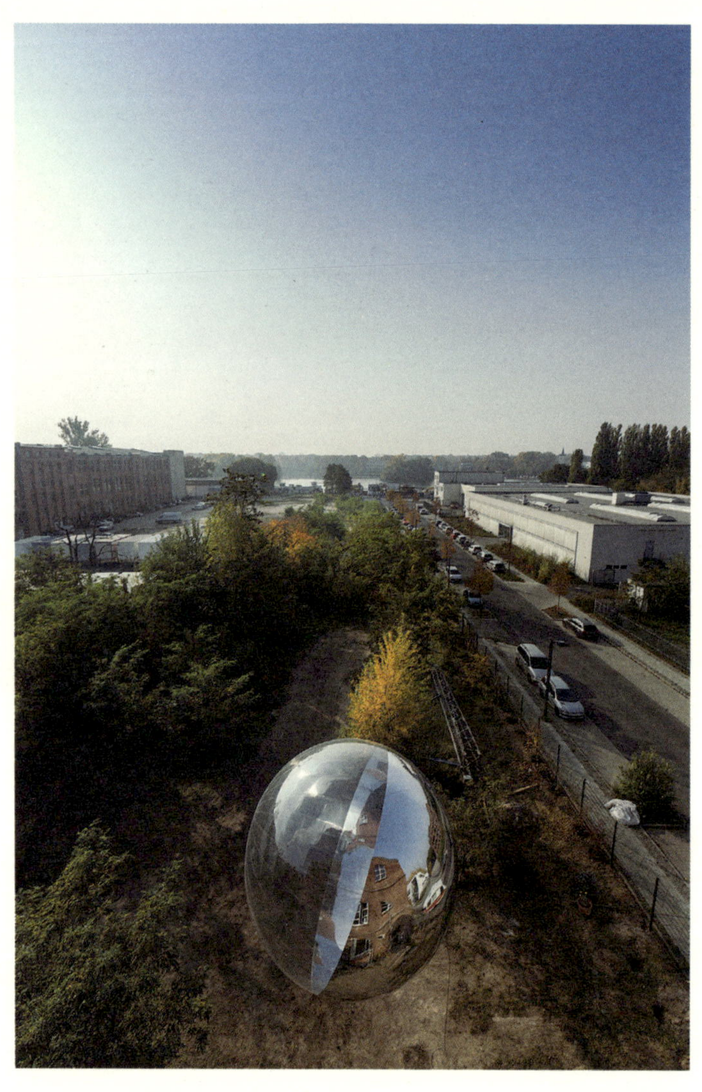

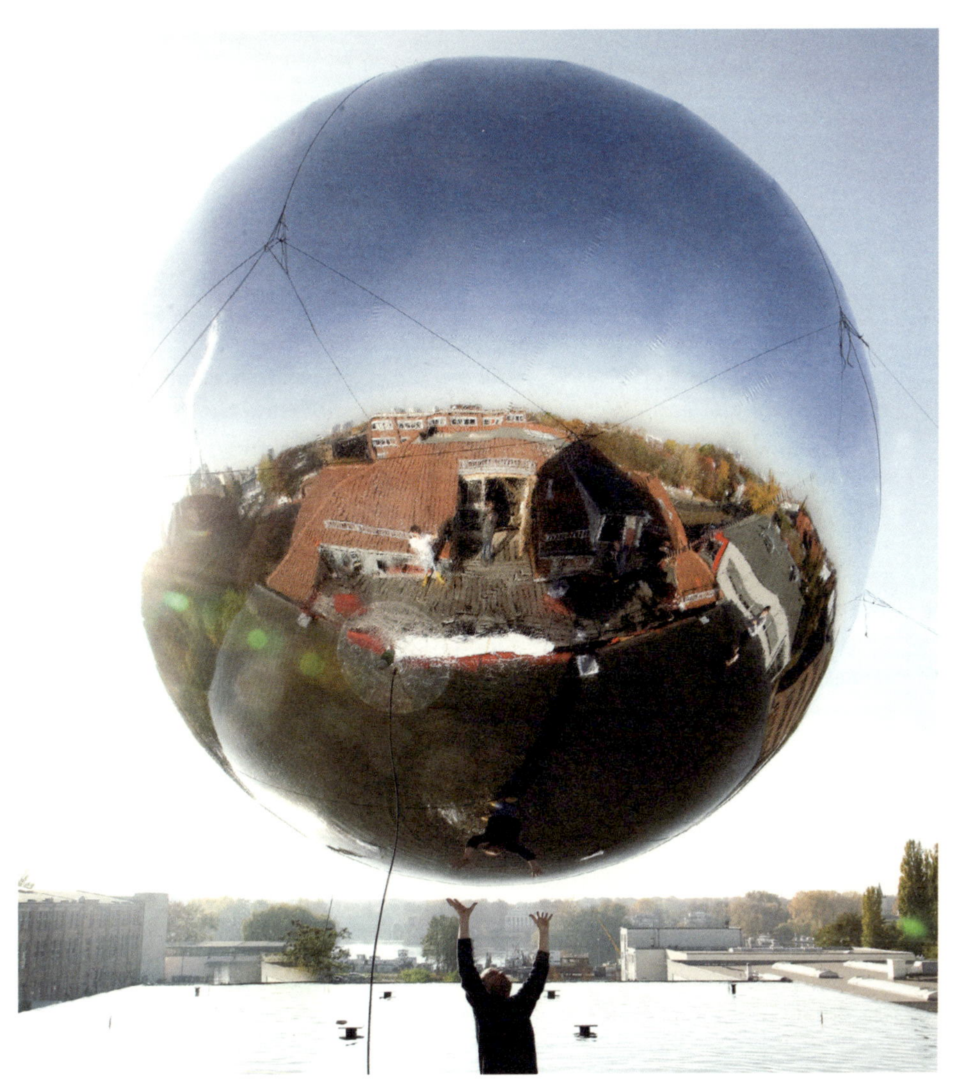

Thermodynamic Constellation

"While fossil fuel based industries enterprise to colonize other planets, the air, this interface between us and the sun, is controlled by the few and continues to be compromised: carbon emissions fill the air, particulate matter floats inside our lungs while electromagnetic radiation envelops the earth, dictating the tempo of digital capitalism, in the era of global warming. Imagine a different era, defined instead by interplanetary sensitivity, shared through a new ecology of practices. Towards this, collective ideas must form, by asking: How would it feel to breathe in a post fossil fuel era? And, what are our response-abilities to be on air? How can geopolitical borders be challenged in an age of climate inequality? How to participate in a new epoch beyond the Anthropocene, towards the decarbonization of the air, and independence from fossil fuels? Together, we call for this new epoch, which we have named Aerocene.
Aerocene imagines space as a commons, a physical and imaginative place cleared from corporate control and government surveillance. Aerocene promotes de-securitized, free access to the atmosphere, the last earthly layer created as a result of the interplaying forces of the sun, gravity and the earth mass. Aerocene is a proposal—a scene in, on, for, and with the air."

– The *Aerocene Manifesto*

The launch pad towards this new epoch is an aerosolar balloon, whose only engine is the air and heat of the sun, floating as a result of temperature differentials between internal and external air masses. These self-stabilising aerosolar bodies float differently from any airborne plant or animal. Once inflated with air, they are able to elevate into the sky, thanks only to the sun heating the air in the interior, afterwards relying only on the wind to drift along aerosolar journeys.
A Thermodynamic Constellation provides a launchpad for new era of mobility that we call Aerocene. The spheres that comprise the installation, are prototypes for aerosolar sculptures that are able

to float around the world, free from borders, free from fossil fuels. They are modelled versions of bigger structures that would be able to achieve long-distance flights, floating at altitudes between 20 km and 40 km. Tomás Saraceno was the artist in residence at the French Centre National d'Études Spatiales (CNES) in 2014–15, and the design of this sculpture is inspired by scientific experiments that agency started in the late 1970s by launching infrared radiation balloons (Montgolfière InfraRouge, MIR) into the upper levels of the atmosphere. They are made of two different lightweight materials: transparent and mirror foils. The mirror part of these sculptures would reflect part of the sun's radiation, thus preventing the air envelopes from overheating. This insulation is important during daytime flight. The transparent half helps to maintain the temperature inside the envelope (and hence its buoyancy) during the night, since it absorbs the infrared radiation emitted from the earth's surface—the solar heat that the planet accumulated over a day. Floating like this would reveal a fluctuating trajectory, a woven choreography in the air, free from borders, free from fossil fuels.

As a static sculpture, it speculates about what kinds of nomadic socio-political structures might emerge if we could navigate the rivers of the atmosphere, floating airborne aboard structures like this, across borders, without carbon emissions. These aerosolar journeys reimagine the ways in which borders are set up by humans, the power of national institutions to decide who can transit, policies that dramatically affect vulnerable subjects, humans and nonhuman life forms. To move like this would be to become airnomads, moving from *Homo œconomicus* to *Homo flotantis*, who is attuned to planetary rhythms, conscious of living with other humans and nonhumans and who learned to float in the air, adrift with the wind, within its elemental being.

Thermodynamic Constellation
2020
Mylar transparent and metalized, mirrored acrylic plate, membrane pump with pressure control, overpressure release valve, PE tube, PES rope
Dimensions: 2.5m / 5m / 4m diameter

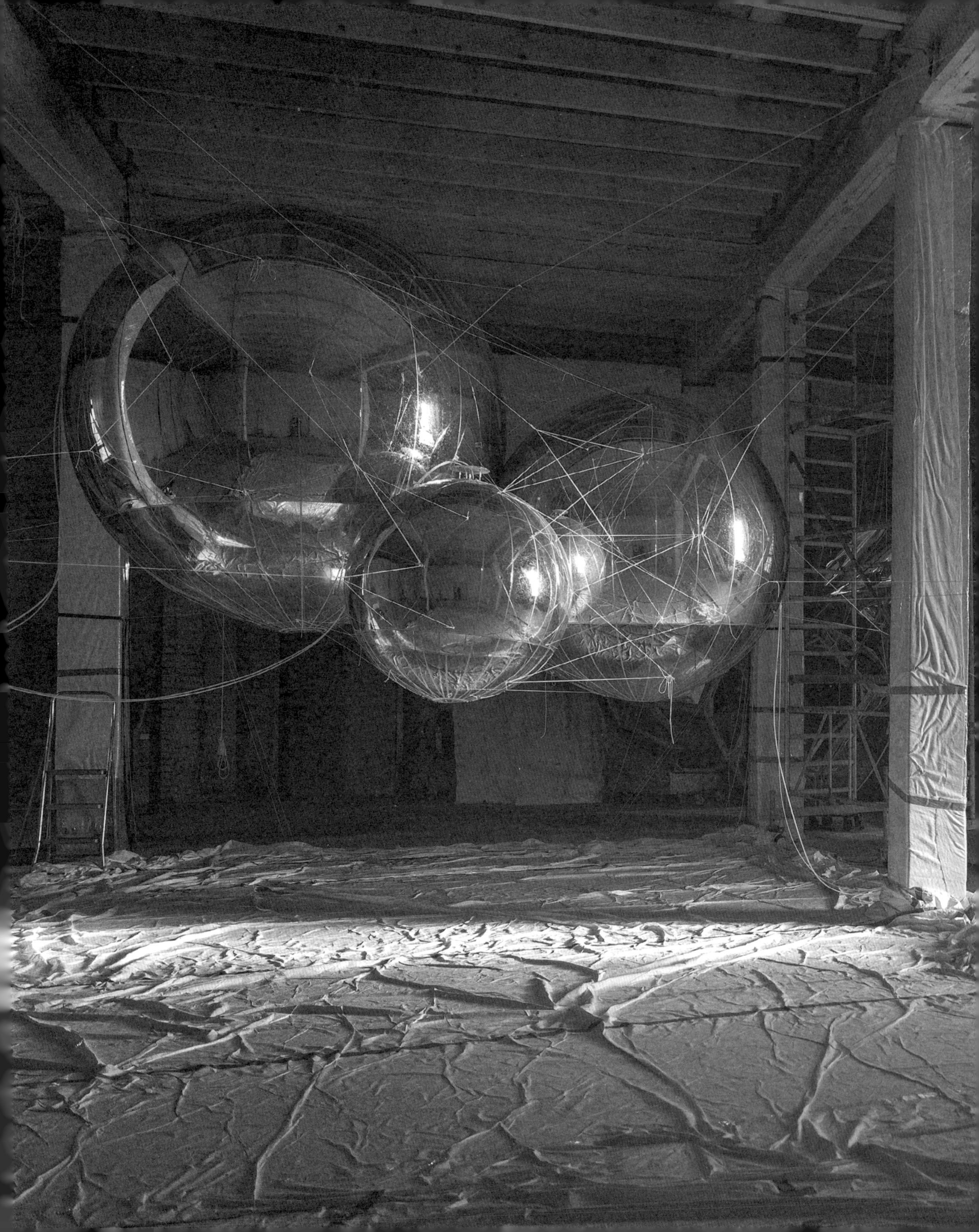

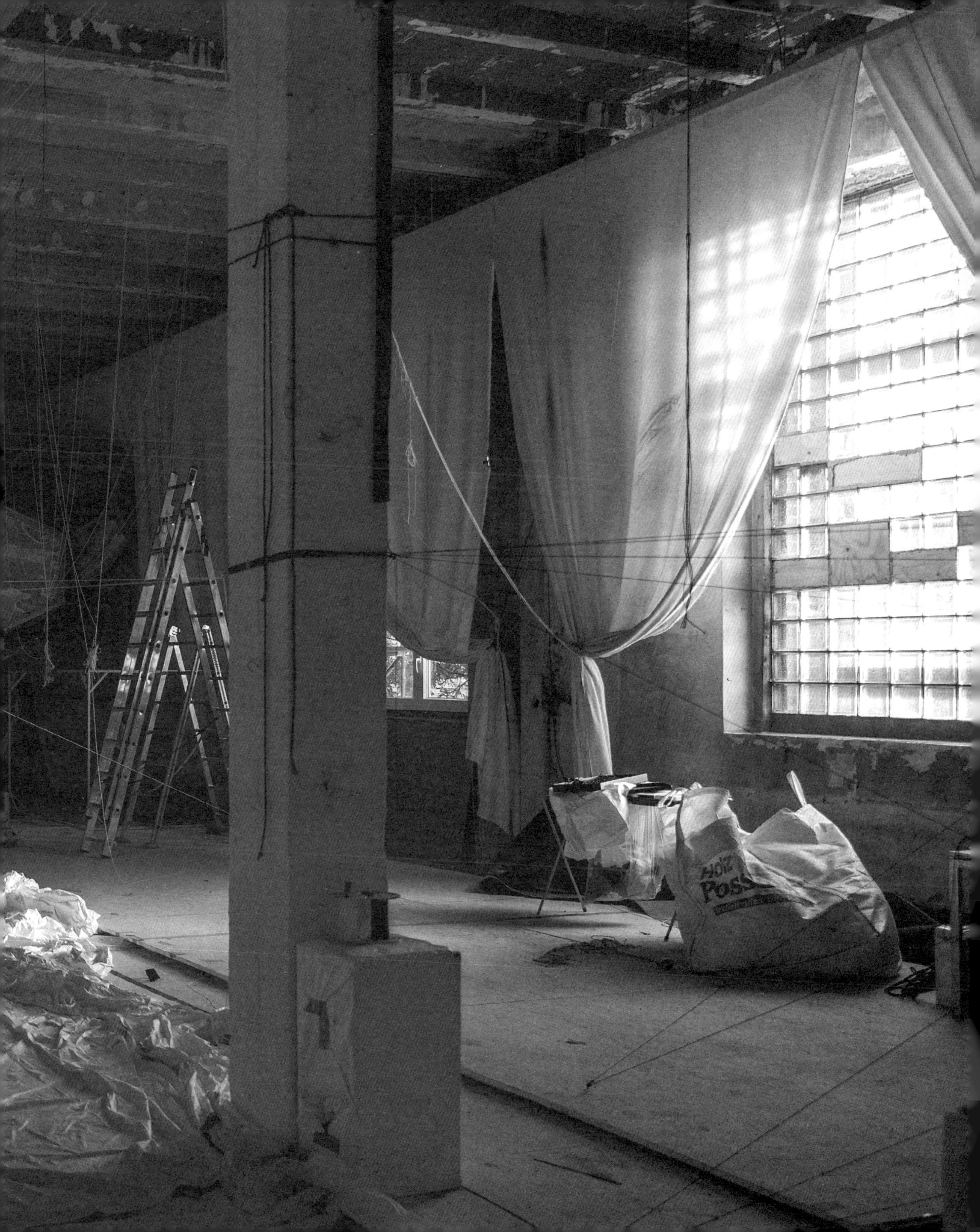

ROOM I

Liquified animals are burned to propel us
toward unforeseen futures.
They take over the sky after being cast out
from the depths of the earth.
Tension between air, water, and land,
beware of geological revenge
when taking without asking.

Suit: Atmospheric Spider/Web
Species: Cyrtophora citricola
Notation: A♯
Plant: Coffea arabica

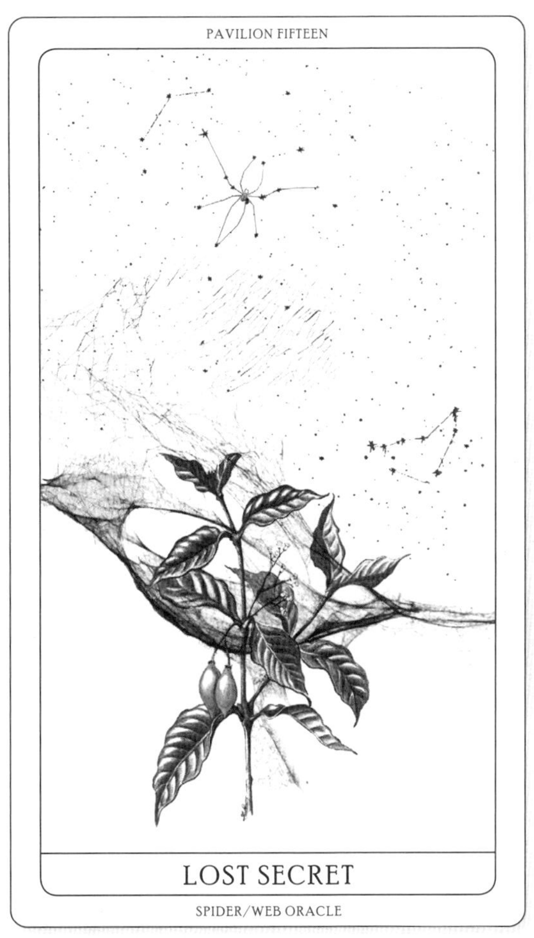

LOST SECRET

SPIDER/WEB ORACLE

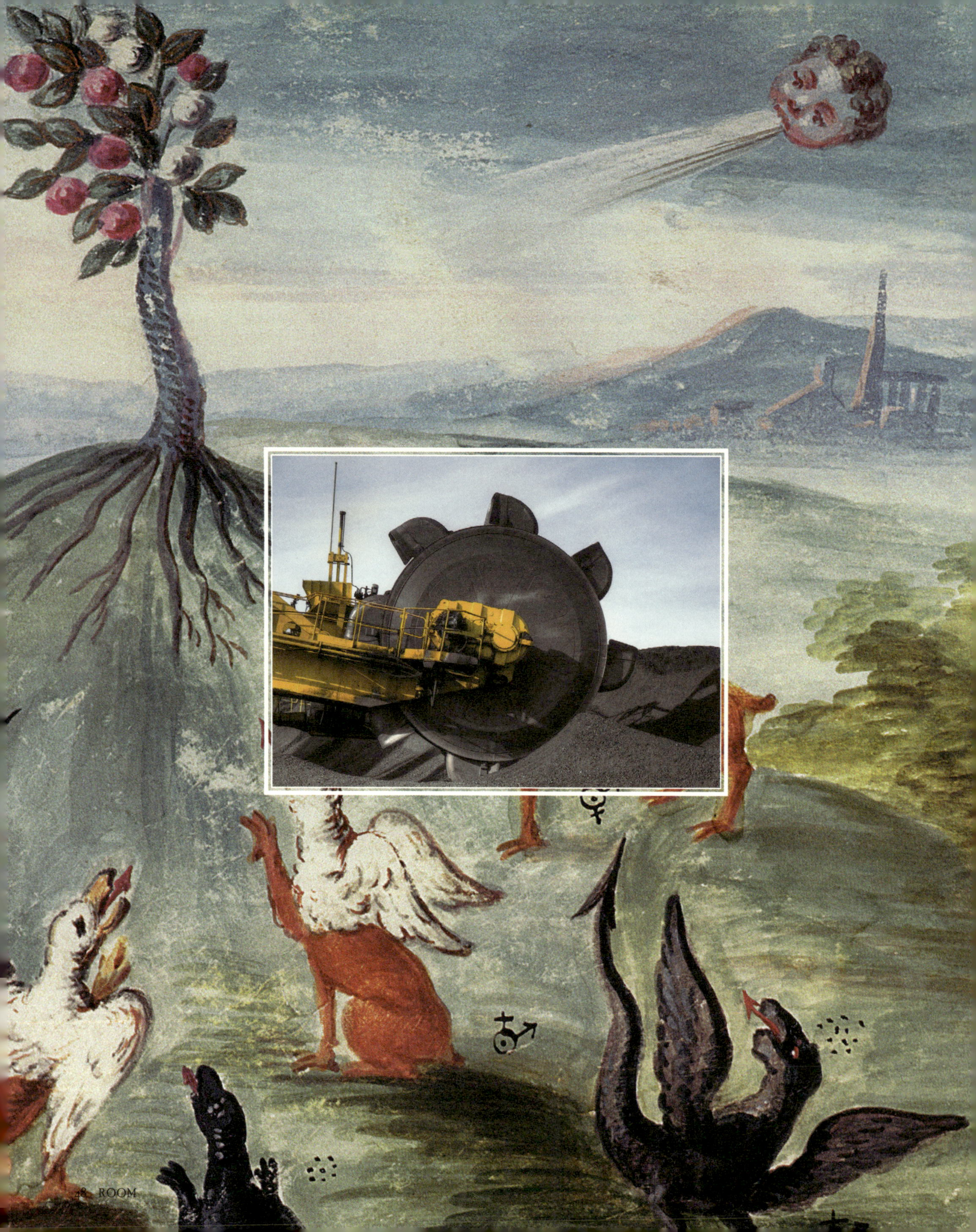

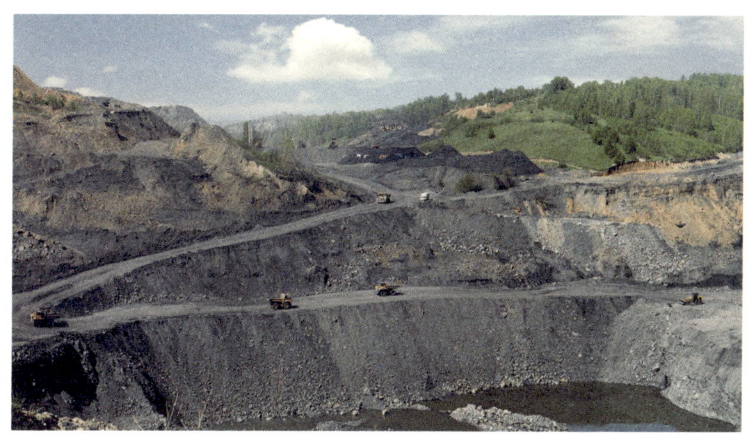

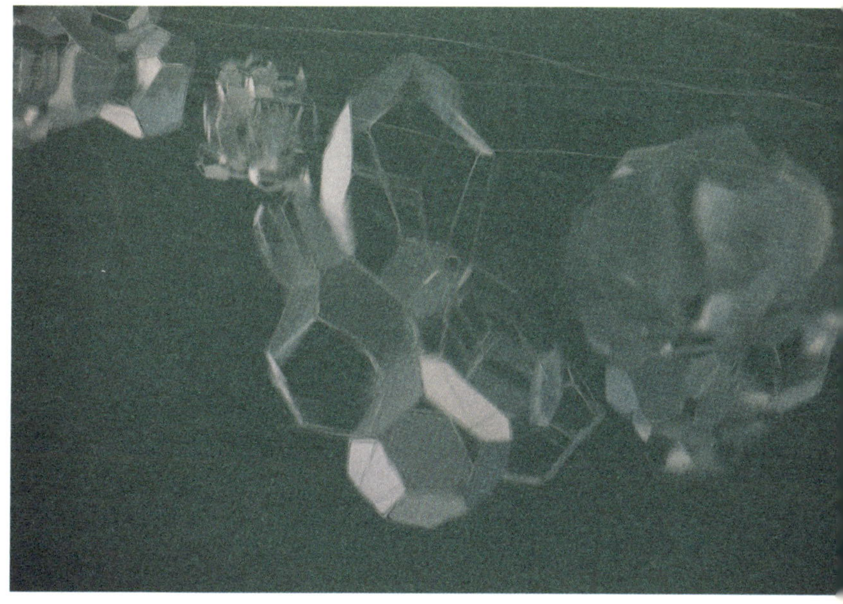

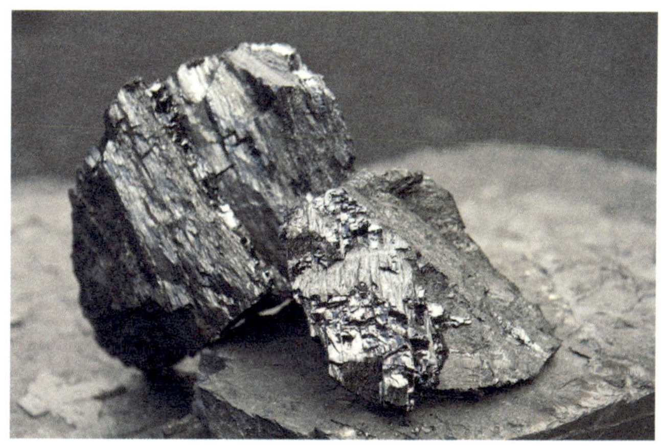

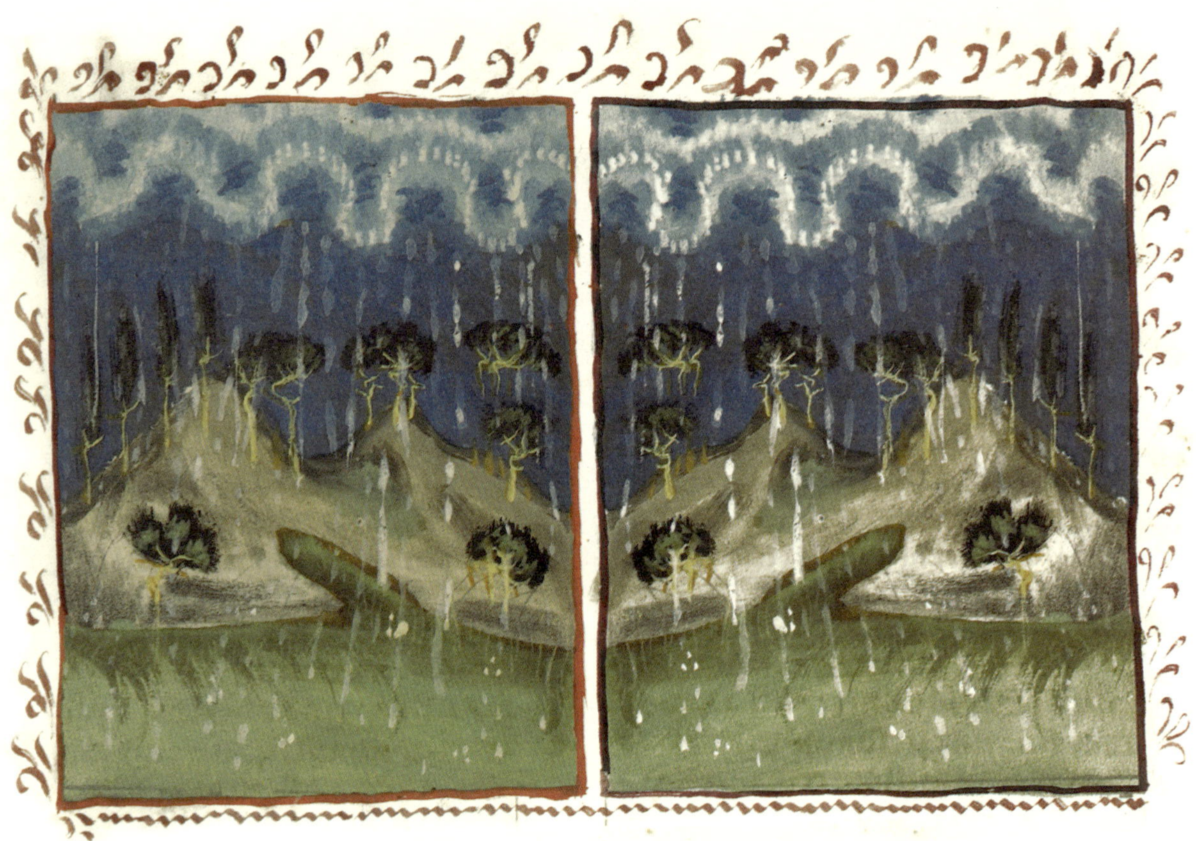

"It's going to rain tonight."

"It's raining now," I said.

"The radio said tonight."

I drove him to school on his first day back after a sore throat and fever. A woman in a yellow slicker held up traffic to let some children cross. I pictured her in a soup commercial taking off her oilskin hat as she entered the cheerful kitchen where her husband stood over a pot of smoky lobster bisque, a smallish man with six weeks to live.

"Look at the windshield," I said. "Is that rain or isn't it?"

"I'm only telling you what they said."

"Just because it's on the radio doesn't mean we have to suspend belief in the evidence of our senses."

"Our senses? Our senses are wrong a lot more often than they're right.

This has been proved in the laboratory. Don't you know about all those theorems that say nothing is what it seems? There's no past, present or future outside our own mind. The so-called laws of motion are a big hoax. Even sound can trick the mind. Just because you don't hear a sound doesn't mean it's not out there. Dogs can hear it. Other animals. And I'm sure there are sounds even dogs can't hear. But they exist in the air, in waves. Maybe they never stop.[1] High, high, high-pitched. Coming from somewhere."

"Is it raining," I said, "or isn't it?"

"I wouldn't want to have to say."

"What if someone held a gun to your head?"

"Who, you?"

"Someone. A man in a trench coat and smoky glasses. He holds a gun to your head and says, 'Is it raining or isn't it? All you have to do is tell the truth and I'll put

away my gun and take the next flight out of here.'"

"What truth does he want? Does he want the truth of someone traveling at almost the speed of light in another galaxy? Does he want the truth of someone in orbit around a neutron star? Maybe if these people could see us through a telescope we might look like we were two feet two inches tall and it might be raining yesterday instead of today."

"He's holding the gun to your head. He wants your truth."

"What good is my truth? My truth means nothing. What if this guy with the gun comes from a planet in a whole different solar system? What we call rain he calls soap. What we call apples he calls rain. So what am I supposed to tell him?"

"His name is Frank J. Smalley and he comes from St. Louis."

"He wants to know if it's raining now, at this very minute?"

"Here and now. That's right."

"Is there such a thing as now? 'Now' comes and goes as soon as you say it. How can I say it's raining now if your so-called 'now' becomes 'then' as so on as I say it?"[2]

"You said there was no past, present, or future."

"Only in our verbs. That's the only place we find it."

"Rain is a noun. Is there rain here, in this precise locality, at whatever time within the next two minutes that you choose to respond to the question?"

"If you want to talk about this precise locality while you're in a vehicle that's obviously moving, then I think that's the trouble with this discussion."

"Just give me an answer, okay, Heinrich?"

"The best I could do is make a guess."

"Either it's raining or it isn't," I said.

"Exactly. That's my whole point. You'd be guessing. Six of one, half dozen of the other."

"But you see it's raining."

"You see the sun moving across the sky. But is the sun moving across the sky or is the earth turning?"

"I don't accept the analogy."

"You're so sure that's rain. How do you know it's not

1 This conception of sound has been on my mind lately, as I have been exploring how to communicate with nonhuman entities. In our *Arachnophilia* project, we communicate with spiders by learning their vibrational messages. I now wonder how we might communicate even with plants, with air, with the earth. What voices are we unable to hear? They truly do "never stop."

2 "Actuality is when the lighthouse is dark between flashes: it is the instant between the ticks of the watch: it is a void interval slipping forever through time: the rupture between past and future: the gap at the poles of the revolving magnetic field, infinitesimally small but ultimately real. It is the interchronic pause when nothing is happening. It is the void between events. Yet the instant of actuality is all we ever can know directly. The rest of time emerges only in signals relayed to us at this instant by innumerable stages and by unexpected bearers. [. . .] If it is a signal it is a past action, no longer embraced by the 'now' of present being. The perception of a signal happens "now," but its impulse and its transmission happened 'then.'" George Kubler, *The Shape of Time: Remarks on the History of Things* (New Haven and London: Yale University Press, 1962), 17.

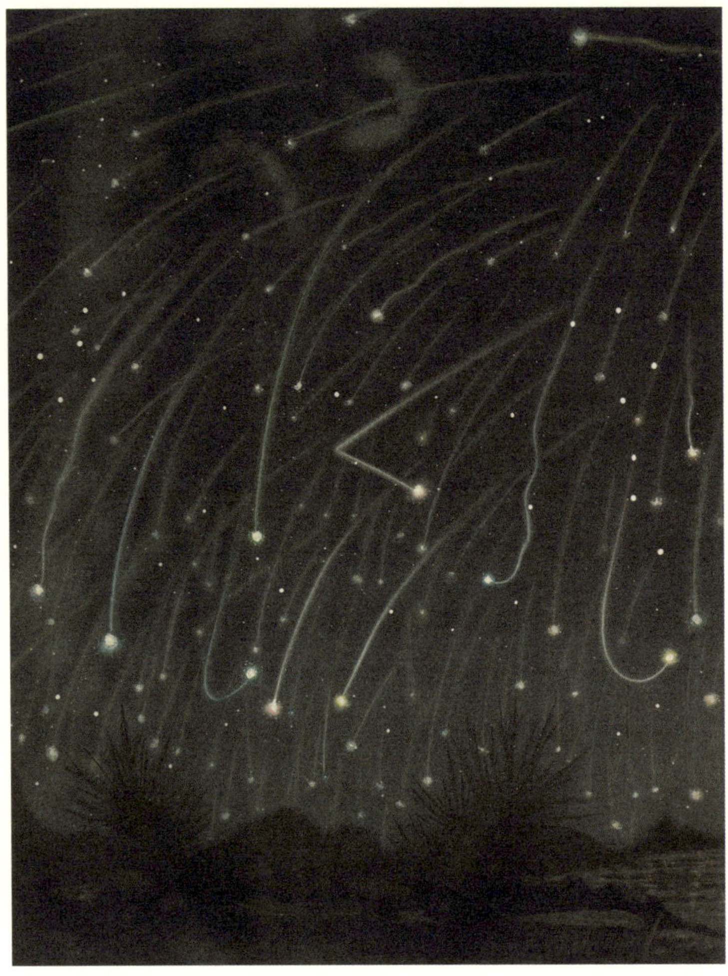

sulfuric acid from factories across the river? How do you know it's not fallout from a war in China?[3] You want an answer here and now. Can you prove, here and now, that this stuff is rain? How do I know that what you call rain is really rain? What is rain anyway?"

"It's the stuff that falls from the sky and gets you what is called wet."

"I'm not wet. Are you wet?"

"All right," I said. "Very good."

"No, seriously, are you wet?"

"First-rate," I told him. "A victory for uncertainty, randomness and chaos. Science's finest hour."

"Be sarcastic."

"The sophists and the hairsplitters enjoy their finest hour."

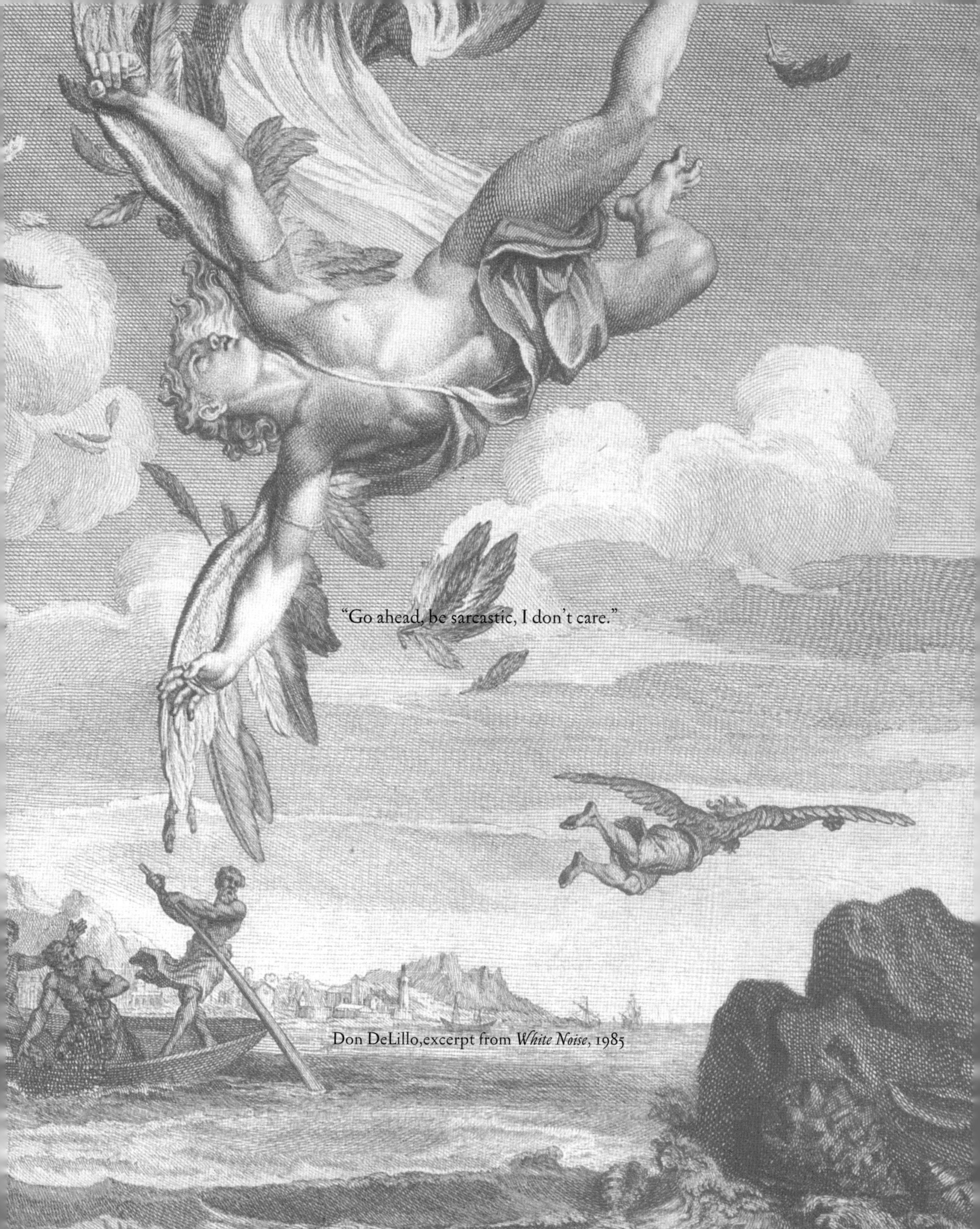

Don DeLillo, excerpt from *White Noise*, 1985

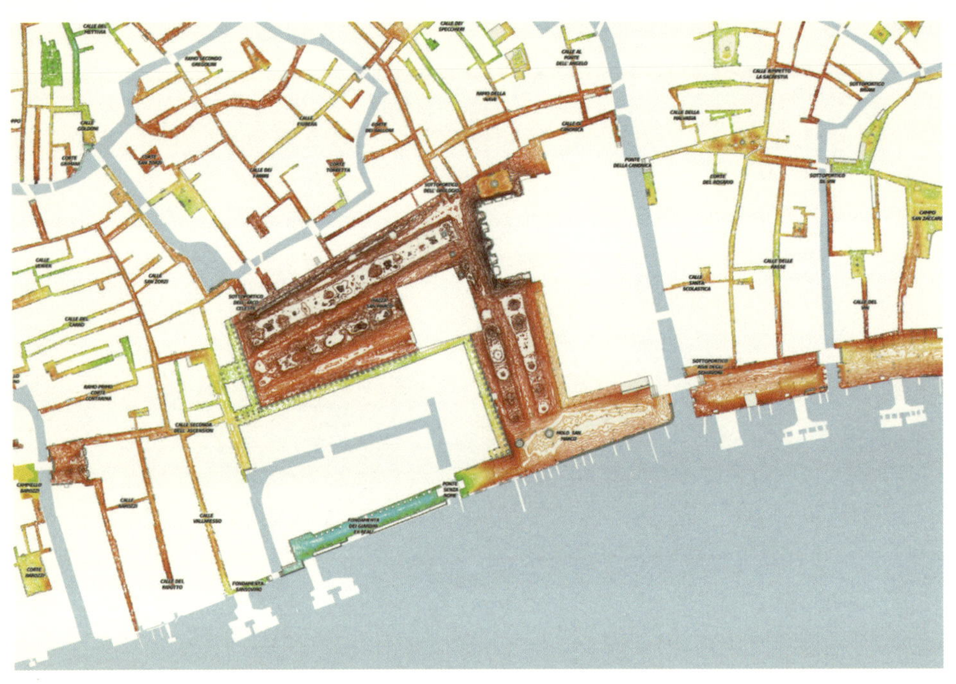
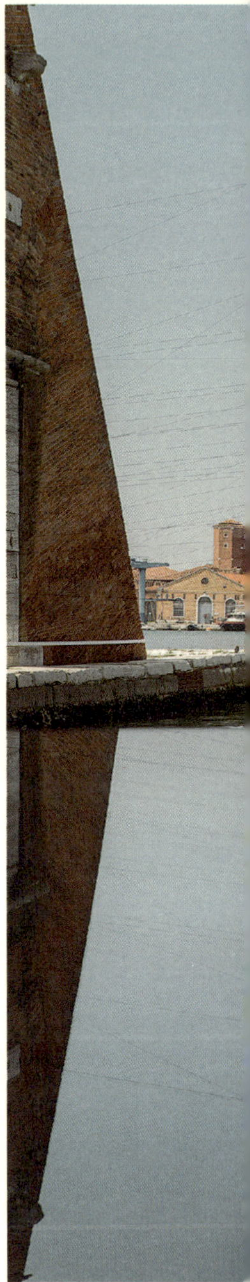

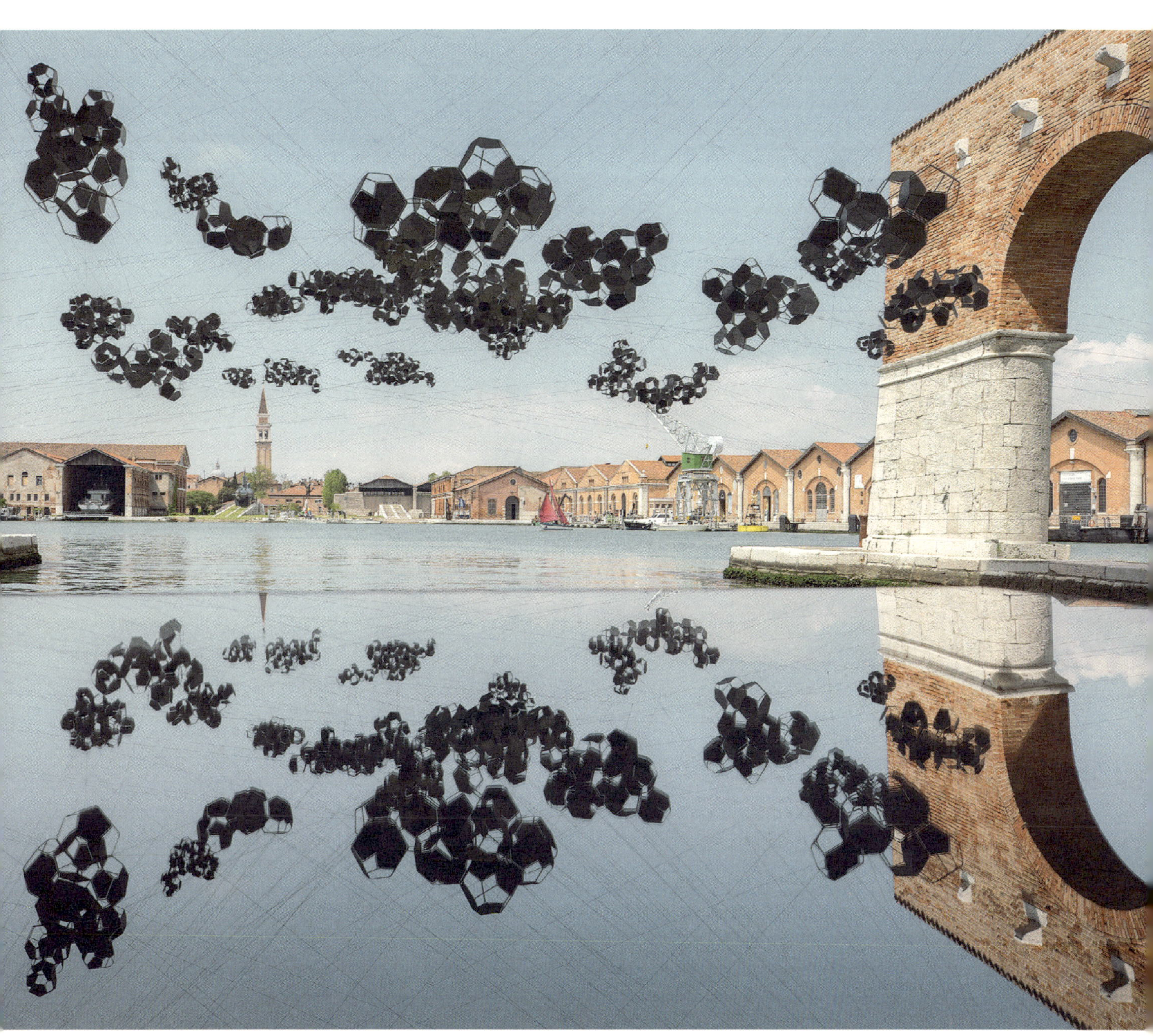

In the far north of Canada, indigenous peoples claim that the sun no longer sets where it used to, and that the stars are out of alignment. The weather is changing in strange and unpredictable ways. Warm, unstable winds blow from new directions; severe flooding threatens towns and villages. Even the animals are changing their patterns of life, struggling to adapt to the uncertain conditions. This is how the world is described in *Inuit Knowledge and Climate Change*, by Nunavut filmmaker Zacharias Kunuk and environmental scientist Ian Mauro, a series of interviews with Inuit

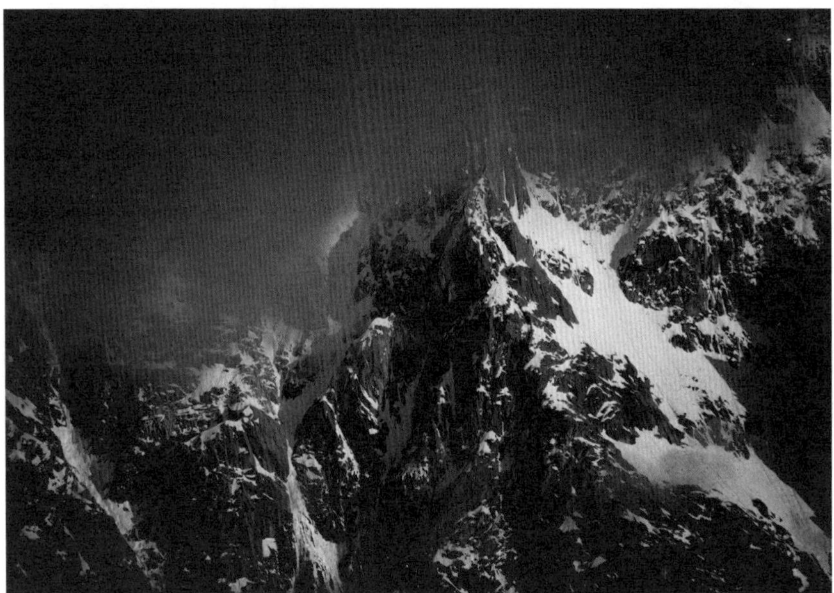

elders in which they recount their experiences of the world around them—experiences informed by decades of observing the climate firsthand.[1] The sun is setting in a different place, they say, often kilometers from where it used to. The earth itself is off-kilter.

When the film was screened at the Copenhagen Climate Change Conference (COP15) in December 2009, it caused many scientists to complain that while the Inuit viewpoint was important, their claim that the earth had actually moved—had tilted on its axis—was dangerous, and would lead to them being discredited. But the direct experience of the Inuit is upheld by scientific theory: at high latitudes, the appearance of the sun is hugely affected by the snow covering the ground, which reflects and refracts it in myriad ways.[2] Changes in the snow and ice correspond to changes in visibility. At the same time, the atmosphere is indisputably filling up with particulate matter, the impurities of jet liners and the exhaust of fossil fuel fires. The bright red sunsets seen over dirty cities are the result of the smog and smoke the city itself exhales. In this way, the sun above the Arctic is distorted, and appears to set further and further away. The sky, like everything else, is seen through the lens of climate change. Not knowing why doesn't make it not so.

"Over the years, nobody has ever listened to these people. Every time [the discussion is] about global warming, about the Arctic warming, it's scientists that go up there and do their work. And policy makers depend on these findings. Nobody ever really understands the people up there," Kunuk reported.[3] In this regard, the knowledge of the Inuit is much akin to the Kenyan victims of torture, whose embodied evidence was ignored until it was validated in the language of their oppressors, through formal documentation and analysis. Scientific and political knowledges cannot escape the horizon of their own experience any more than embodied ones can, but it doesn't mean they're not looking at the same thing and seeking ways to articulate it.

Some of the most spectacular sunsets seen in Europe in recent times occurred after the eruption of Eyjafjallajökull, the Icelandic volcano that filled the heavens with ash in April of 2010. These sunsets are also caused by aerosols in the atmosphere, particularly sulfur dioxide. As sunset approaches, ash and sulfur dioxide produce ripples of white cloud on the horizon, before the blue light scattered by atmospheric particles combines with the extended red of sunsets to produce a unique tone known as volcanic lavender.[4] The sunsets appeared across the continent as the ash cloud moved south and west over several days. Volcanic ash was known to interfere with jet engines, but despite several incidents over decades, few studies had been performed. As a result, the whole of European airspace shut down. Over the course of eight days, over one hundred thousand flights were cancelled, almost half the world's air traffic, and ten million passengers were stranded. Apart from the sunsets, the most unsettling thing about the Eyjafjallajökull event was its silence. For the first time in decades, the skies over Europe were quiet. The poet Carol Ann Duffy noted its stillness:

Britain's birds
Sing in this spring, from Inverness
to Liverpool,
From Crieff to Cardiff, Oxford,
London Town,
Land's End to John O'Groats;
the music silence summons,
That Shakespeare heard, Burns,
Edward Thomas; briefly, us.[5]

Others commented on the archaic strangeness of a sky without contrails. It was a strangeness that crept up on us slowly, an inversion of the event. While the media reported on the "chaos" of travel disruptions, we sat in sunlight beneath clear blue skies. The eruption was a hyperobject: an event of almost inconceivable violence, present everywhere but experienced locally as an absence, like climate change, like Roni Horn's paradox of the weather: "The nice is occurring in the immediate and individual, and the wrong is occurring systemwide."

James Bridle, excerpt from *New Dark Age: Technology and the End of the Future*, 2018

1. Zacharias Kunuk and Ian J. Mauro, *Inuit Knowledge and Climate Change* (Igloolik: Isuma, 2010), documentary, http://www.isuma.tv/inuit-knowledge-and-climate-change/movie.

2. Susan Schuppli, "Can the Sun Lie," in *Forensis: The Architecture of Public Truth*, ed. Forensic Architecture (Berlin: Sternberg Press: 2014): 56–64.

3. Kevin van Paassen, "New Documentary Recounts Bizarre Climate Changes Seen by Inuit Elders," *Globe and Mail* October 19, 2010, theglobeandmail.com.

4. *SpaceWeather.com*, Time Machine, weather forecast, July 2, 2009.

5. Carol Anne Duffy, "Silver Lining," Sheer Poetry, 2010, sheerpoetry.co.uk.

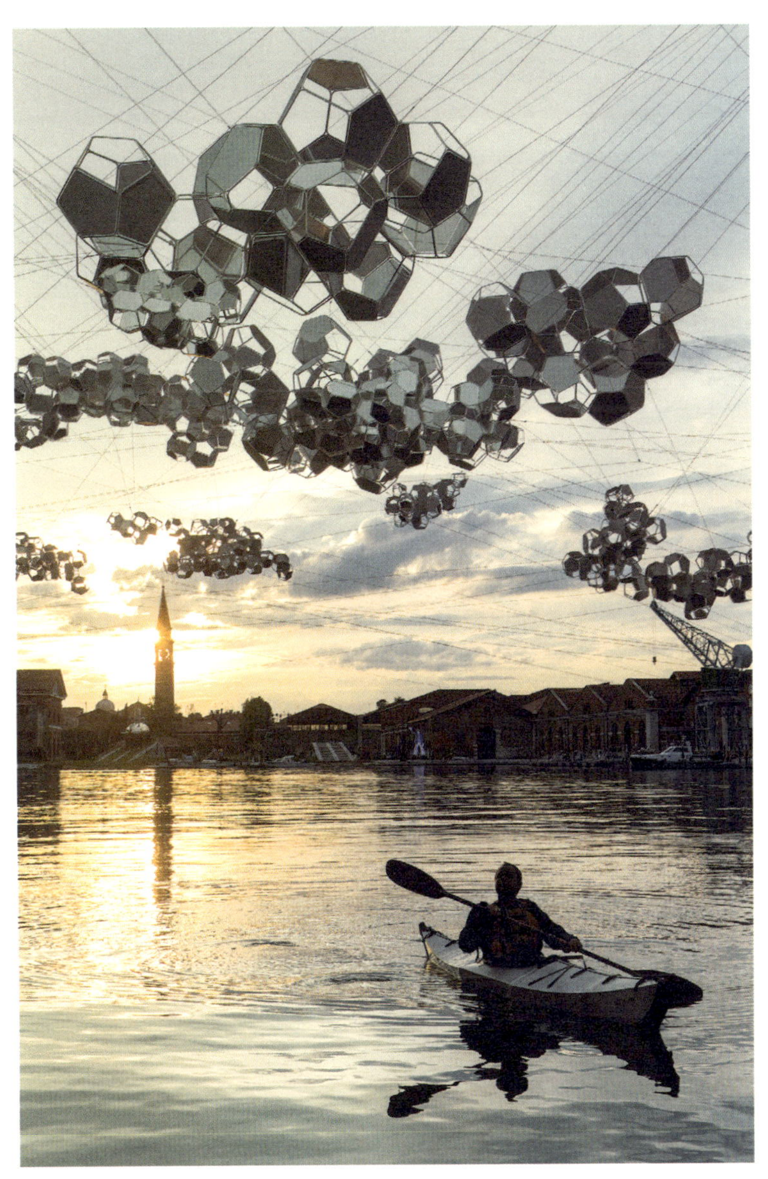

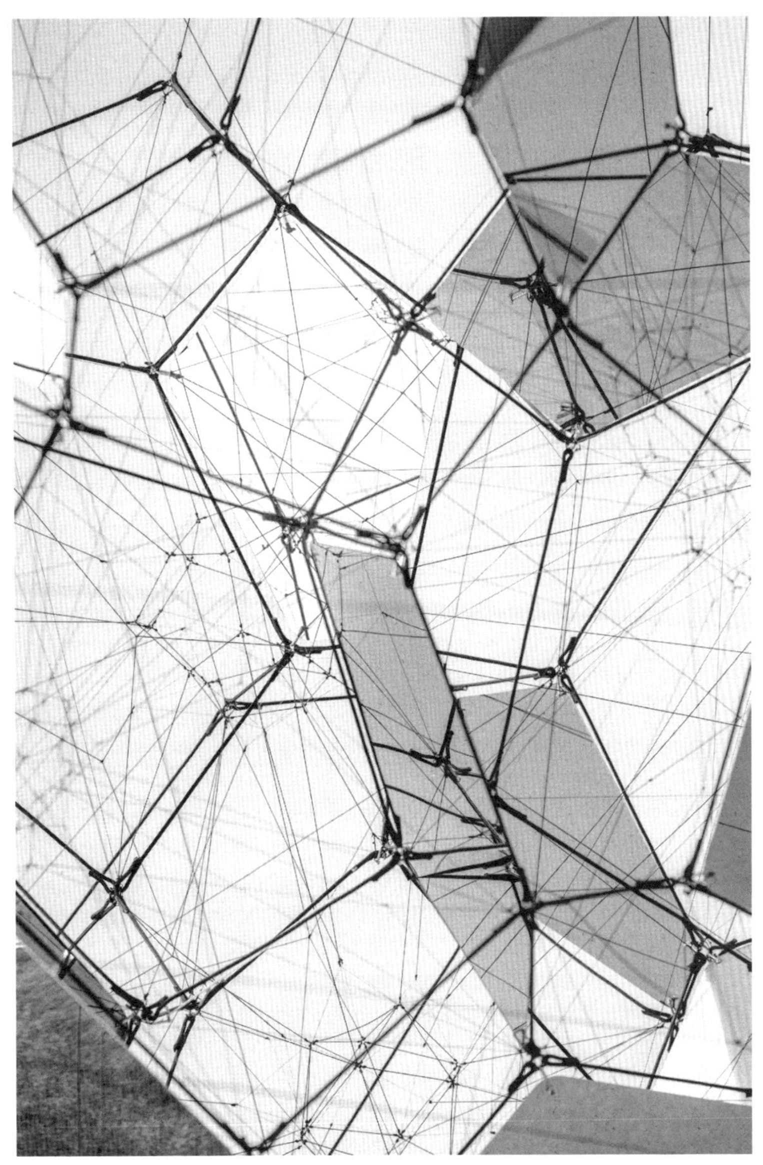

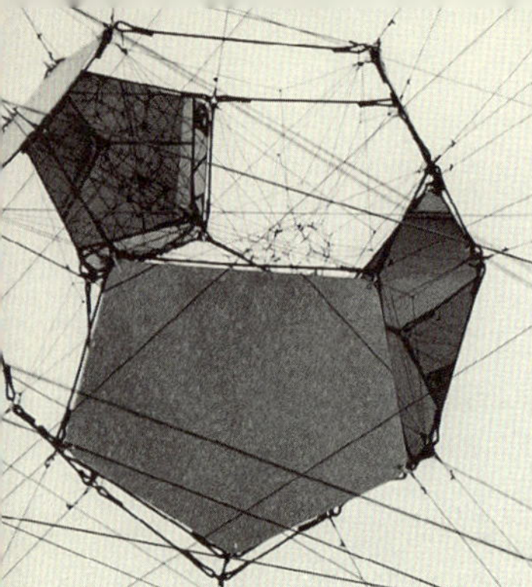

Connectome

Enter an atmosphere filled with complex geometrical systems assembled to form alighted clouds. Irregular structures reminiscent of a Weaire-Phelan structure of foam and soap bubbles whose remarkable shapes act as an invitation to engage from diverse bearings, as mirrored planes trace the sun's rays in a play of light and shadow, where there is neither up nor down anymore, no inside or outside. Composed of habitat-like geometries reminiscent of Saraceno's utopistic Cloud Cities, the installation reveals the elemental properties that, though the very essence of our lives, seem to perpetually recede from view. Sunlight, air, ash, black carbon, organochlorine pesticides, sulfur dioxide—particles that populate what once was simply wind and rain, that throw into question the very fiber of our world.

Held together in mutual tension, the installation bridges the air between spider/web and cosmic web, its structural allusions spanning scales from the micro to the macro. It is a web of reciprocal alliances, where if one thread were to move, the resultant vibration, reverberating across the whole structure, would produce a greater frequency than could be produced by one thread alone. Immersed in an upturned environment, the senses are challenged to reconsider and reflect on what has precedence in the contemporary world and why. Placing viewers in communication with beyond human architectures and modular logics that illustrate the ability of distinct *Umwelten* to coexist, this installation offers visitors a chance to picture themselves in a harmonious universe— through the activation of their bodies in space as well as their very literal reflections in the mirrored panels.

These reflective planes may catch glimpses of a society collectively able to break off from an extractive rapport with the earth, a meditation on a future in which alternatives to travel without the use of noisy, gas sputtering engines become not only possible, but the standard. Floating pacifically above our heads, these intricate systems of interwoven ropes stretching from land to sky, restore attention towards the ocean of air in which we all live.

Connectome
2020
Metal, polyester rope, nylon rope, mirror panels, monofilament
Various dimensions

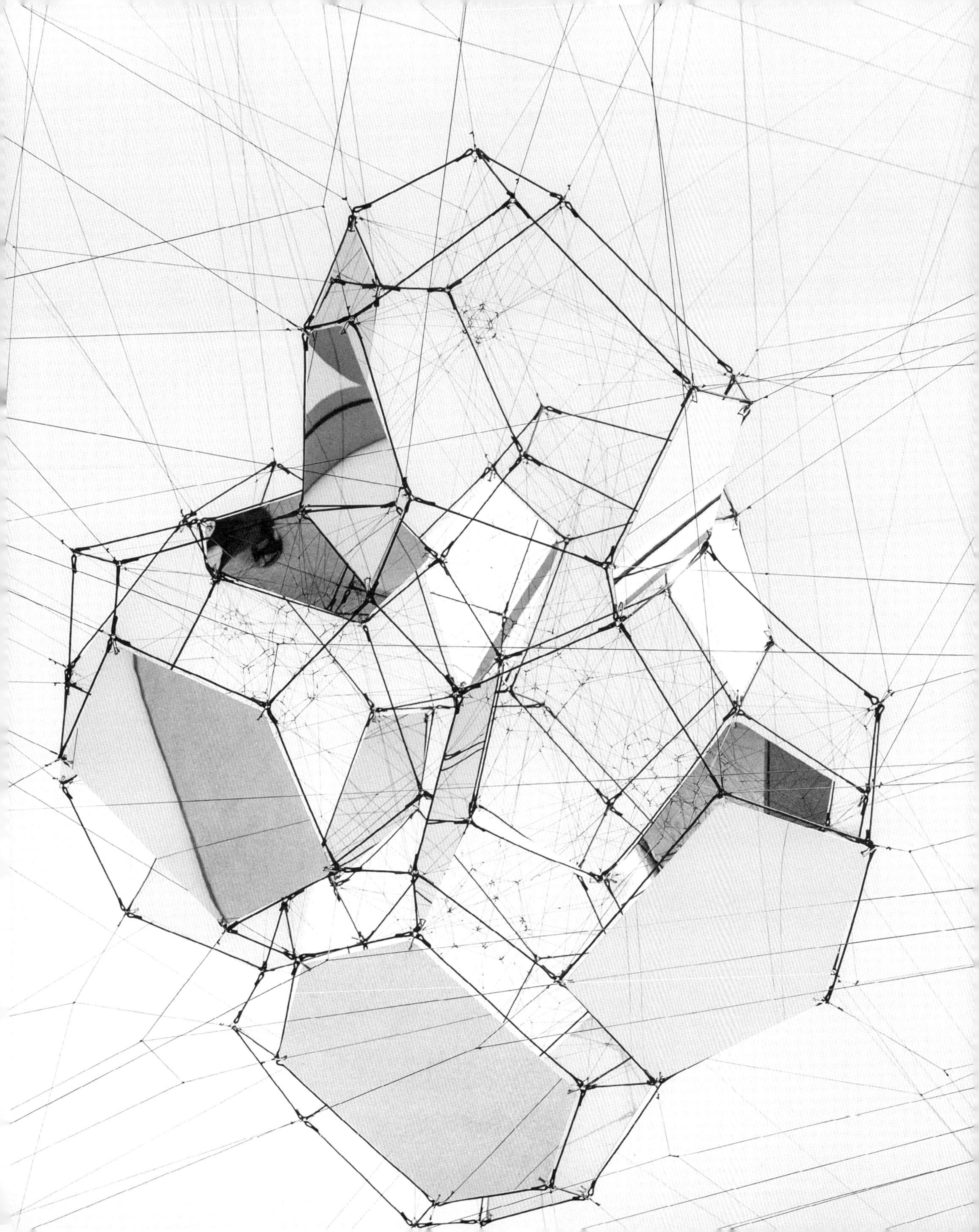

ROOM II

Fluttering leaves, branches flexing east
if Levant is blowing. If it is a light
breeze, enjoy the swing,
if it is Near Gale, be centered and still,
but if the storm is coming, be ready to leave.
Release a thread to ask the wind.

Suit: Ballooning Spider/Web
Species: Pardosa lugubris
Notation: F#
Plant: Typha angustifolia

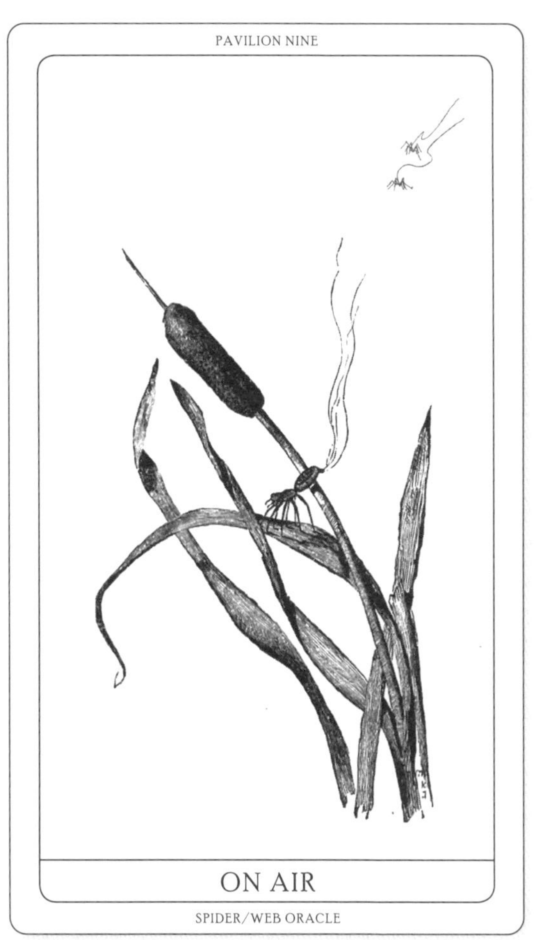

PAVILION NINE
ON AIR
SPIDER/WEB ORACLE

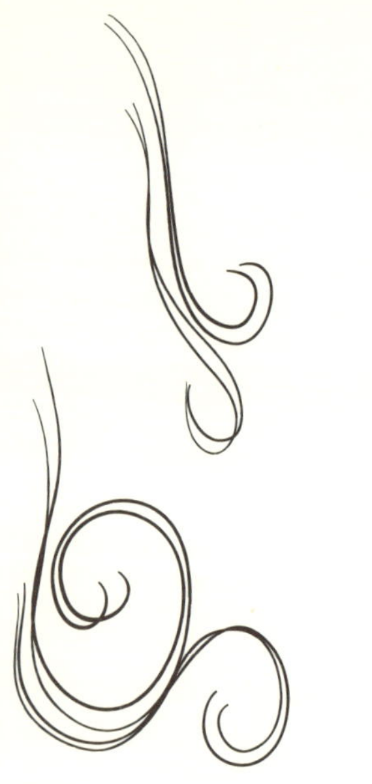

Soft and softlier hold me, friends!
  Thanks if your genial care
Unbind and give me to the air.
  Keep your lips or fingertips
    For flute or spinet's dancing chips;
     I await a tenderer touch,
      I ask more or not so much:

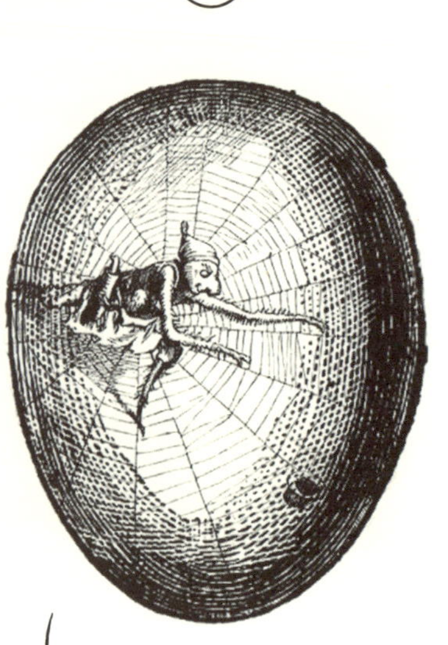

       Give me to the atmosphere—
       Where is the wind, my brother—where?
      Lift the sash, lay me within,
      Lend me your ears, and I begin.
       For gentle harp to gentle hearts
       The secret of the world imparts;
      And not today and not tomorrow
      Can drain its wealth of hope and sorrow;
     But day by day, to loving ear
     Unlocks new sense and loftier cheer.

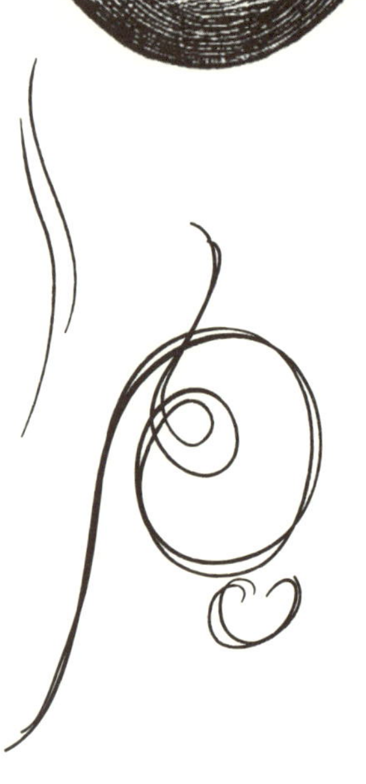

    I've come to live with you, sweet friends,
    This home my minstrel-journeyings ends.
   Many and subtle are my lays,
  The latest better than the first,
For I can mend the happiest days
And charm the anguish of the worst.

Ralph Waldo Emerson, *Maiden Speech of the Aeolian Harp*, 1868

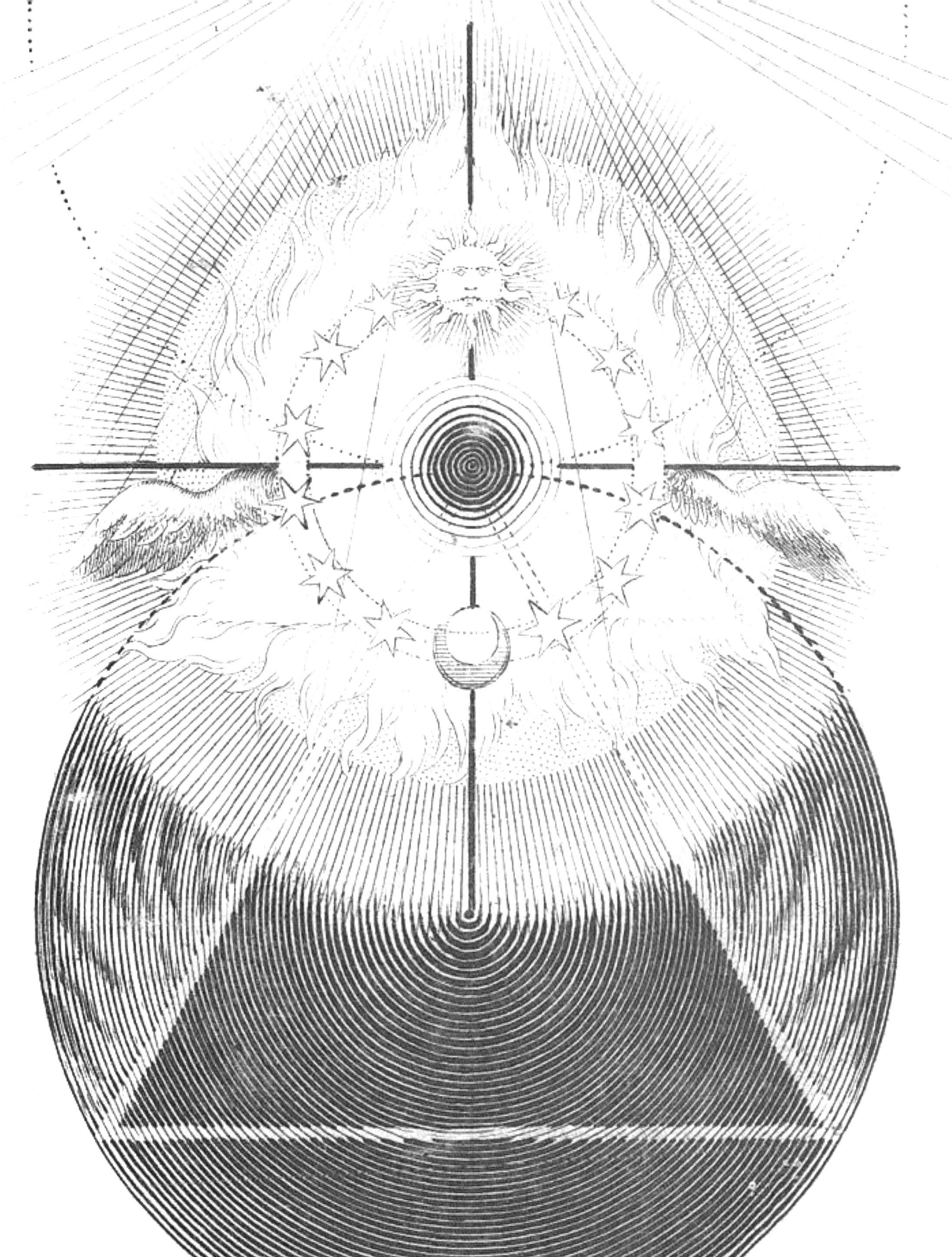

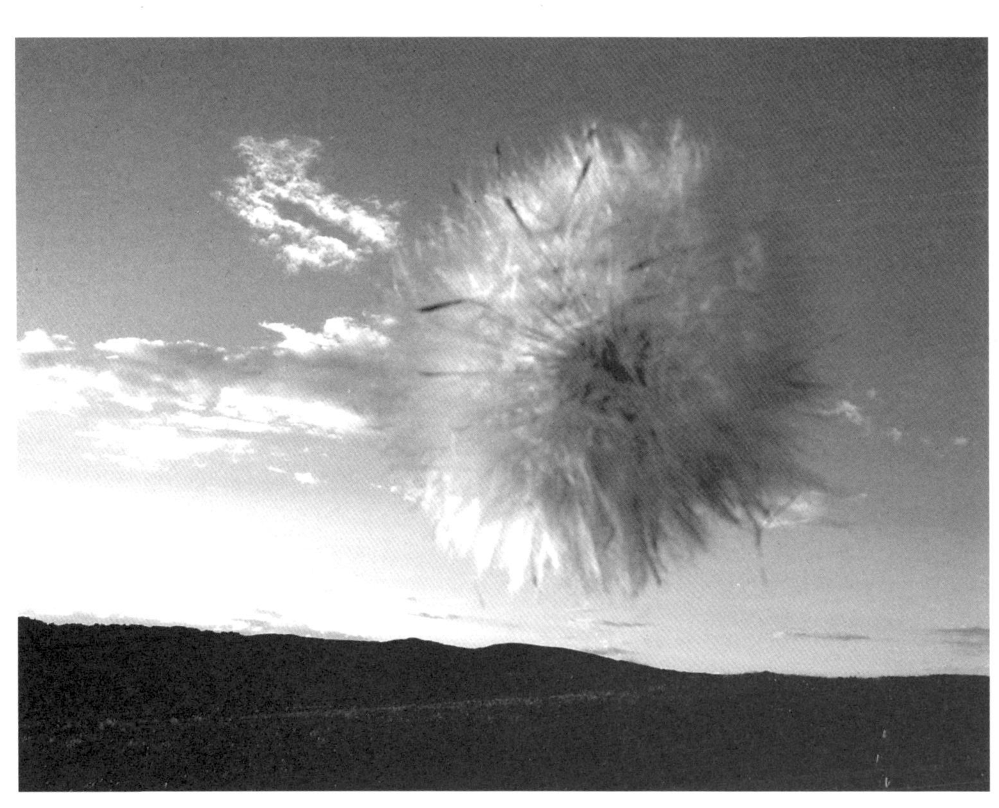

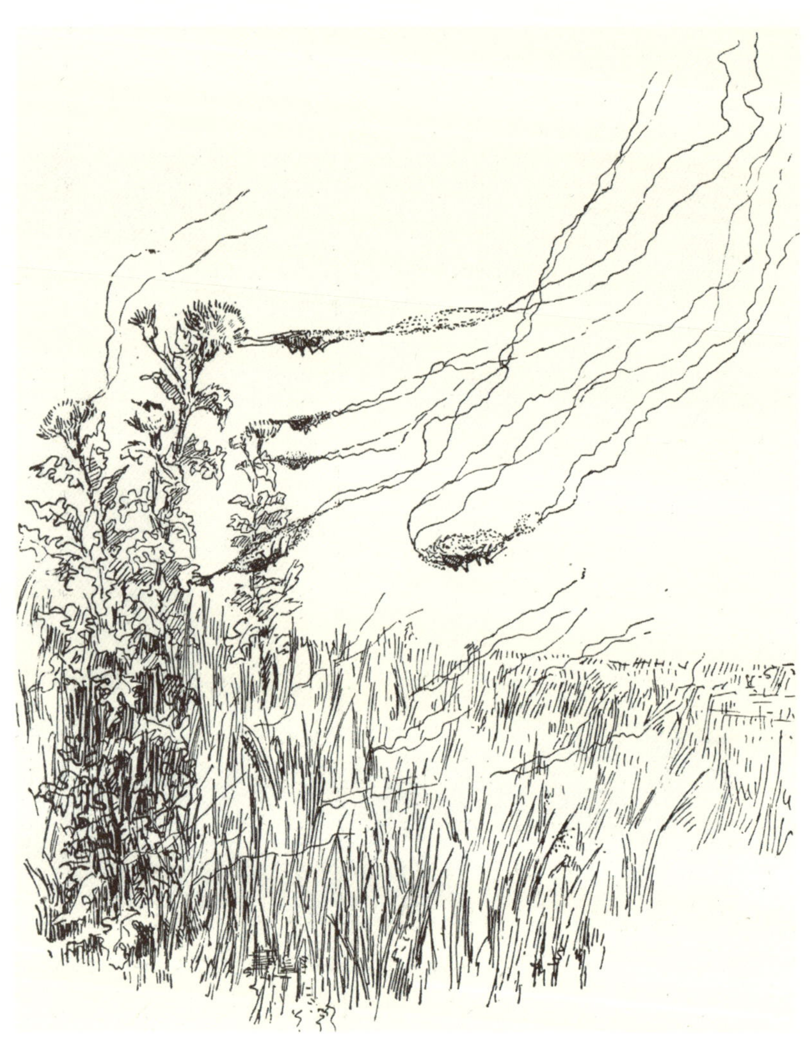

Beyond the boundary layer, thousands of feet into the troposphere, it's likely that only a small proportion of these animals—those without wings (such as spiders and mites), those that become too cold, and those suffering from exhaustion—are passively carried. From the tiniest to the largest, migrating insects are out there actively flying, flapping their wings, maintaining or varying their altitude and direction despite the strength of the winds around them. Sometimes they hover, sometimes they glide, sometimes they free-fall, sometimes they soar. They do what they can to evade birds in the daytime and bats at night. Rarely do they drift along like pollen in a breeze. Or plankton in the ocean.

No, aerial plankton is not a good name for these animals. They don't live in this medium; they occupy it temporarily. And their residency is full of calculation and action. Their exodus is triggered by the impulse to find new habitats and to encounter new hosts. Sometimes their flights are short, repeated dispersals; sometimes they are vast migrations from which the traveler may or may not return. In either case, there is little passivity. Takeoff is oriented to wind and light. If the animal is strong enough, flight is often against or across the wind. Butterflies and locusts streaming in formation may suddenly interrupt a low-level journey with a dramatic collective rise to catch a current at thousands of feet. Even tiny insects appear to seek out thermal drafts. In the upper reaches of the air column, the minute ones take paths strongly determined by the wind, but inside the airstream they hold steady, beating their wings, adjusting their direction and altitude. And then they alight, often prompted by scent or reflecting light, using their bodies to bring themselves to earth.

Forty years ago, Cecil Johnson, the author of a classic text on insect migration and dispersal, pointed out that many, perhaps most, individual insects die on these voyages, but "this is the price such species pay for finding their habitats."

Johnson conjured an image of a planet under surveillance, "the surface of the earth is thus scanned very effectively as millions of individuals, flying on air currents, continuously encounter suitable and unsuitable situations." When the situation does not suit, they soon take off again in search of a better location for feeding or breeding (or some other activity obscure to us), following "a direction determined either by the wind or themselves." It is a fact of planetary life, a great "diffusion system" that transports immense populations of animals "day after day, year after year, century after century." What happens to the notion of an invasive species in the face of this continuous and irrepressible traffic of short- and long-range travel, dispersal, and migration? What is left of a notion that everything has its own place, that everything belongs somewhere and nowhere else, that boundaries are inviolable, that with vigilance and chemicals this hyperabundance of willful and random life can be brought under control? Perhaps this was what Glick glimpsed three thousand feet above Durango, face-to-face with the pink bollworm moth, its flapping wings gleaming in the high-altitude sunshine.

Stop. If you're inside, go to a window. Throw it open and turn your face to the sky. All that empty space, the deep vastness of the air, the heavens wide above you. The sky is full of insects, and all of them are going somewhere. Every day, above and around us, the collective voyage of billions of beings.

That's the letter A: the first thing not to forget. There are other worlds around us. Too often, we pass through them unknowing, seeing but blind, hearing but deaf, touching but not feeling, contained by the limits of our senses, the banality of our imaginations, our Ptolemaic certitudes.

Hugh Raffles, excerpt from "Air," in *Insectopedia*, 2010

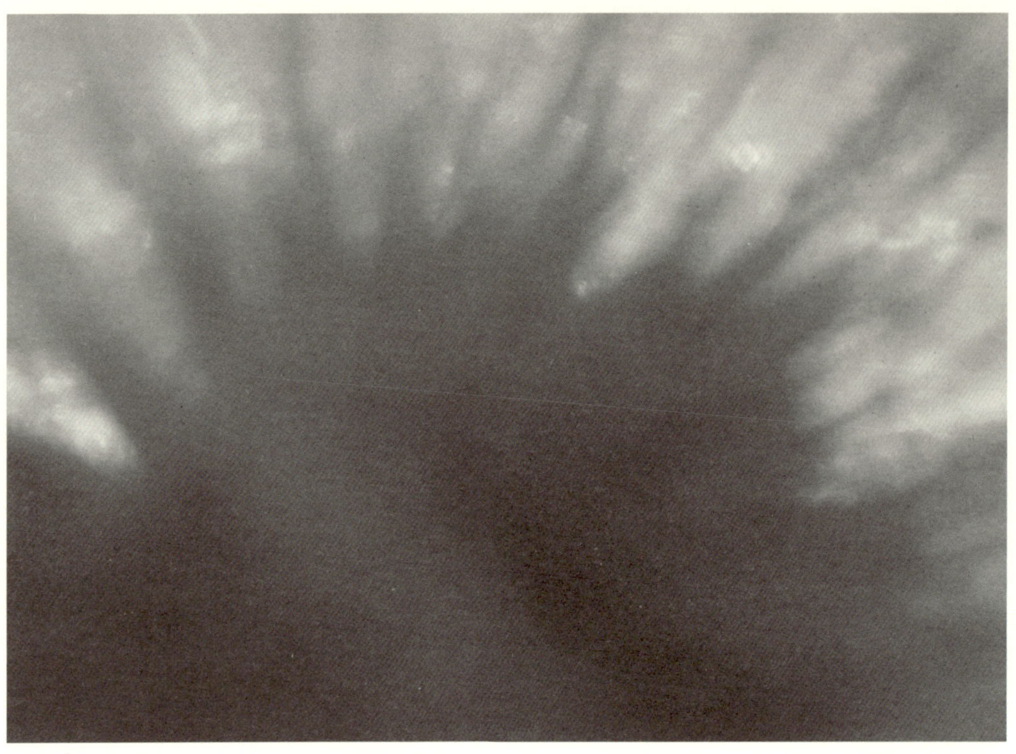

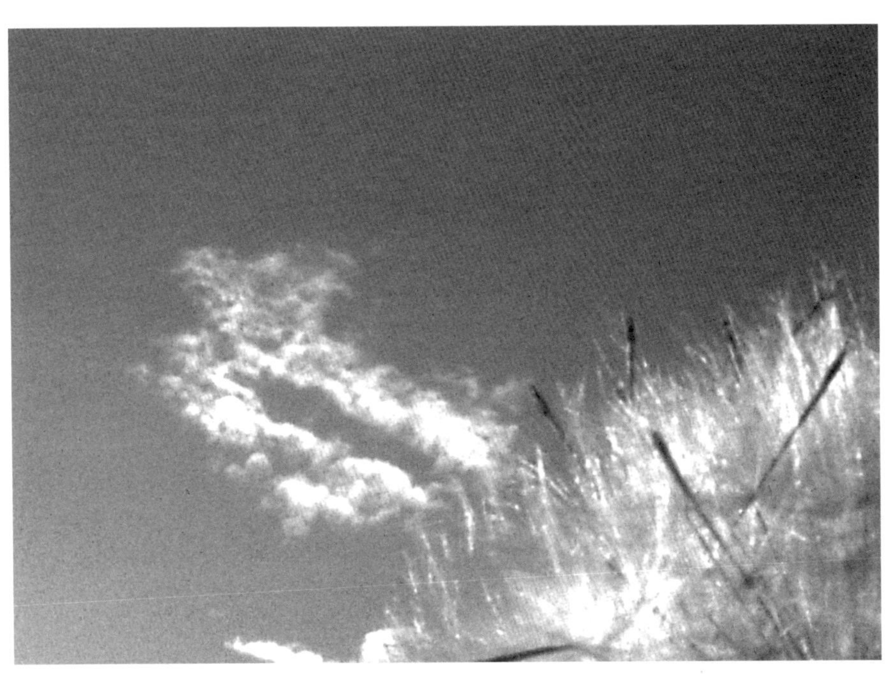

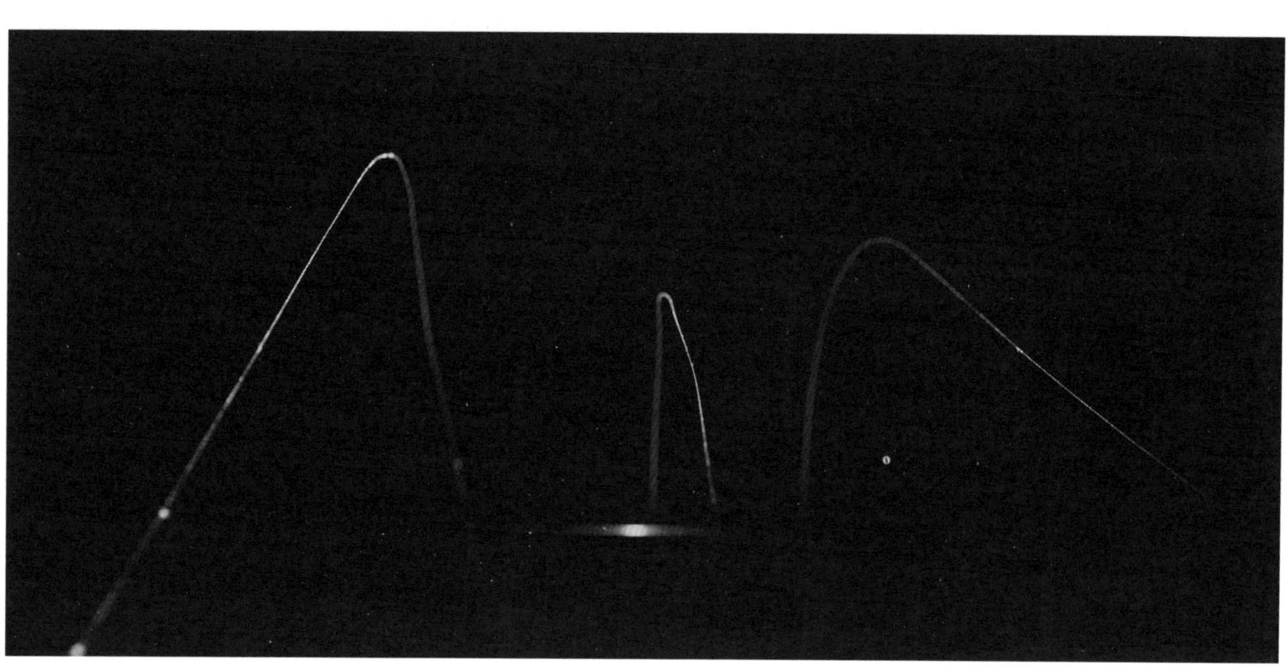

Sounding the Air

Sounding the Air is an aeolian instrument, a musical instrument that is "played" with the wind. Its sound
is produced by five threads of spider silk that drift and resonate with the air. Real-time video captures the
gestures of these "strings," translating them into sonic frequencies and patterns.
The work thus constitutes a collective creation improvised by an ensemble of forces and bodies: the radiant
heat of human bodies, or the flurries and tremors created by the flux and breath of participants, but also
the endless intra-actions of different aerial elements—dust, silk, heat, wind, spiders and electrostatic forces.
Together they create a cascade of influences that transform the rhythms of the fluctuating silk threads.
In this immersive sonic environment, every subtle movement alters the compositional whole. Thrown into
this acoustic dialogue, each of us becomes musicians in an atmospheric jam, collectively inventing an improvised score.
Sounding the Air draws inspiration from the phenomenon of spider "ballooning," a behavior in which some
spiders use airborne dispersal to move between locations. They release several silk threads into the air
which carry them away on updrafts of wind. Individuals or colonies are able to travel long distances on
those aerial kites of gossamer silk, buoyed by thermal updrafts and electrostatic force. Those flights allow
us to speculate about the possibility of a collective aerial flight and of interspecies attunement and collaboration with the forces of the atmosphere.

Sounding the Air
2020
Spider silk, carbon fiber, microphone, transducer, speakers, lights, computer, camera

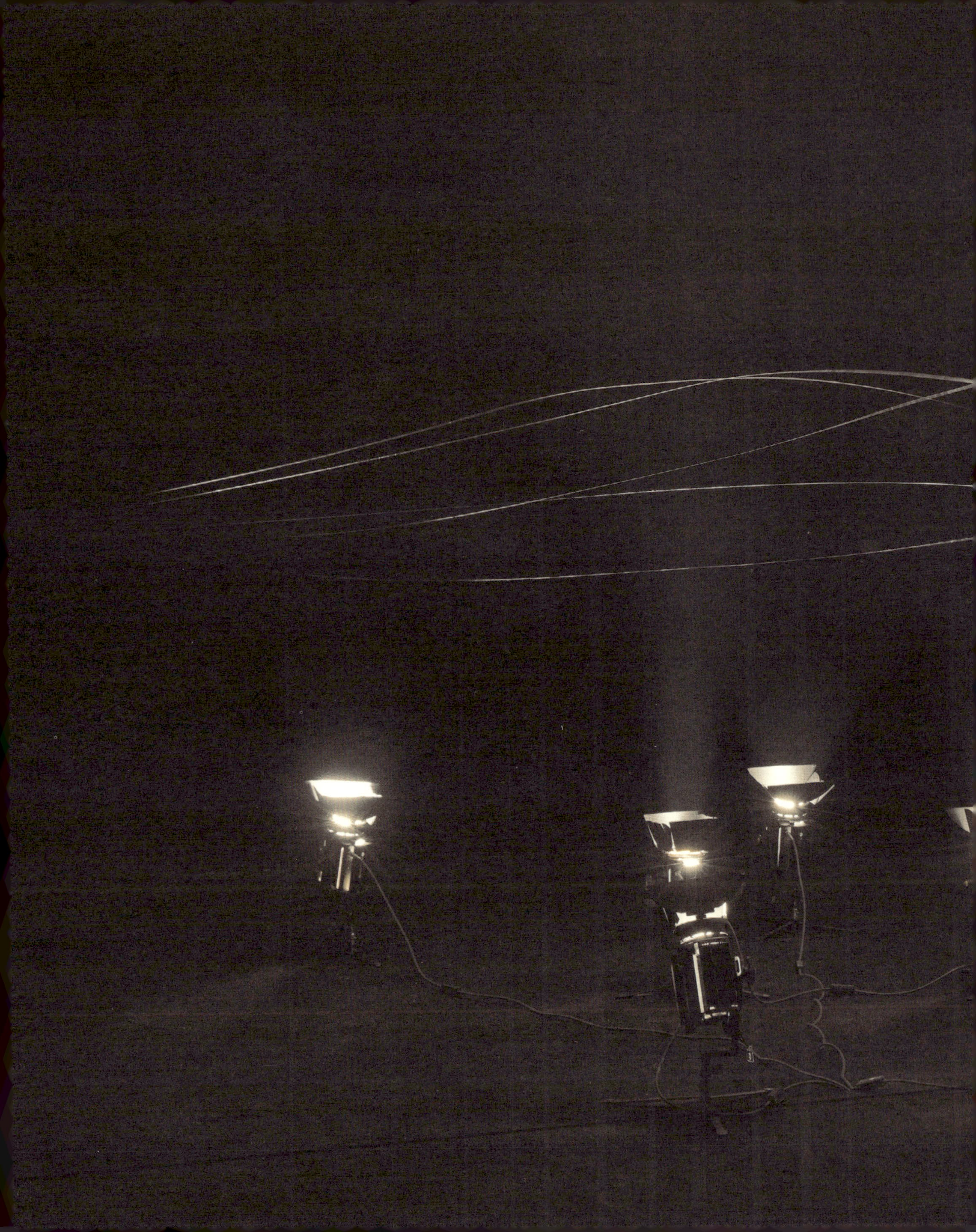

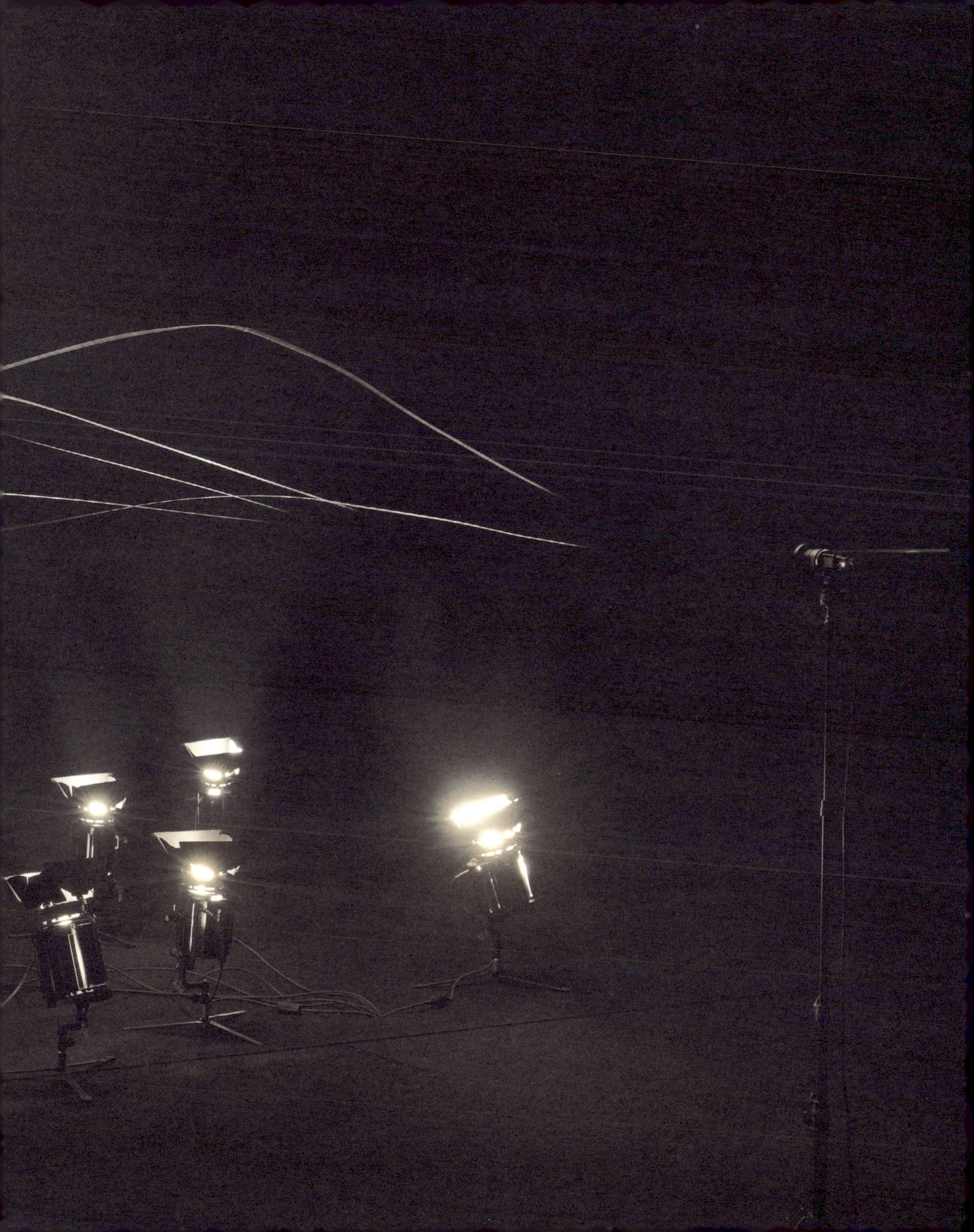

ROOM III

What you see is my mind, my body.
I cannot eat until I weave
the mouth that feeds me.
These threads belie the geometries of extinction,
telling stories against extraction,
mind the stories you are spelling out
in your trajectories.

Suit: Communal Orb Spider/Webs
Species: Parawixia bistriata
Notation: G#

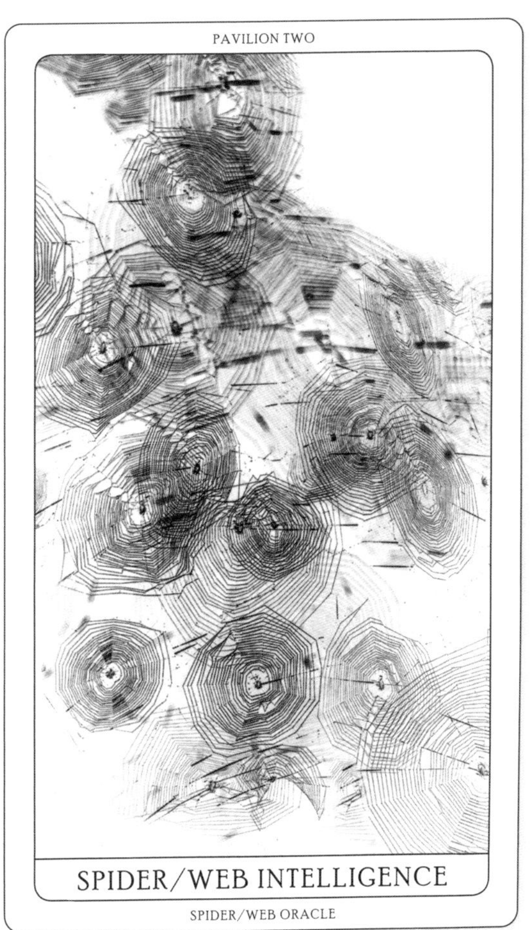

PAVILION TWO
SPIDER/WEB INTELLIGENCE
SPIDER/WEB ORACLE

I couldn't have been born in
any city but this one, a great
European capital filled with beautiful,
highly detailed architecture, a castle
overlooking the river, the city a spread
of gilded and copper garlic-like
domes, gargoyles, steeples, trains,
lampposts resembling moons
entrapped by black vines, skylights
like dew on buildings, factories,
workshops, cabarets, a forest of iron,
stone, glass. I certainly can't imagine
myself existing in an American or
Siberian village, a desert, a valley.
I have only seen such places in books,
I have never left the city in which I was
born. I'm given many invitations to
visit villas in foreign countries, castles,
the seaside, but I worry I would
disappear as soon as I stepped out
of this city, like a cloud of smog.

I feel part wrought iron, part human and, I won't lie, part vermin.

I have eight legs, and the upper body of a normal man. Black hair, elegant nose and melancholy green eyes, a good set of fake teeth made out of elephants' tusks—I had my real ones removed, like so many gentlemen of my city, so I could enjoy rich food and drink without continual visits to a dentist. I had my fake ones designed to be sharper than my originals, more fang-like. The style has been emulated by many men, young and old.

I bring to mind a spider, an umbrella, a marionette. The way I move I resemble a large hand with a few extra fingers. I only have one set of genitals—thank goodness! The delicacy and sensation of having a pair between each leg would be unbearable.

The spaces between my other legs resemble armpits, but slightly firmer. They are hairy. I have the hair removed with wax, so there will be less ambiguity when viewing my naked form. I take great care of my feet, each nail covered in clear, shiny polish, each sole dipped in scented powder.

My anus is directly underneath me, my buttocks a circle in the center of my legs, much like a lavatory on which my torso permanently sits. A chamber pot is much easier for me to use than a modern toilet, and the cafés I patronize regularly provide me with one. Afterwards, I wipe myself with a wet cloth.

I take great care with my appearance. I have suits especially made to fit the proportions of my body, though some, including my doctor, have suggested it would be more comfortable for me to wear a gown. I never wear unmatching shoes, though some people would imagine I would want to, in order to show off my vast collection of footwear. I buy four pairs of each shoe I desire, and wear them all at once. I could be a stone arabesque that crawled off a building, or a complex contraption belonging to a barber, a photographer or a mathematician. I could be one of many things that exist in the modern city, I play various roles in many fantasies.

It's impossible to imagine my parents, I believe I simply rose out of the city, out of a steamy grate, like Venus out of the ocean. There are many men in the city, deformed by the guns and cannons of the last war, who have only one or two limbs left, or none at all—in a sense they are my fathers. If there is nothing shocking about a man with one limb, what is so shocking about a man with eight?[1]

A soldier with one arm and no other limbs lives on a small wooden wagon outside the metro near my apartments. I always gave him coins until one day he asked if he could have two of my legs instead. He laughed, but his eyes looked so envious, so hungry, that I never stopped to give him anything again. I scurried away on my infinitely precious eight feet, an abundance of flesh.

From what I was told, I was left on a church doorstep,

like a gargoyle that had fallen from its façade. I was brought to an orphanage, but I was too exceptional to stay in an orphanage long, news spread of me quickly. A handful of kind, curious patrons hired a nanny to raise me, tutors to educate me, a doctor to watch my health carefully. I was a particular favorite among wealthy women. No one person possessed me, I was considered a child of the city.

[...]

How I love cockroaches, lice, fleas, pigeons, moths, rats, mice, spiders, sparrows and of course, *Cimex lectularius*. It is thanks to me such dwellers in this city have a safe haven. Using my vast funds, I created a zoo where a selection of so-called vermin can exist in fascinating proliferation, in a closed-off area of the city, where glass tunnels have been built so that human citizens may walk through unmolested and unbitten. Visitors bring them rotten meat, stale bread, old clothes and bedding. Some find

1   This is not the only time in the story Grudova suggests that modernity is what gives birth to this kind of human-critter hybrid, though only modernity once it has been taken to its most extreme conclusions, a kind of accelerationist doctrine on extra-human relations. Anna Tsing similarly discusses the relationship between modern acceleration and the emergence of "feral landscapes," which she writes, "replace not just the last wilderness areas but also the last peasant ecologies, with their comparatively long-term accommodations between humans and nonhumans." Anna Tsing, "The Buck, the Bull, and the Dream of the Stag: Some Unexpected Weeds of the Anthropocene," *Suomen Antropologi*, vol. 42, no. 1 (Spring 2017): 9.

it relaxing, even addictive, to watch the creatures propagate, consume, die, to see them exist in a space where they can do each without restraint, without poison, brooms, traps, felines and dogs.

From a distance, my zoo resembles a great gallery or train station. It has many glass roofs, and grand pediments with friezes depicting rodents and insects. At the entrance, there is a bronze statue of me, a rat in one hand, a moth in the other.

I love the moth house, for those creatures consume everything. The moths were enclosed in a structure resembling a greenhouse. Every morning a man who wears an outfit similar to a beekeeper's opens one of the glass panels and throws in a bag of stale bread and a pile of coats. In such profusion, the swarms of moths resemble swathes of brown fabric or vicious and strange tropical trees which sway to an unknown breeze.

Inside the rat house is a model in miniature of our city, the very same buildings and streets, so that one may watch the rats, so manlike with their hands and whiskers, go about their business of breeding, eating and digesting.

The cockroaches and mice keep themselves hidden under old mattresses and couches. If one taps the glass of their cage with a cane or a fist, they move from one hiding place to another, storms of brown and grey. I always bring along a pair of opera glasses, to view the fleas and bed bugs.

The spider house is quiet. It has so many webs it resembles an arctic landscape in its whiteness.

It is still except for the morning feeding, when flies and other small creatures are sacrificed. There is a great difference to me between a spider that needs blood, and so must kill, and the unnecessary crushing of spiders, simply because we do not like the sight of their webs in our windowsills.[2] The spinning of webs in the zoo is barely perceptible to the viewer, but the spiders communicate with each other by playing their webs like string instruments, a harmonious music you can hear when all else is silent.[3] They are common household spiders, from the windowsills and corners of my city. Some auspicious women visit the zoo specifically for the spiders, almost praying to them, telling them their secrets and their ailments, as if their words will be absorbed into the webs.[4] I heard that some younger women bring, hidden in precious boxes, the pulp of their menstruation to give to the spiders, believing that doing so will bring them love, marriage, children, and even death. The zookeeper has shown me such boxes, like the ones rings are held in, but stained with blood. He keeps them in his office, after dropping the blood clots into the spiders' home.

Camilla Grudova, excerpt from "Notes from a Spider," in *The Doll's Alphabet*, 2017

2 A beautiful reminder that we cannot impose human value systems onto nonhuman creatures—and that even if we do, we are the ones that will often be found wanting.

3 A question I've been exploring: How quiet must you be to hear the spider's voice?

4 We can see in the history of many animistic and esoteric practices an elevation of the nonhuman—and the spider, specifically—to a level of almost divine wisdom—for example, the spider oracles of various cultures, including the Mambila people of Cameroon and Nigeria. Such trust derives from the spider ability to perceive abiotic and biotic tremors and vibrations that we cannot; living in a world of vibration, they are tapped into knowledge unavailable to human senses.

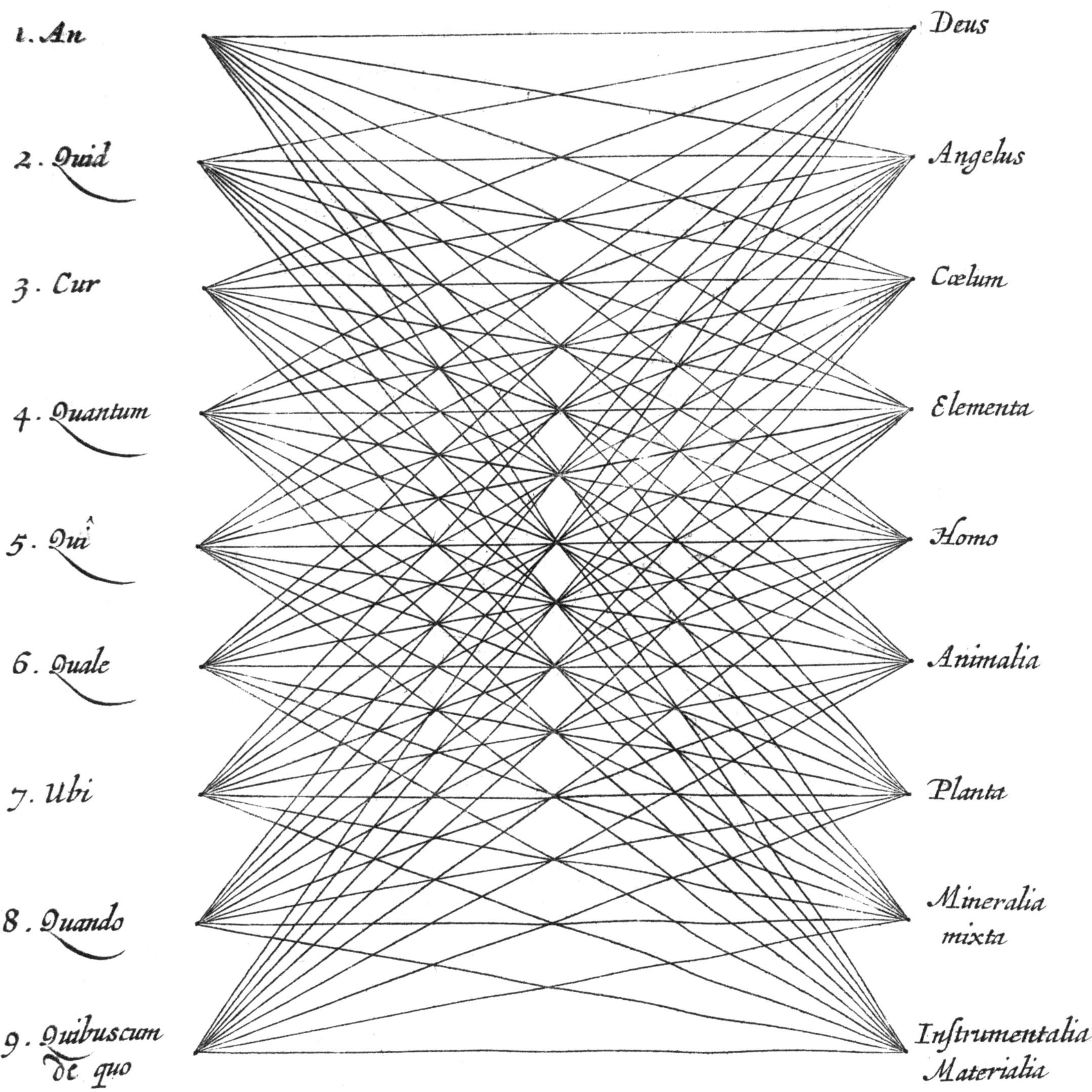

1. An
2. Quid
3. Cur
4. Quantum
5. Qui
6. Quale
7. Ubi
8. Quando
9. Quibuscum de quo
Deus
Angelus
Cælum
Elementa
Homo
Animalia
Planta
Mineralia mixta
Instrumentalia Materialia

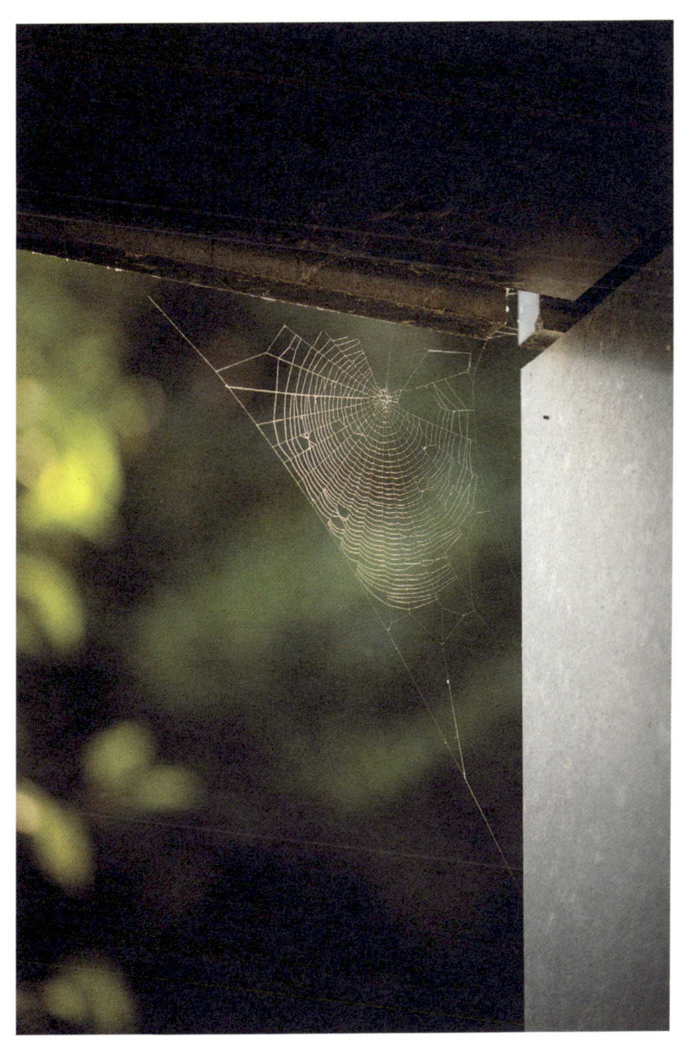

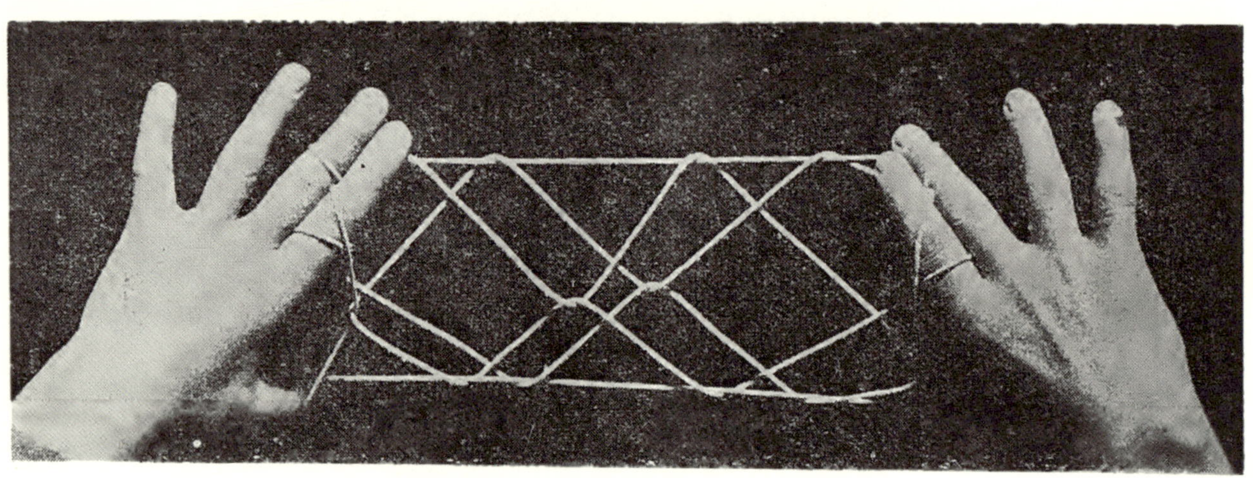

Reclaiming means recovering what we have been separated from, but not in the sense that we can just get it back. Recovering means recovering from the very separation itself, regenerating what this separation has poisoned. The need to struggle and the need to heal, in order to avoid resembling those we have to struggle against, are thus irreducibly allied. A poisoned milieu must be reclaimed, and so must many of our words, those that—like "animism" and "magic"—carry with them the power to take us hostage: do you "really" believe in. . .?

[. . .]

It may be better to revive more compromised words, which have been restricted to metaphoric use only. "Magic" is such a word, as we freely speak of the magic of an event, of a landscape, of a musical moment. Protected by the metaphor, we may then express the experience of an agency that does not belong to us even if it includes us, but an "us" as it is lured into feeling.

I would propose that we need to forfeit this protection in order to relieve ourselves of the sad, monotonous little critical or reflexive voice whispering that we should not accept being mystified, a voice that relays that of the inquisitors. This voice may tell us about the frightening possibilities that would follow if we gave up critique, the only defense we have against fanaticism and the rule of illusions. But it is first of all the voice of the epic story that still inhabits us. "Thou shall not regress!" We would admit many daring propositions as long as—like Breton's—they reflect a version of the epic, as long as they warrant that only selected types (artists, philosophers, and so forth) are authorized to explore what mystifies others.

Magic undercuts any such version of the epic. And this is precisely why neo-pagan witches call their own craft "magic": naming it so, they say, is itself an act of magic, since the discomfort it creates helps us notice the smoke in our nostrils. Worse, they have learned to cast circles and invoke the Goddess—she who, the witches say, "returns," she to whom thanks will be given for the event that makes them capable of doing what they call "the work of the Goddess."

In so doing, they put us to the test! How can we accept regression, or conversion to supernatural beliefs? The point, however, is not to wonder whether we have to "accept" the Goddess that contemporary witches invoke in their rituals. If we said to them, "But your Goddess is only a fiction," they would doubtless smile and ask us whether we are among those who believe that fiction is powerless. What the witches challenge us to accept is the possibility of giving up criteria that claim to transcend assemblages, and that reinforce, again and again, the epic of critical reason. What they cultivate, as part of their craft (it is a part of any craft), is an art of immanent attention, an empirical art about what is good or toxic—an art which our addiction to the truth has too often despised as superstition. They are pragmatic, radically pragmatic, experimenting with effects and consequences of what, as they know, is never innocuous and involves care, protections, and experience.

The witches' ritual chant—"She changes everything she touches, and everything she touches changes"—could surely be commented on in terms of assemblages, since it resists the dismembering attribution of agency. Does change belong to the Goddess as "agent" or to the one who changes when touched? But the first efficacy of the refrain is in the "she touches." The indeterminacy proper to assemblages is no longer conceptual. It is part of an experience that affirms the power of changing to be NOT attributed to our own selves nor reduced to something "natural." It is an experience that honors change as a creation. [. . .]

A rhizome rejects any generality. Connections do not manifest some truth about what is common beyond the rhizomatic heterogeneous multiplicity—beyond the multiplicity of distinct pragmatic significations associated with "magic" as related to what we call politics, healing, education, arts, philosophy, sciences, agriculture, or to any craft requiring or depending upon a capacity to lure us into relevant metamorphic attention. The only generality here is about our milieu and its compulsion to categorize and judge—and spiritualism is here a probable judgment— or to negate whatever would point to the metamorphic dimension of what is to be achieved. Rhizomatic connections may be a non-general answer to this generality. Each "magic" craft needs connections with others in order to resist infection by the milieu, the divisive power of social judgment, to smell the smoke that demands we decide whether we are heirs to the witches or the witch hunters.

But connections may also be needed to heal and to learn. Where the dangerous art of animating in order to be animated is concerned, what connects may be practical learning about the needed immanent (critical) attention. Not about what is good or bad in itself, but about what Whitehead called "realization." Again, no mode of realization may be taken as a model, only as calling for pragmatic reinvention. In order to honor the making of connections, to protect it against models and norms, a name may be required. Animism could be the name for this rhizomatic art.

Reclaiming animism does not mean, then, that we have ever been animist. Nobody has ever been animist because one is never animist "in general," only in terms of assemblages that generate metamorphic transformation in our capacity to affect and be affected—and also to feel, think, and imagine. Animism may, however, be a name for reclaiming these assemblages, since it lures us into feeling that their efficacy is not ours to claim. Against the insistent poisoned passion of dismembering and demystifying, it affirms that which they all require in order not to enslave us: that we are not alone in the world.

Isabelle Stengers, excerpt from "Reclaiming Animism," *e-flux Journal*, 2012

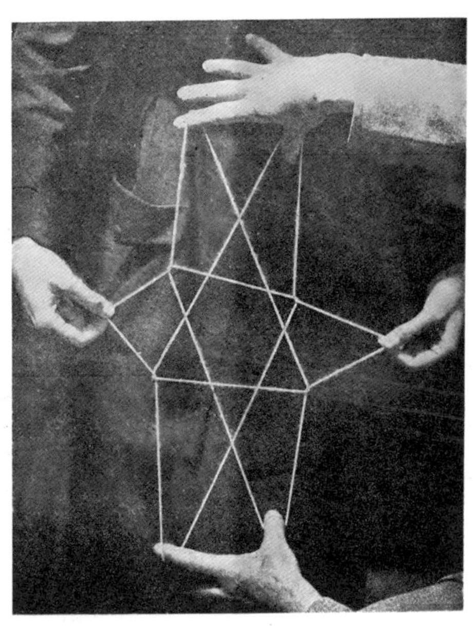

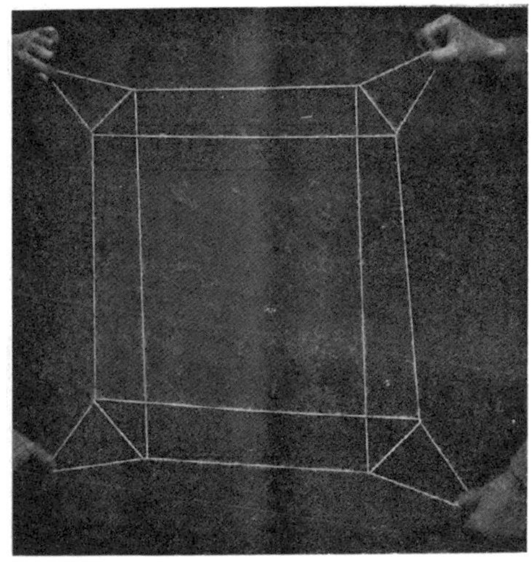

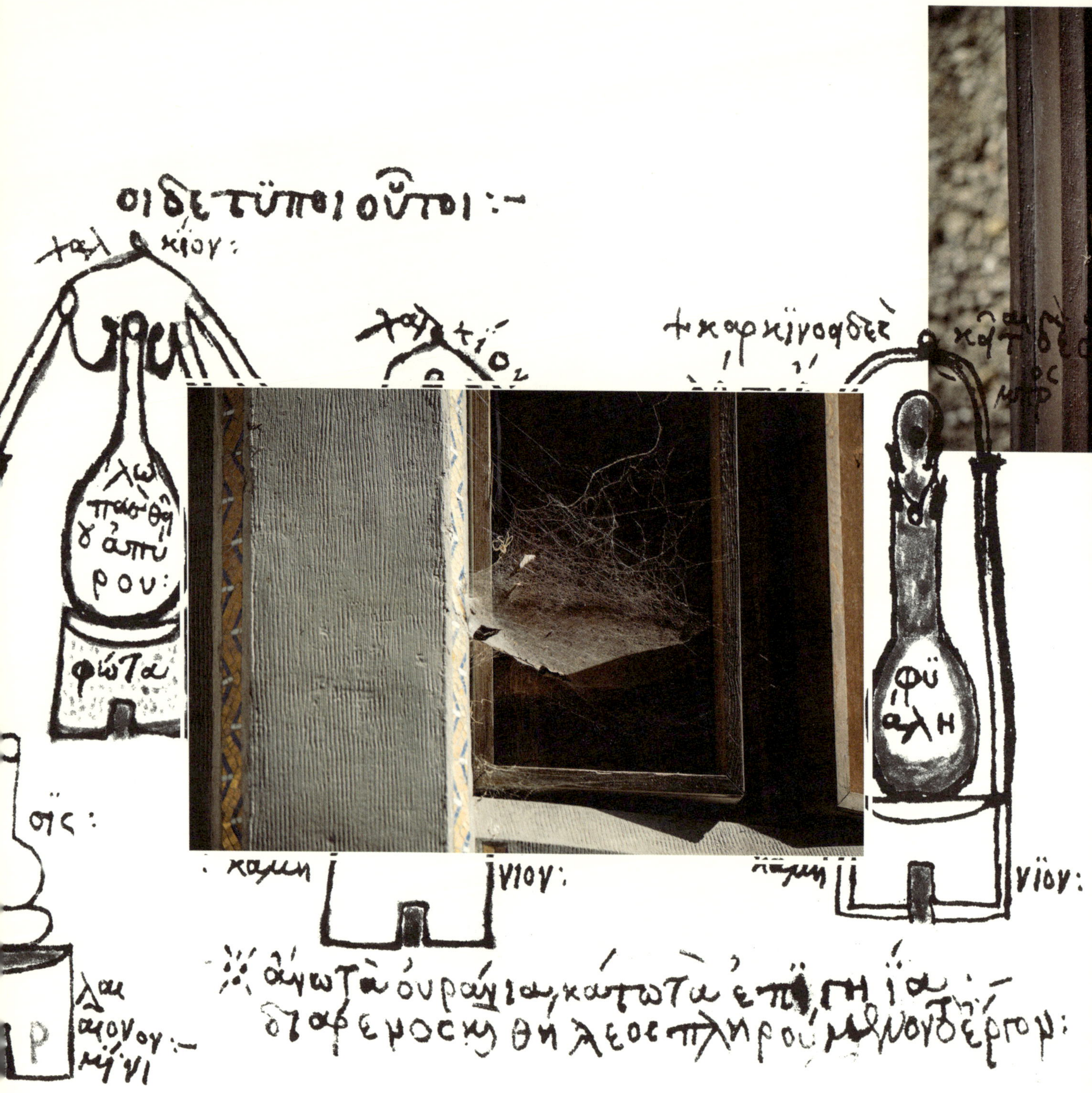
ΟΙ ΔΕ ΤΥΠΟΙ ΟΥΤΟΙ:–
κιου:
χαλκιου
καρκινοςδε
φωτα
φϊαλη
κομη
υιον:
κομη
υιον:
ανωτα ουρανια, κατω τα επι γη ια
διαφερος

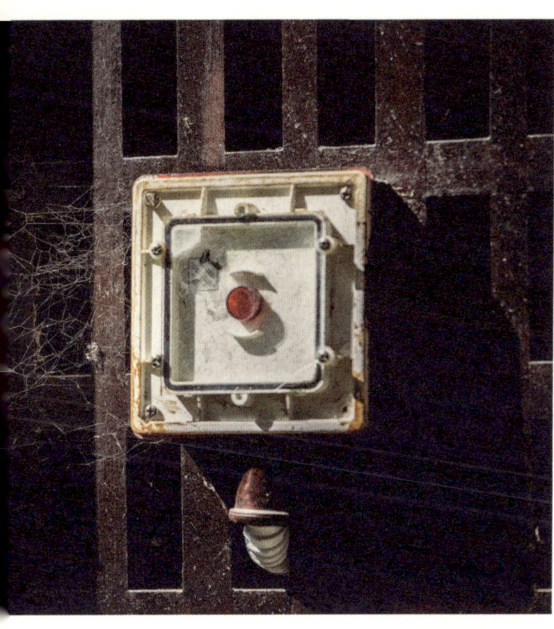

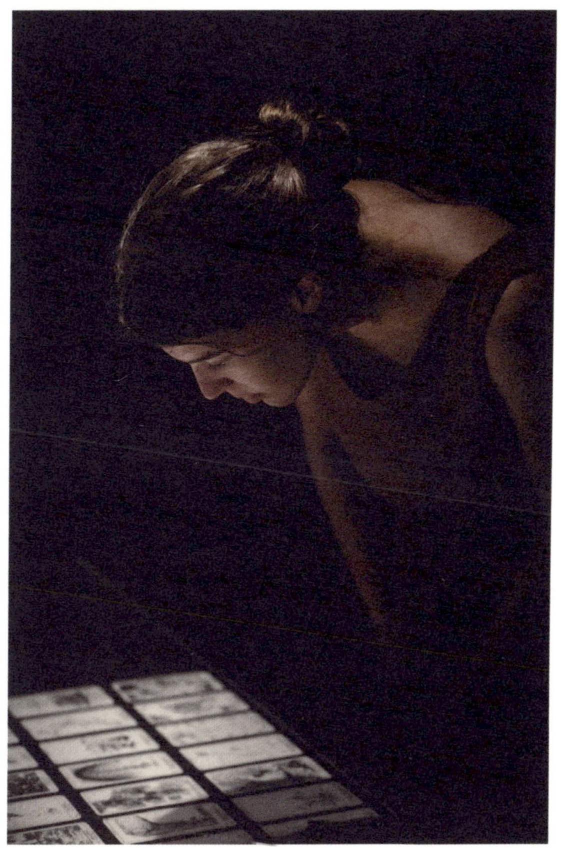

Webs of At-tent(s)ion

Webs of At-tent(s)ion is made up of a myriad of hybrid spider/webs—sculptures interwoven by different spider species, in which individual threads and sensory worlds combine to form a floating landscape. These spider/webs are an extension of the spiders' senses—they become their ears, eyes and mouths—while at the same time providing homes for their bodies. Through the filaments of the spider/webs, spiders send and receive vibrations, and perhaps even thoughts: they offer a way for these creatures to connect to the world. Some of these spider/webs have been amplified with special microphones that allow us to listen to the rhythm of their vibrations. The webs are like a musical instrument through which earthly and cosmic tremors resound.
The multiple entanglements and connections between spiders also create sensorial and living connections with nonhuman animals and ecosystems, inviting us to reflect on our coexistence with this ever-present species. We are all invited to take part in this giant jam session, a way to shift our attention to worlds in tension and suspension. By doing so, we attune with nonhuman voices that join with our own in endless webs of connectivity. The installation challenges the idea of a hierarchical tree of life, instead proposing a rhizomatic *web* of life, highlighting the hybridities between and among species and worlds.

Webs of At-tent(s)ion
2020
Spider silk, glass, carbon fiber, metal, lights, silicone
Various dimensions

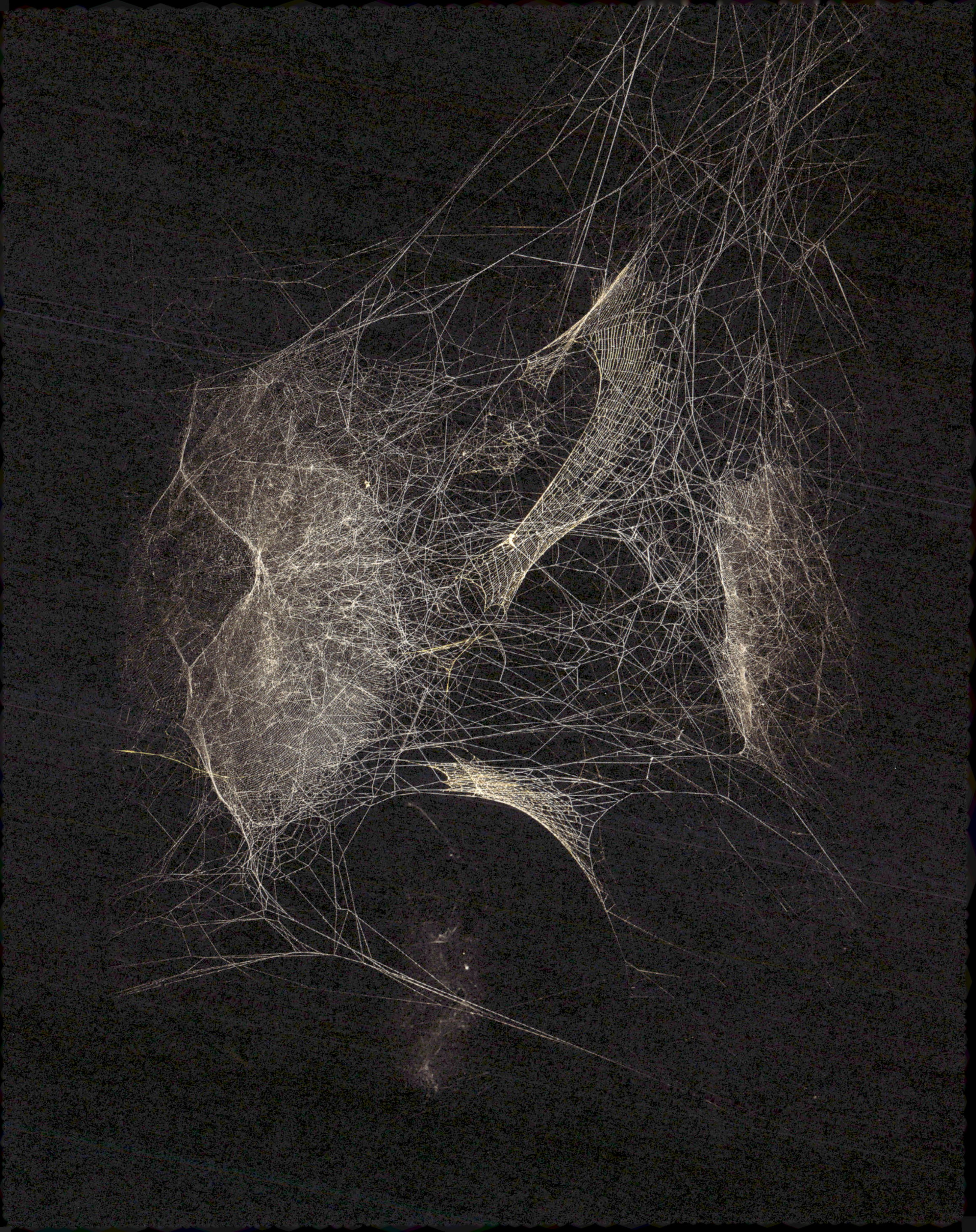

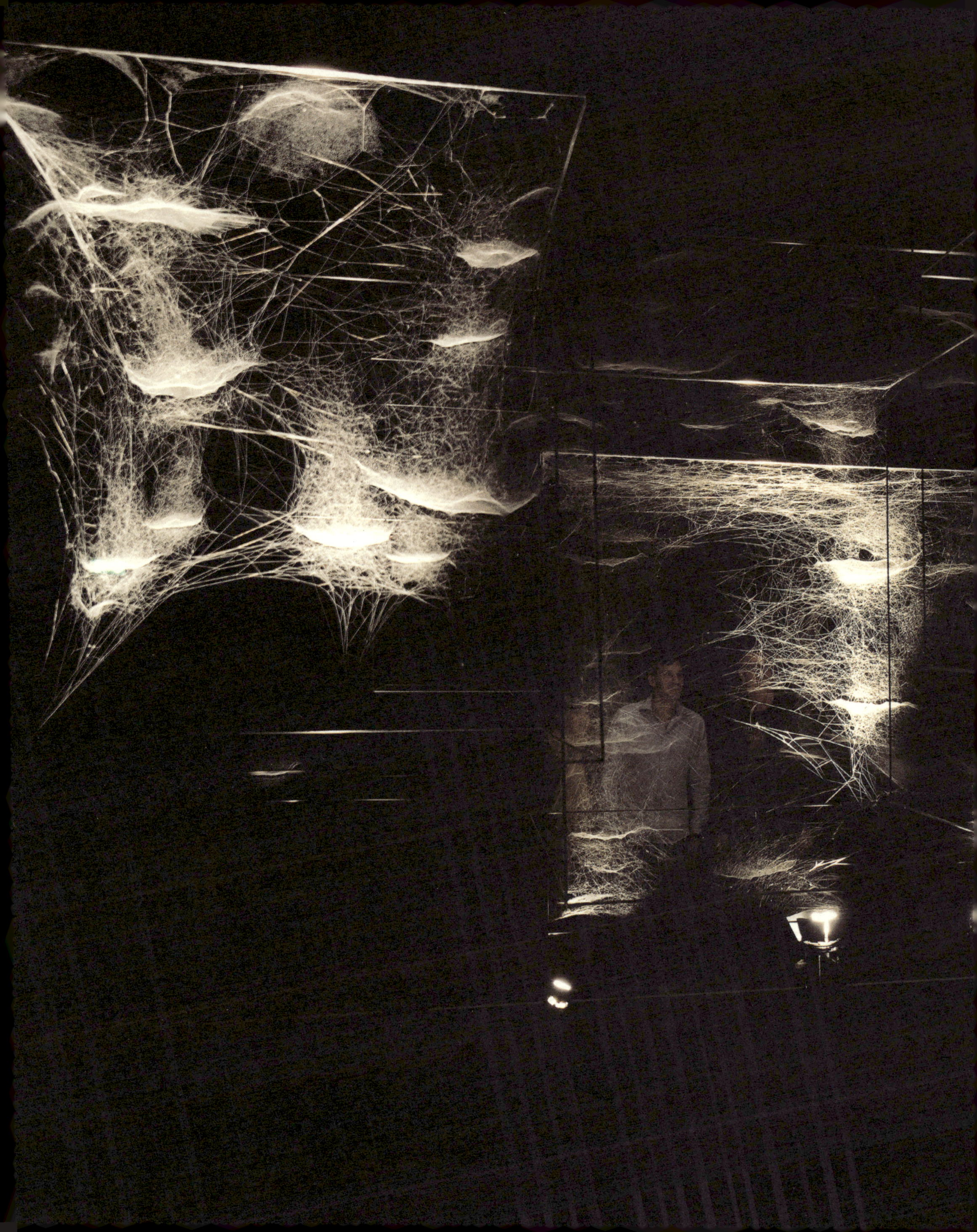

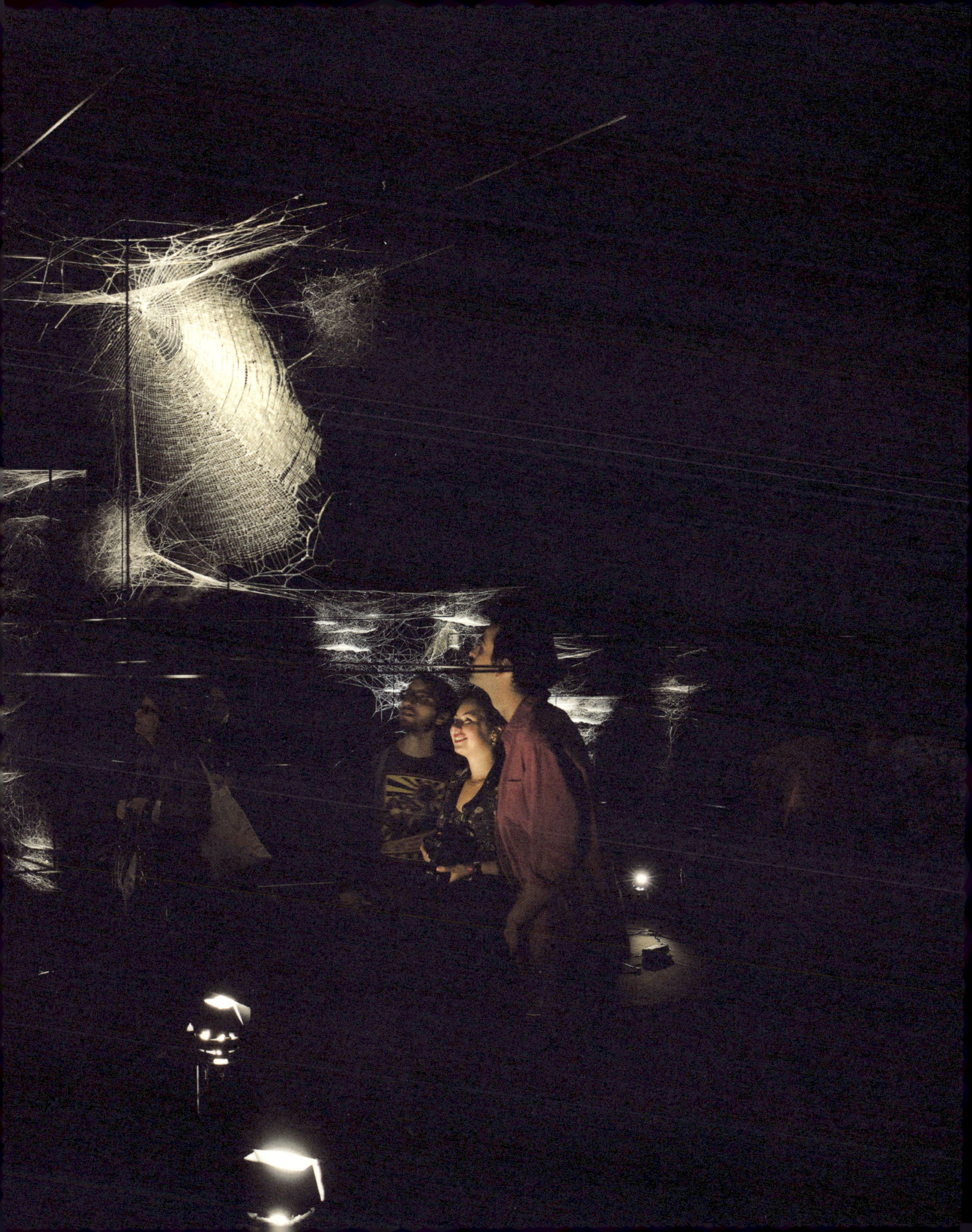

ROOM IV

Traces of living bodies woven
in a suspended membrane, biotic multitudes
and carbon residues trapped by its sticky threads.
To know your future assemblage,
choose one web to ask,
but remember that not only the living
have stories to tell.

Suit: Cosmic Spider/Web
Species: Dark and Ordinary Matter
Notation: D#

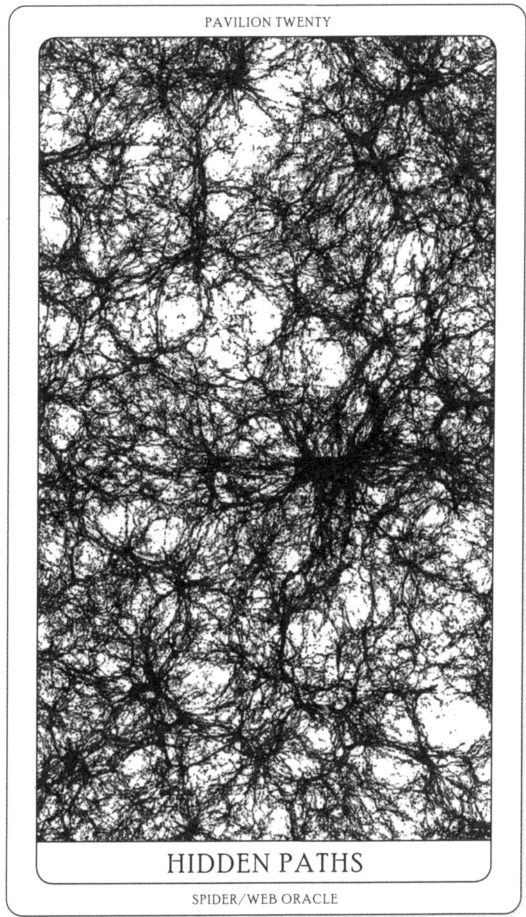

PAVILION TWENTY
HIDDEN PATHS
SPIDER/WEB ORACLE

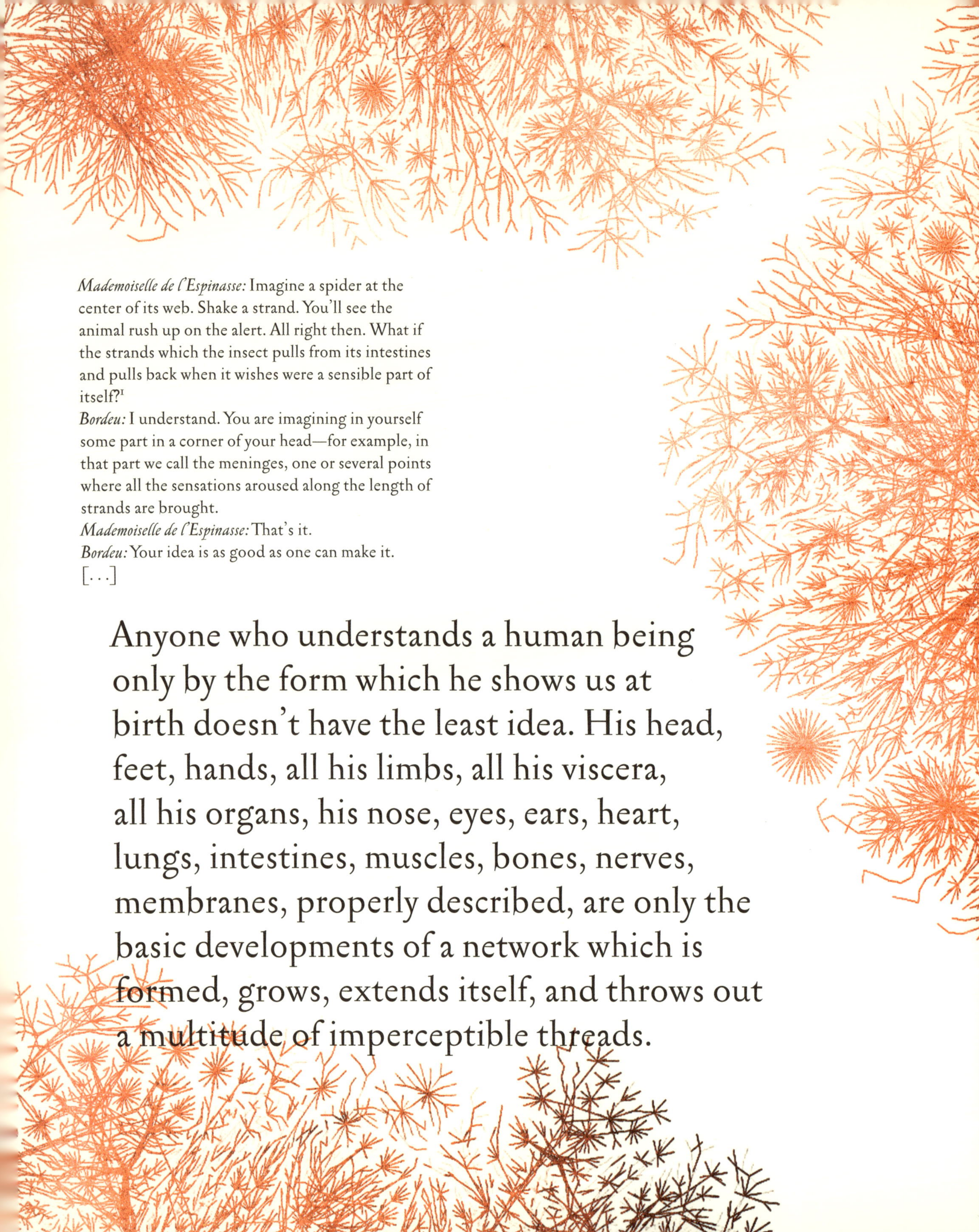

Mademoiselle de l'Espinasse: Imagine a spider at the center of its web. Shake a strand. You'll see the animal rush up on the alert. All right then. What if the strands which the insect pulls from its intestines and pulls back when it wishes were a sensible part of itself?[1]

Bordeu: I understand. You are imagining in yourself some part in a corner of your head—for example, in that part we call the meninges, one or several points where all the sensations aroused along the length of strands are brought.

Mademoiselle de l'Espinasse: That's it.

Bordeu: Your idea is as good as one can make it.

[...]

Anyone who understands a human being only by the form which he shows us at birth doesn't have the least idea. His head, feet, hands, all his limbs, all his viscera, all his organs, his nose, eyes, ears, heart, lungs, intestines, muscles, bones, nerves, membranes, properly described, are only the basic developments of a network which is formed, grows, extends itself, and throws out a multitude of imperceptible threads.

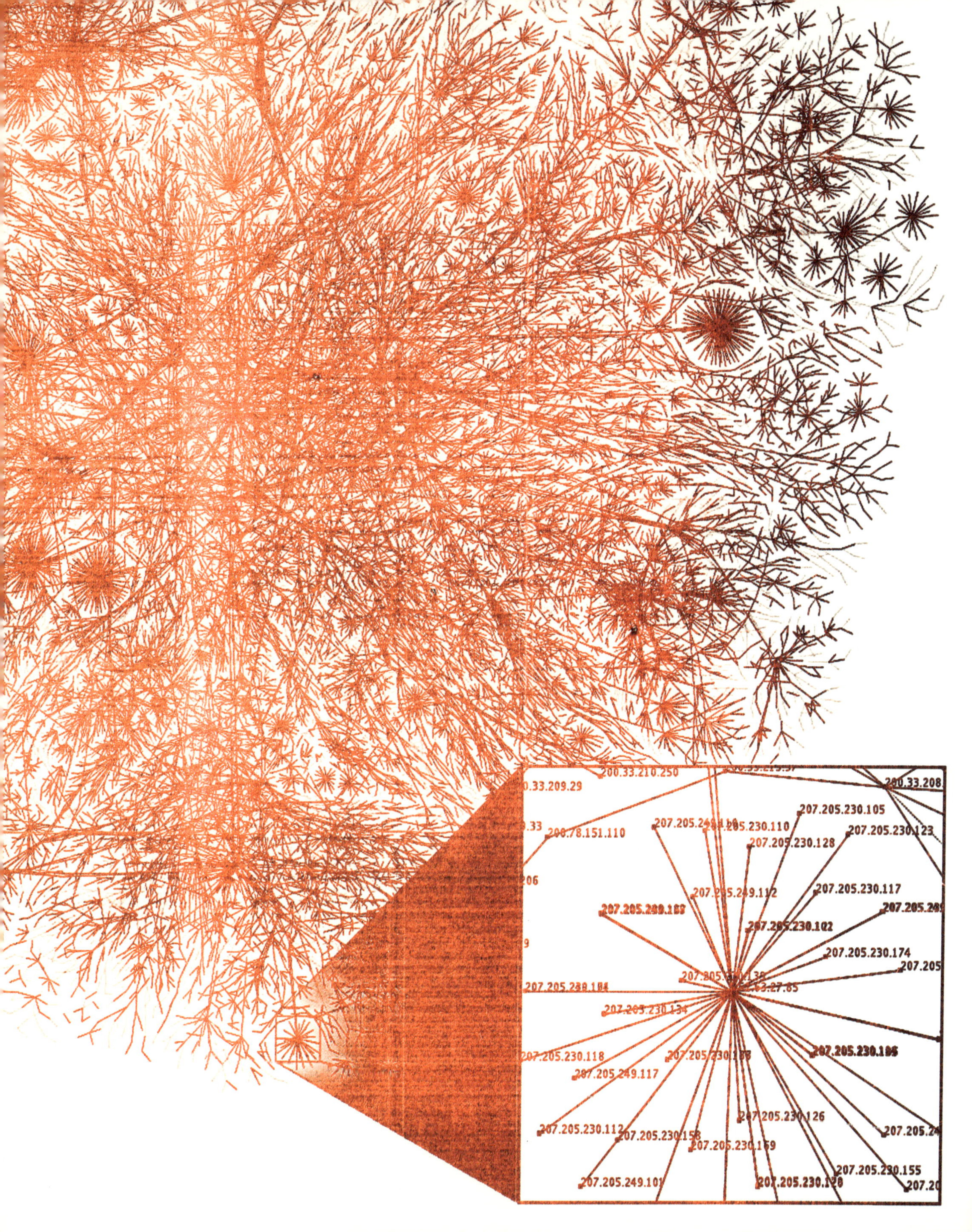

200.33.210.250
200.33.209.29
200.33.208
207.205.230.105
207.205.230.110
207.205.230.123
.33
200.78.151.110
207.205.230.128
206
207.205.249.112
207.205.230.117
207.205.230.163
207.205.249
207.205.230.102
207.205.230.174
207.205
9
207.205.230.130
207.205.230.184
63.27.85
207.205.230.134
207.205.230.118
207.205.230.195
207.205.249.117
207.205.230.126
207.205.230.112
207.205.230.158
207.205.24
207.205.230.159
207.205.230.155
207.205.249.101
207.205.230.120
207.20

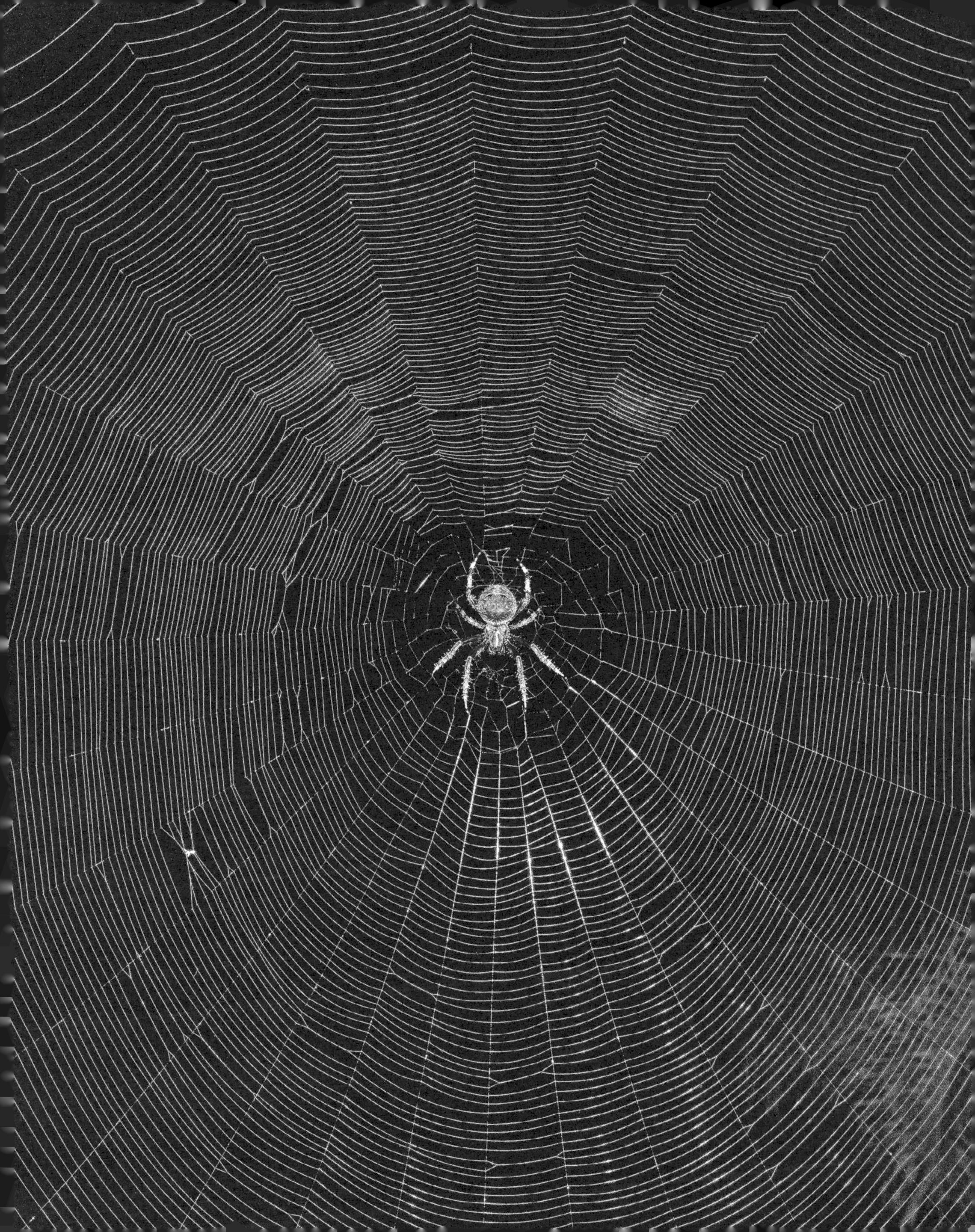

Mademoiselle de l'Espinasse: That's my web, and the central point of all these threads is my spider.
Bordeu: Exactly.
Mademoiselle de l'Espinasse:

Where are the strands? Where's the spider located?

Bordeu: The strands are everywhere. There is no part on the surface of your body where they don't end up. And the spider is lodged in a part of your head— the one I mentioned to you—the meninges, which we can hardly touch without knocking the entire machine unconscious.
Mademoiselle de l'Espinasse: But if an atom sets one of the spider's strands vibrating, the spider then is alarmed and disturbed. It flees or runs up.

At the center it is informed about everything which goes on in any point of the immense dwelling it has woven.

Why don't I know what's going on in mine or in the world, since I am a pack of sensitive points which all impinge on me and since I impinge on everything?
Bordeu: It's because the impressions grow weaker in proportion to the distance they travel.
Mademoiselle de l'Espinasse: If we strike the lightest blow at the end of a long girder and if I place my ear on the other end, I hear the blow. If one end of the girder was touching the earth and the other end was in Sirius, the same effect would be produced. If everything is linked, contiguous—that is, as in the real existing girder—why do I not hear what goes on in the immense space which surrounds me, above all if I really open my ears?
Bordeu: And who has told you that you do not hear it more or less? But the distance is so great, the impression so faint, the passage so confused. You are surrounded and deafened by such violent and different sounds. [. . .] Let's go back to your network and its formation. [. . .]
Mademoiselle de l'Espinasse: Each strand of this sensitive network can be injured or tickled along its entire length. The pleasure or pain is here or there, in one location or another on one of the long legs of my spider, for I always come back to my spider. It's the spider which is located at the common origin of all the legs and which establishes that the pain or pleasure is at such and such a place without experiencing the pleasure or pain itself.
Bordeu: It's this continual, invariable interaction between all impressions and the common origin which constitutes the unity of the animal.
Mademoiselle de l'Espinasse: And it's the memory of all these successive impressions which creates for each animal the history of his life and of its individuality.
Bordeu: And it's the memory and the comparisons which necessarily come after all these impressions which create thought and reason.
Mademoiselle de l'Espinasse: Where is this comparison made?
Bordeu: At the center of the network.
Mademoiselle de l'Espinasse: What about the network itself?
Bordeu: It does not have in its center any sense unique to it.
It cannot see or hear, and it doesn't suffer. It's produced and fed. It arises from a soft, insensitive, inert substance which serves as a pad on which it sits, listens, judges, and pronounces."

Denis Diderot, excerpt from *D'Alembert's Dream*, 1769

1 Diderot actually predicted what evolutionary biologists would discover centuries later: that a spider's web is a sensible part of itself, that the spider/web is a model of extended cognition. See Hilton Japyassú and Kevin Laland, "Extended Spider Cognition," *Animal Cognition*, vol. 20, no. 3 (2017): 375–395.

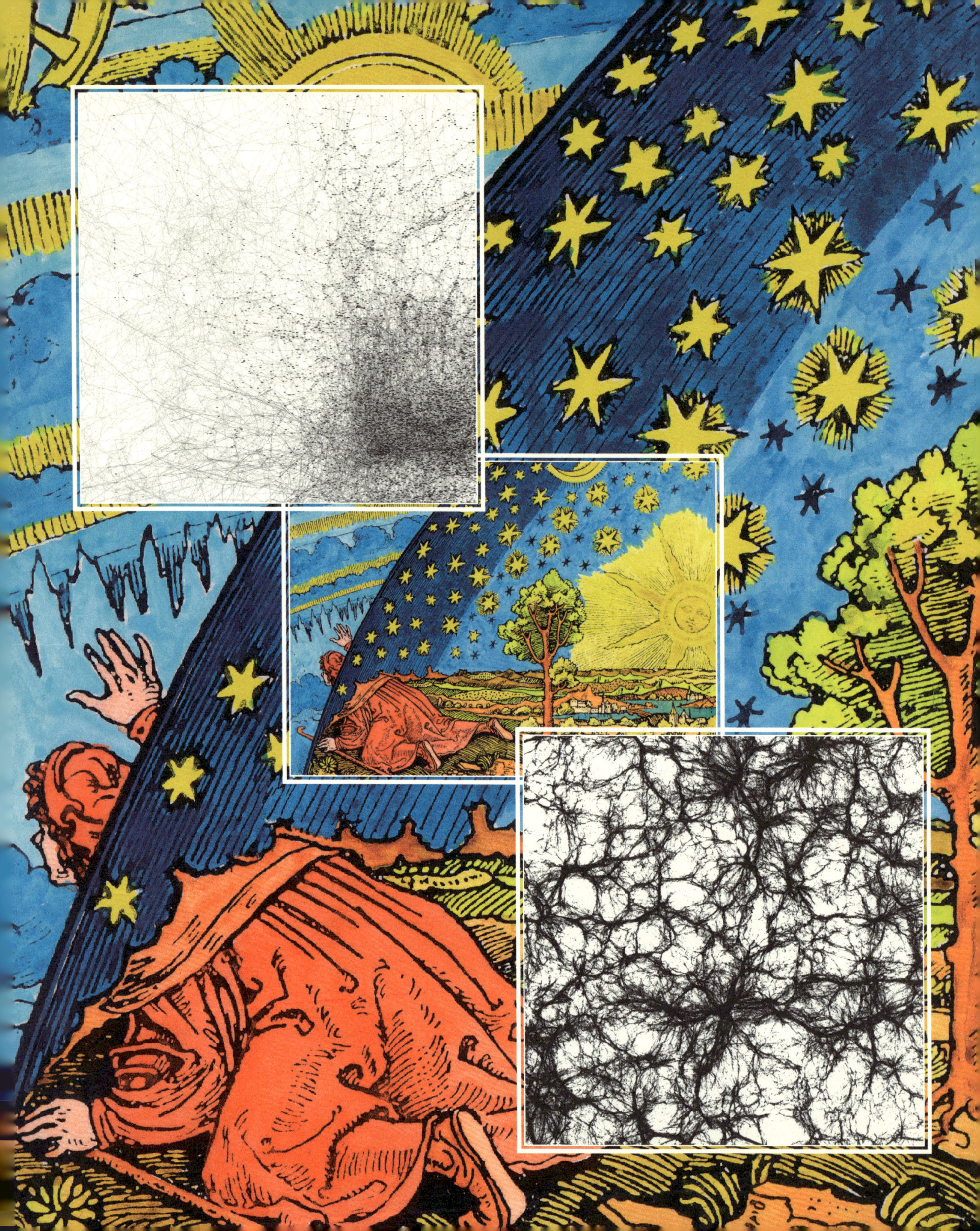

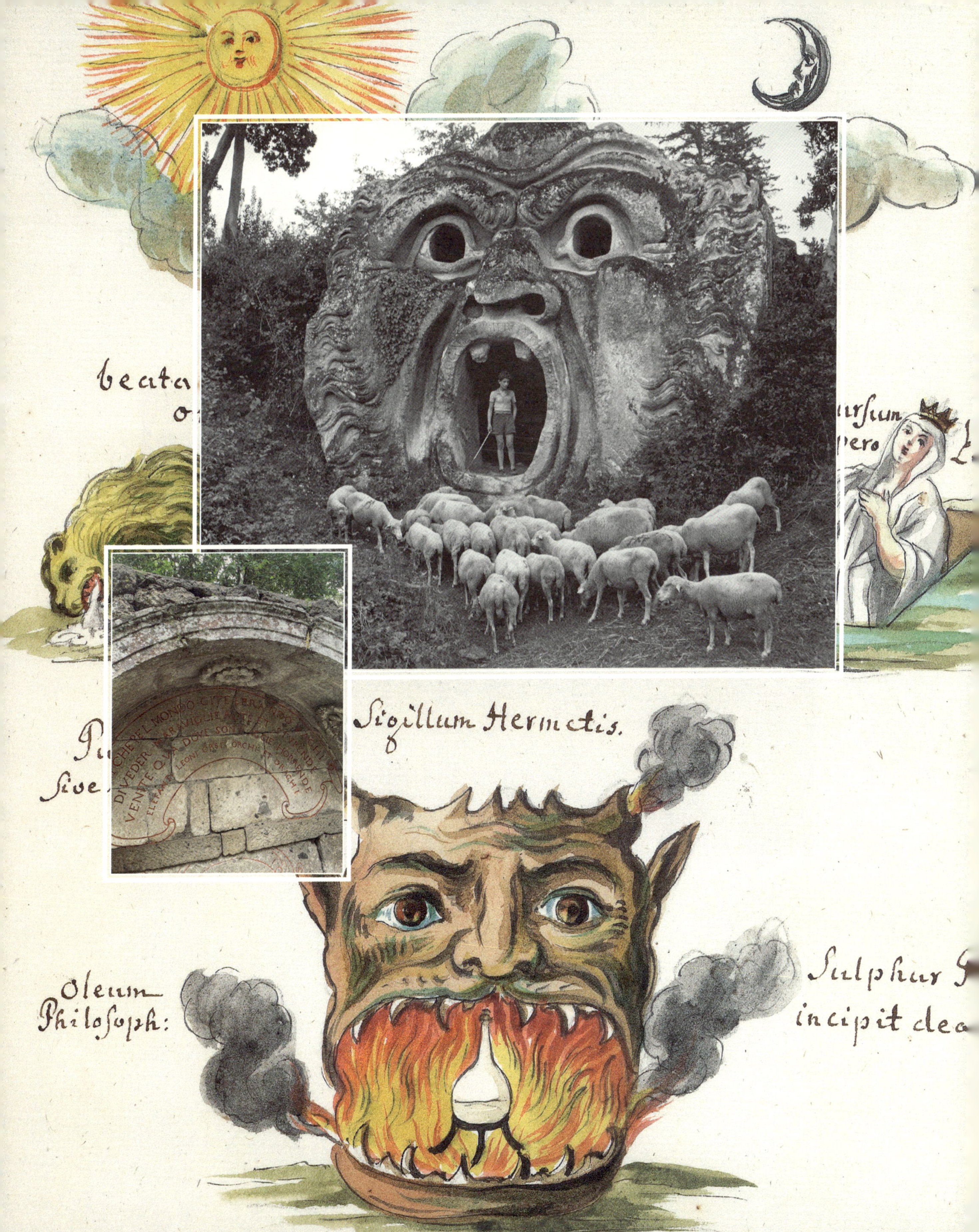
beata
Sigillum Hermetis.
Oleum
Philosoph:
Sulphur
incipit dea

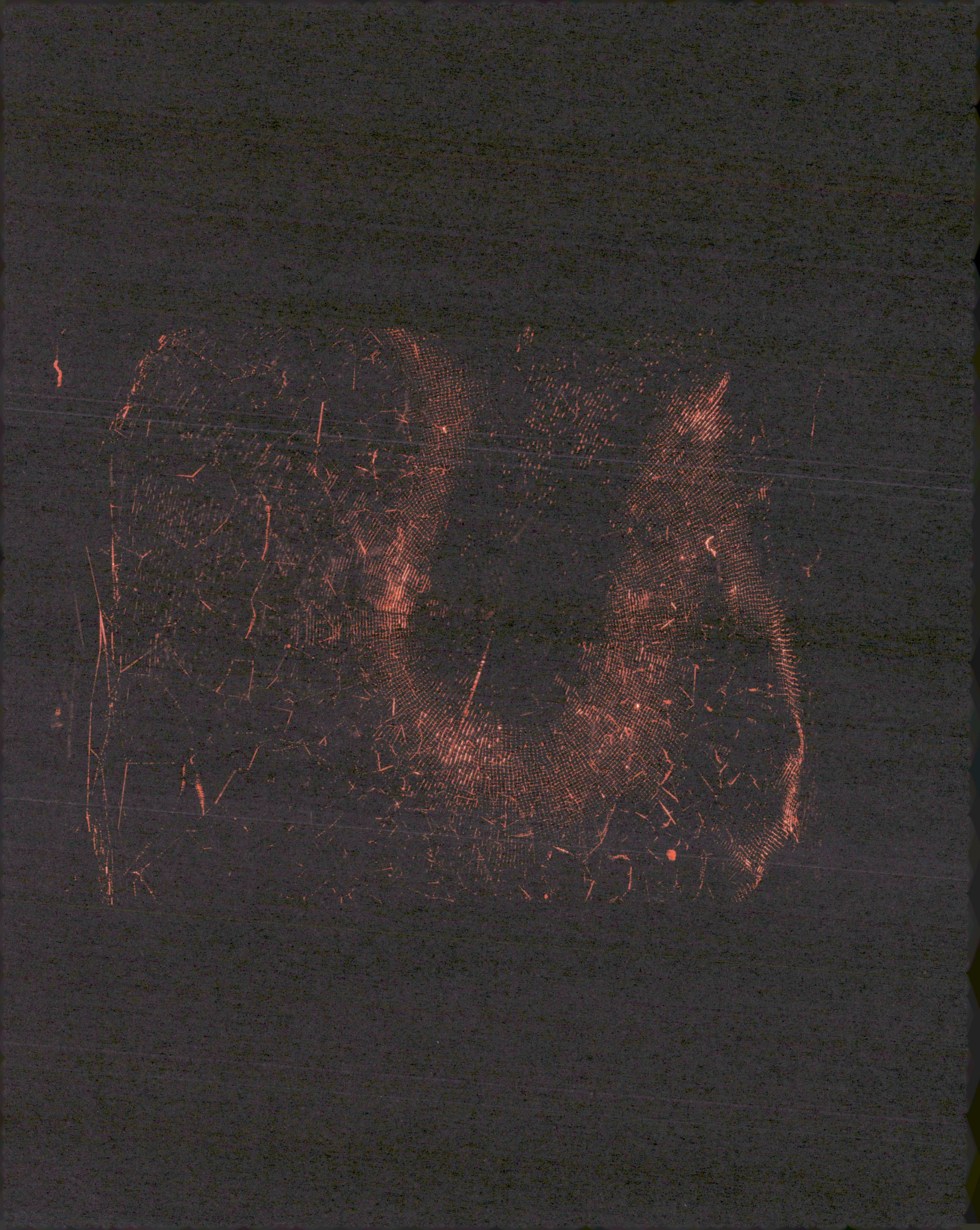

Spider webs actively spring towards prey thanks to electrically-conductive glue spread across their surface, Oxford University scientists have discovered.

The researchers found that the electrostatic properties of the glue that coats spider webs cause them to reach out to grab all charged particles, from pollen and pollutants to flying insects. They also showed that the glue spirals can distort Eearth's electric field within a few millimeters of the web, which may enable insects to spot the webs with their antennae "e-sensors."

The study, published in *Naturwissenschaften*, shows how a quirk of physics causes webs to move towards all airborne objects, regardless of whether they are positively or negatively charged. This explains how webs are able to collect small airborne particles so efficiently and why they spring towards insects.

According to the researchers, common garden spider webs around the world could be used for environmental monitoring as they actively filter airborne pollutants with an efficiency comparable to expensive industrial sensors.

"The elegant physics of these webs make them perfect active filters of airborne pollutants including aerosols and pesticides," said Professor Fritz Vollrath of Oxford University's Department of Zoology, who led the study. "Electrical attraction drags these particles to the webs, so you could harvest and test webs to monitor pollution levels—for example, to check for pesticides that might be harming bee populations."

"Even more fascinating, you would be able to detect some airborne chemicals just by looking at the shape of the webs! Many spiders recycle their webs by eating them, and would include any particles and chemicals that are electrically drawn to the web. We already know that spiders spin different webs when on different drugs, for example creating beautiful webs on LSD and terrible webs on caffeine. As a result, the web shapes alone can tell us if any airborne chemicals affect the animal's behaviour."

Working with Dr Donald Edmonds from Oxford University's Department of Physics, Professor Vollrath showed that webs like that of the garden cross spider also cause local distortions in earth's electric field since they behave like conducting discs. Many insects are able to detect small electrical disturbances, including bees that can sense the electric fields of different flowers and other bees.

"Pretty much all flying insects should be capable of sensing electrical disturbances," said Professor Vollrath. "Their antennae act as 'e-sensors' when the tips are connected to the body by insulating materials, meaning the charge at the tip will be different from the rest of the insect. As insects approach charged objects, the tips of their antennae will move by a small amount, which they may be able to feel. Bees already use e-sensors to sense flowers and other bees, so it now remains to be seen whether they might also use them to avoid webs and thus becoming dinner."

Electrical disturbances caused by spider webs are extremely short-ranged, so it is not yet clear whether insects would be able to sense them before the web snaps out to grab them.

Either way, it is clear that electrostatic charges play an important role in the insect world. "People often underestimate the static electricity that builds up in airborne objects, but it is important at all scales," said Professor Vollrath. "The Hindenburg disaster might have been caused by a discharge of static electricity, and helicopters have been known to explode if they discharge suddenly when landing.

Everything that moves through the air develops
static charge, so it's fascinating to see how
spider webs make use of this to actively catch
prey. It's a great bonus for us that this also
causes them to attract pollutants, making them
a cheap and natural way of tracking pesticides
and air quality around the world."

University of Oxford, "How electricity helps
spider webs snatch prey and pollutants,"
ScienceDaily, 2014

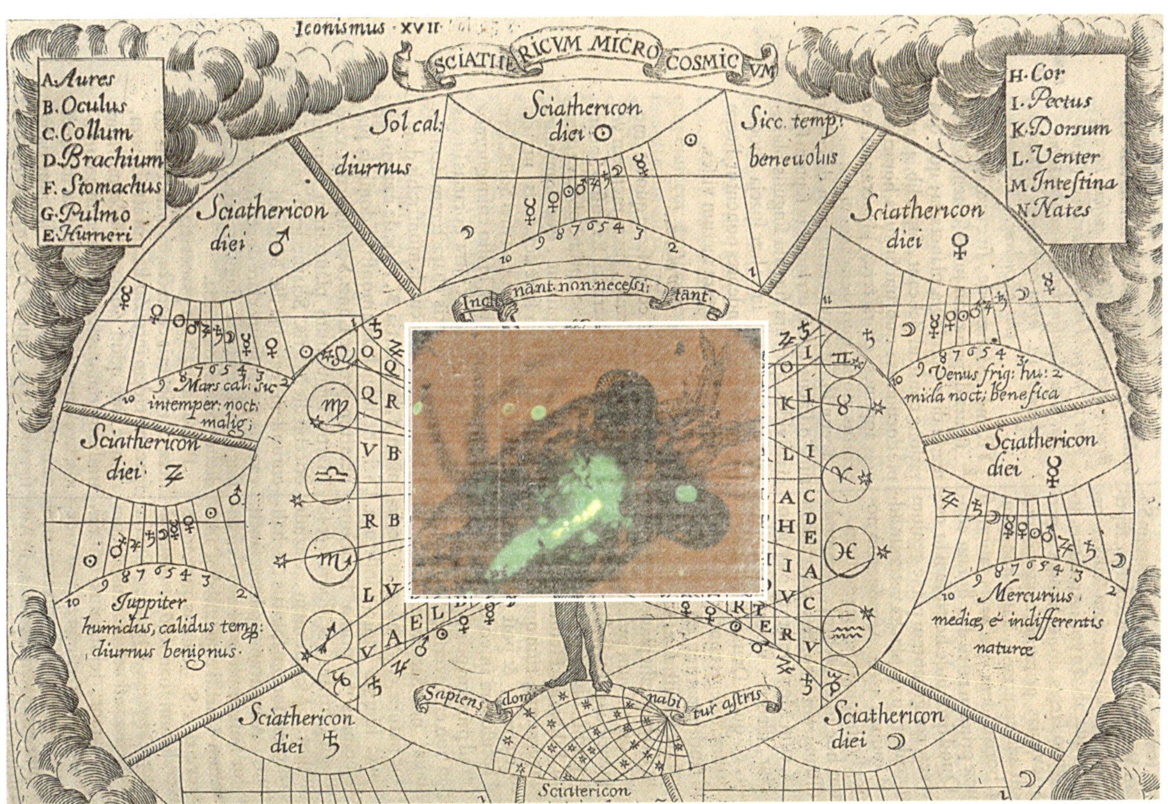

How to Entangle the Universe in a Spider/Web?

The cosmic web is a vibrant superorganism—its filamentary networks of assembling dark matter provide the mesh on which the large-scale structure of the universe is composed.
Ordinary matter is gravitationally attracted to the densest parts of the cosmic web, and there, galaxies and clusters of galaxies are formed, leaving large, relatively empty voids. Similarly, spider silk acts as an active archive of particulate matter, its silvery strands thickening with carbon dust. Some scientists observed that complex, three-dimensional spider/webs resemble computer simulations of the cosmic web. Building on this analogy, Tomás Saraceno invented, for the first time, an original technique for 3D scanning, digitizing and reconstructing spider/webs. In this installation, a laser sheet bi-dimensionally intersects the spider/web; this process transcends its service origins, becoming instead an artwork in its own right. The visual vibratory signals of the laser reveal the hidden architectural entanglements woven by the spider, while also imparting their own effects: with every nanometer that the laser moves, the viewer's sight is transformed, as it becomes visible—with startling clarity—how all three-dimensional space is made up of an infinity of planes. The universe stands before us between dimensions.
Maybe spiders, whose vibratory sensitivities are far more developed than those of humans, can already perceive dark matter, building their complex mazes according to its invisible score.

How to Entangle the Universe in a Spider/Web?
2020
Spider silk, carbon fiber, laser

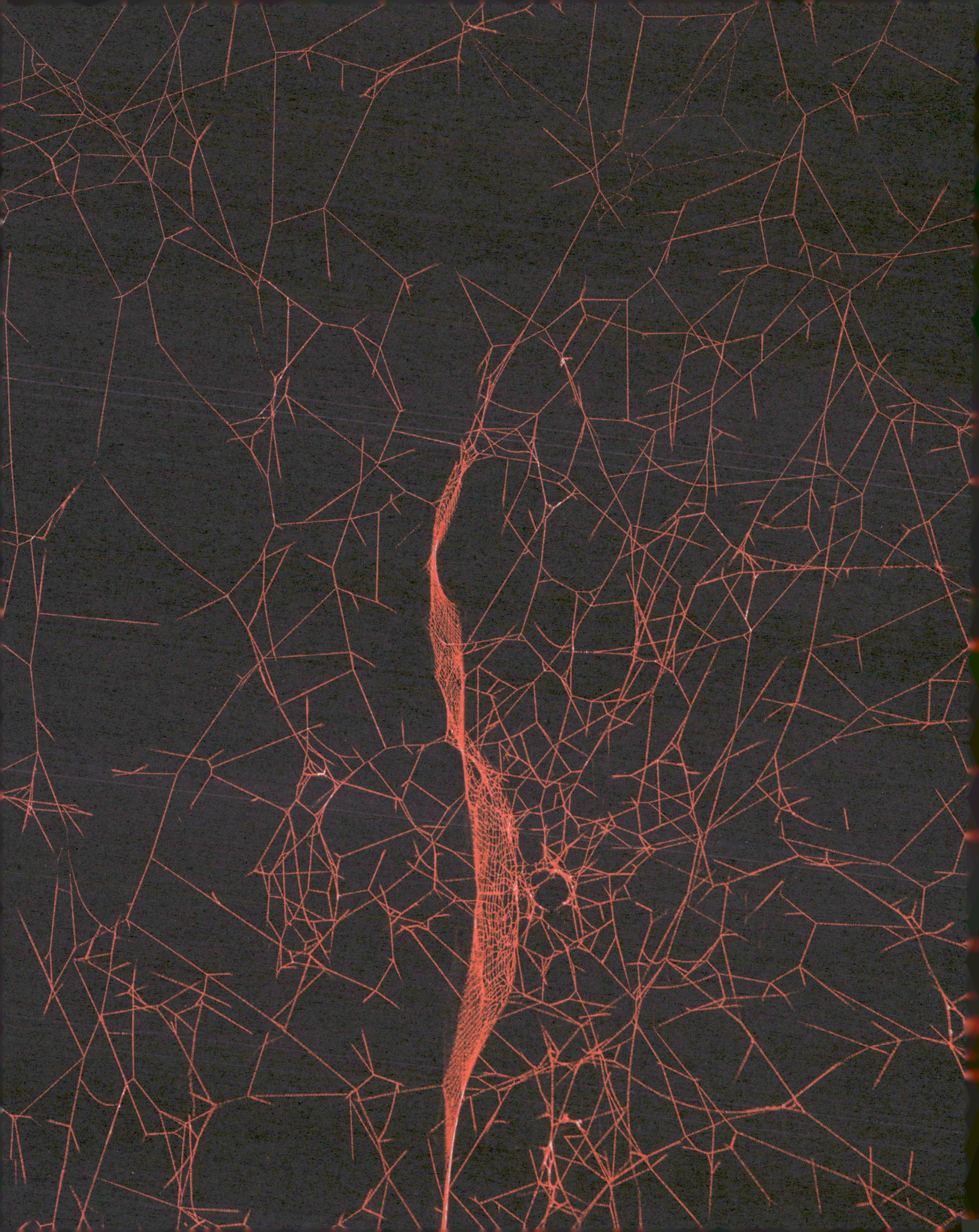

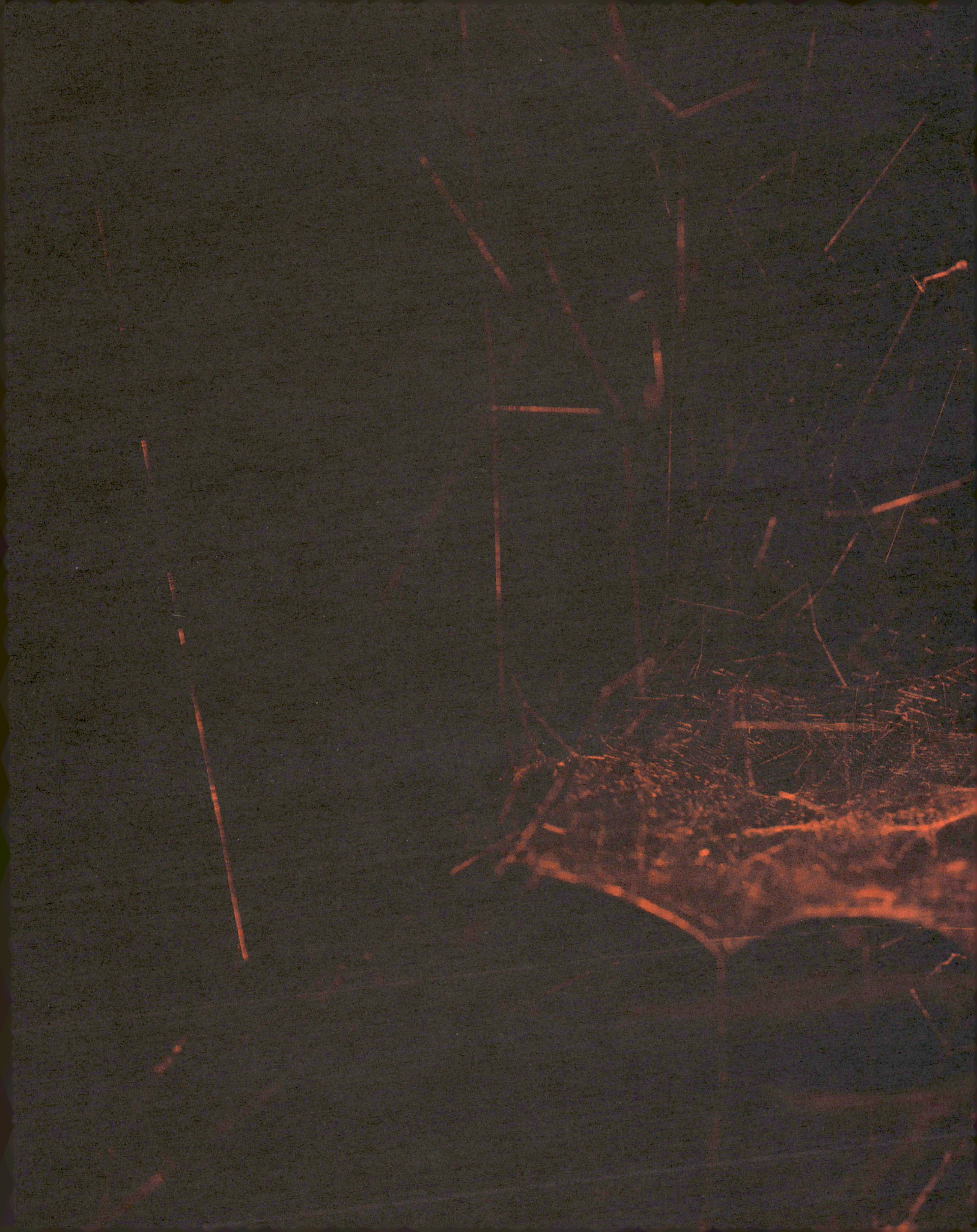

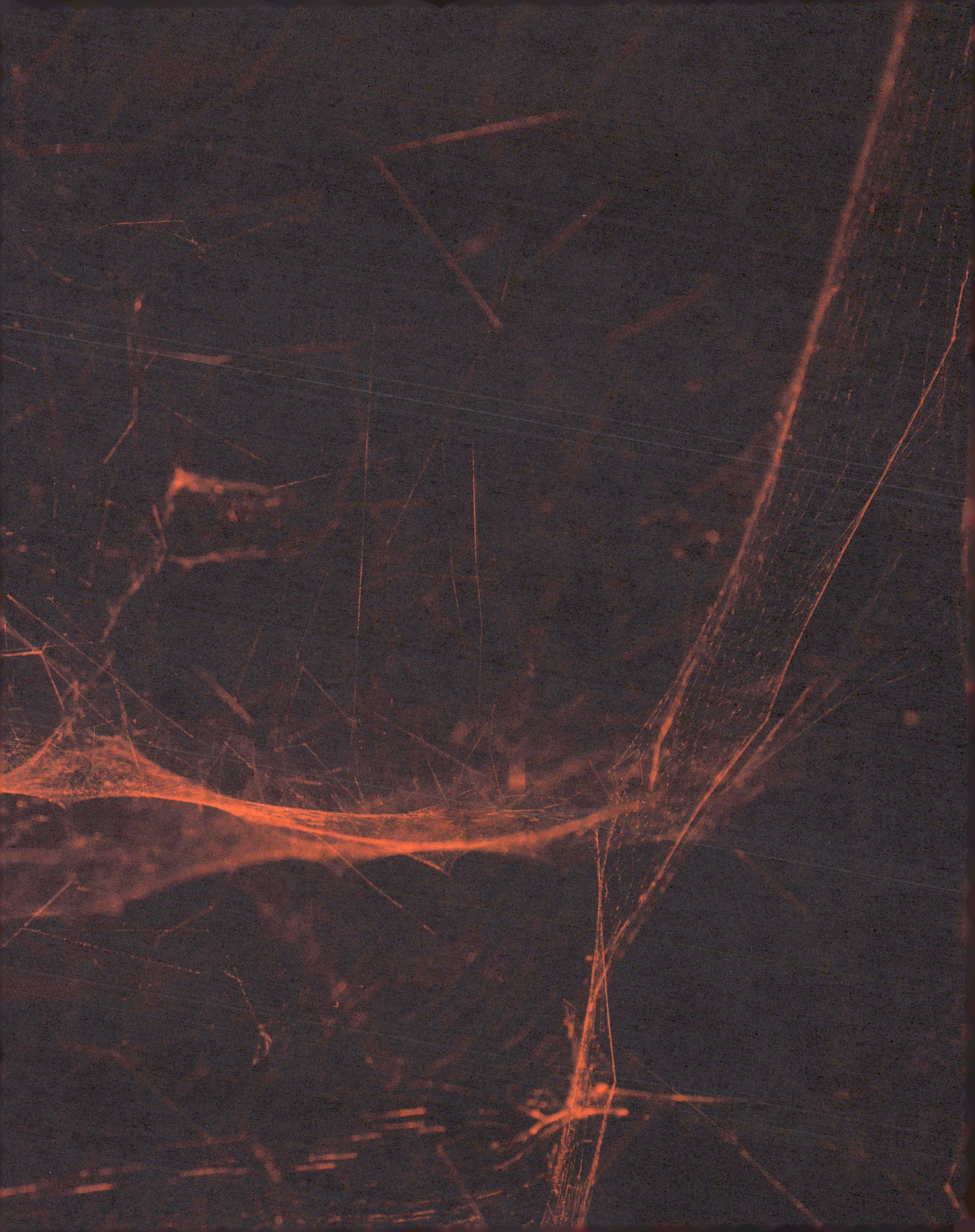

ROOM V

Tectonic plates, a tiger mosquito, a mating ritual,
the waters beneath shaking when a cruise ship
approaches the canal. The web is an instrument
that contains its score, the players are multiple.
At which frequency are you vibrating?

Suit: Orb Spider/Web
Species: Araneus diadematus
Notation: G♭

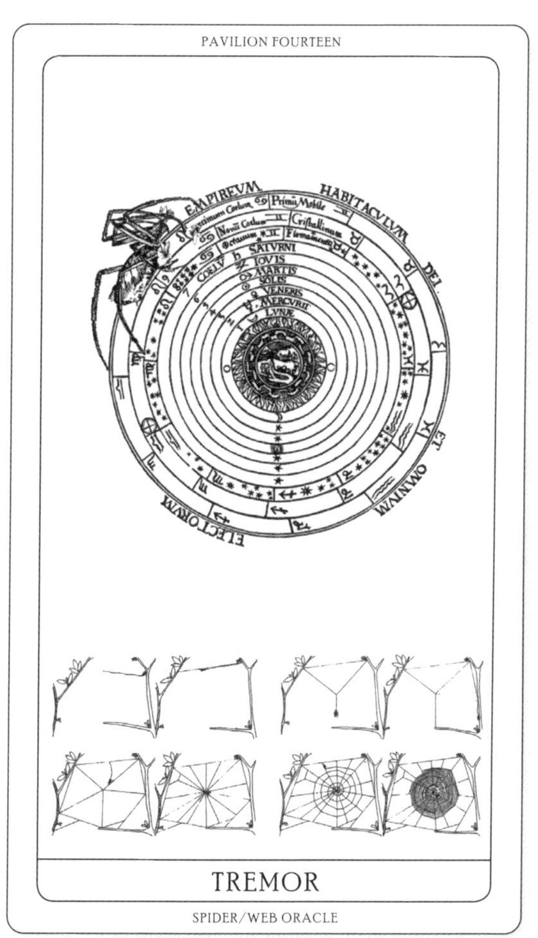

TREMOR

SPIDER/WEB ORACLE

It was the dust speaking. It blew through my books like a dry storm, investigated crevices and took the shapes of the stairs.[1] It rustled by my ears as if it was making words. On the hat's brim the dust jumped up and flew into its co-matter. My eyes and throat and lungs wept. Swirling through the puffs of my labored breaths handfuls of dust funneled back into the old man just enough to plump his lips and tongue and rattle around the throat and give it a dusty voice box, so the skin whispered to me, Don't try not to breathe, comrade. Breathe deep.

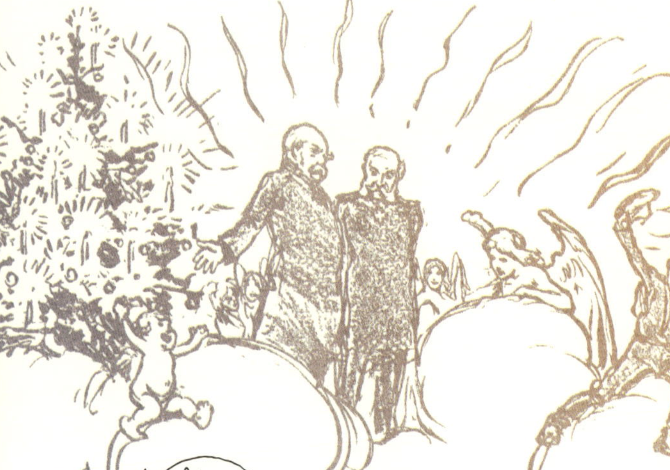

I couldn't have resisted. It could have just drowned me drily. All I could smell was desiccation. I told myself I had no choice but in a situation like that the choice you have is how you go about not having a choice.

I inhaled the dust. In it rushed.

My body must have thought I was dying. Probably I was writhing and twitching alongside the old skin.

I envisage the dust tickling my synapses until they quiver. It gave me new thinking. The dust thought for me, drumming against my tympani.[2] So I have this dilemma. What I'm trying to tell you—for which you may not thank me—is that the dust was and is my comrade. So it's yours too. It was there not only in gratitude but in solidarity.

1 "My encounter with dust is a face-to-face (indeed, surface-to-surface) meeting with myself, with parts of me that, though already dead, lead an uncanny afterlife in combination with other fragmentary and whole entities, be they threads of fabric or dust mites. The very possibility of our mingling harkens back to the shared source of finite existence, against which the act of dusting rebels. There is no depth in the encounter, save for the reciprocal mirroring effect of two surfaces: the dusting duster and the dusted dust. In most cases, nonetheless the mirror is broken, and the former does not recognize her- or himself in the latter. A tremendous psychic investment is necessary to inhibit the flashes of this traumatic recognition and, perversely, to identify vitality with shining, dust-free, lifeless exteriors." Michael Marder, "Dusting the Furniture of Our Minds," *New York Times,* June 1, 2015, https://opinionator. blogs.nytimes. com/2015/06/01/ dusting-the-furniture- of-our-minds/.

2 Vibrational sound as a means of controlling thought . . . The ear is the door to the brain!

A move into the *longue durée*. A politics that could chide the Annales School for a skittish short-term optic, for which the sound of struggle is the crepitus of one landmass against another.

Dissenting dust expounded its position. Cycles of geological insurrection.

Vaalbara, prelapsarian collectivity of stone and surface, Kenorland and Pangea, peace becoming war; the rage of the gap at the unbreached, totalities torqued apart over mere glimmering millions of years. A savaging of scale, Triassic wars of position as Gondwanaland and Laurasia rounded in ruthless continental pugilism, their own components in solidarity, plateaus heaving, shale slipping as masses, subject-objects of history, scree in struggle against the bottomness of holes. A primitive communism of granularity, grassroots democracy before there was grass or roots or anything but hot dirt, until at last there were birds and an epoch of walls.[3]

We are Jillies and Jonnies come lately to insurgency. The coal on the blackleg's legs was taking sides long before the meat beneath it. My body was spasming. Clods with agency as opaque as their substance. Crumbling as syndicalism, the ca'canny of quartz. Flint ultraleftism; dirt voluntarism; glass struggle; regroupment of rock orienting to freedom. Slime against the dry, tooth versus stone in the mysteries of the organism, a baroque new fascism of flesh. The dust remembered onslaughts of the bodied, shock troops of blood-and-sinewed reaction against the revolutionary unliving.

No sides are uncontested. These are traditions not givens. There's a civil war in water, I'm animal disloyal to mainstream quick and it, one, is dissident dust: not even all dirt is revolutionary.
And even for those that are, among the radicals of all matter, there's always an *uchi-geba*, a brutal faction fight.
[...]
Where are we going? I said.
To a meeting.
What radicals have you ever known that didn't have their weekly meetings?
A runnel of high-rises, a canyon of them, and water. We were below a tower block overhang, where a copse of cold dead trees hung stubby and sculptural across the corner of a canal, where sunken bikes and a rust-scaled supermarket trolley were visible through shallow waters below a half-melted bin and a rise of earth and a squat clot of dark cloud. This is where we're supposed to be? I said.
The dust nodded. I knew we looked like rough sleepers.

Who are we waiting for? I said. The dust said, We're the last to arrive.

And I looked again and saw our comrades; a tower block overhang, a copse of trees, sunk metal, water, a misshapen bin, the ground, vapor in the sky. Venue and participants were one.
We began the discussion.

China Miéville, excerpt from "The Dusty Hat," in *Three Moments of an Explosion*, 2016

3   Jussi Parikka writes that dust "forces us to rethink such binaries as one/many," a useful political framework for conceiving of ourselves as collective without losing individual subjectivities, of recognizing the communalism across species without obscuring our differences or leaning into monolith. Jussi Parikka, "Dust and Exhaustion: The Labor of Media Materialism," *CTHEORY*, October 2, 2013, https://journals.uvic.ca/index.php/ctheory/article/view/14790.

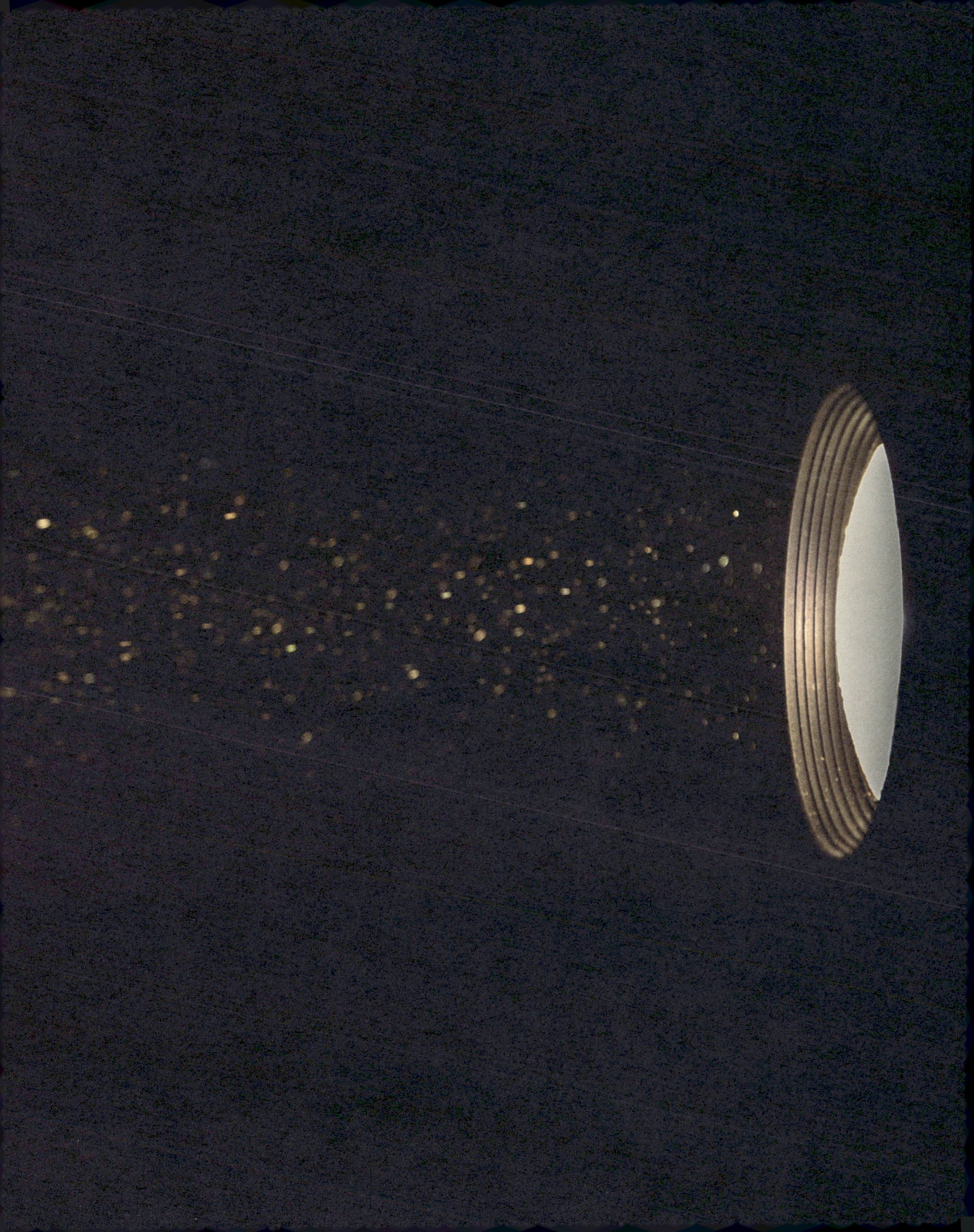

So-called new materialism is a good conceptualization and a methodology to track why non-human particles carry with them wider contexts. The dust particle from the polished iPad is an excess of the admittedly beautiful fetishistic surface; the dust particle is what registers the globalized wage labor relation

human perception, intensity of matter of technological and biological kinds.

In short, this media-biased proposition goes something like this: new materialism is not only about intensities of bodies and their capacities such as voice or dance, of movement and relationality, of fleshyness, of ontological monism and alternative epistemologies of generative matter, and active meaning-making of objects themselves non-reducible to linguistic signification. Not wanting to dismiss any of those perspectives, I just want to remind of the specificity and agency in mediatic matter too. New materialism is already present in the way technical media transmits and processes "culture," and engages in its own version of the continuum of "natureculture" (to use Donna Haraway's term) or in this case, "medianatures."

Instead of philosophical traditions, let us read modern physics, engineering, and communications technology as mapping the terrain of new materialism: the basis for signal-processing, use of electromagnetic fields for communication, and the various non-human temporalities

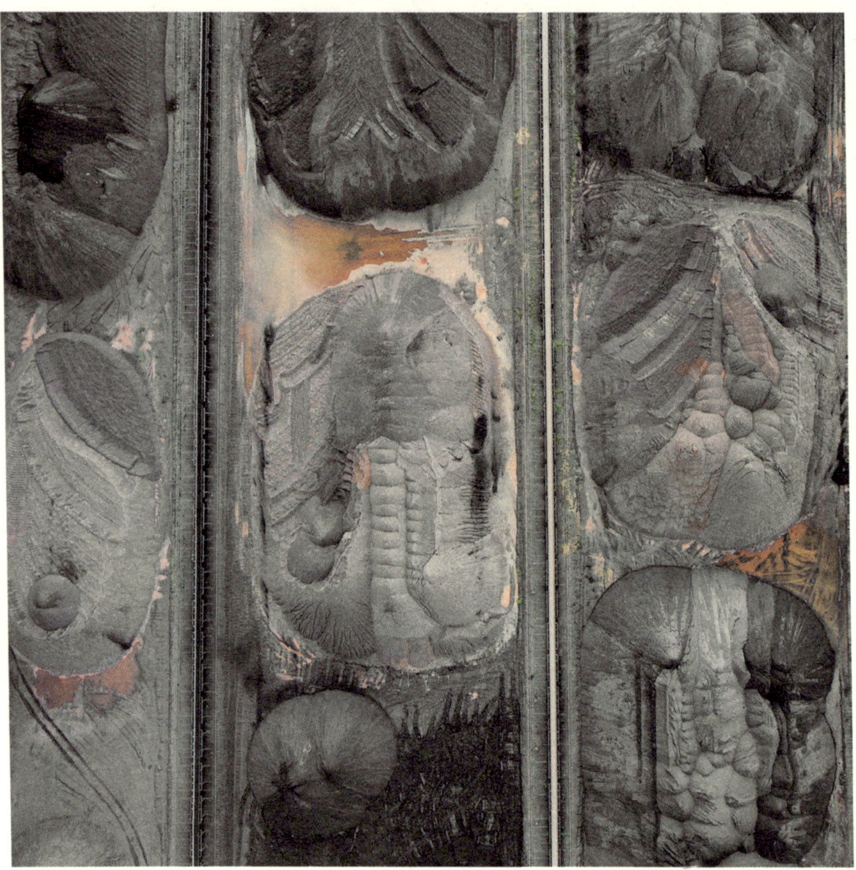

on the soft tissue of the Chinese worker. This is where new materialism can contribute to thinking "depletion design" and media theory more widely. Mixing philosophy with media theory offers an insight to why we are so interested in non-human bodies and objects, processes that escape direct and conscious

of vibrations and rhythmic of, for instance, computing and networks are based in non-solids. But also, let us follow the entanglements of chemicals and flesh together with the more abstract but as real labor relations that define the political economy of digital culture devices.

Besides dust, media history is one

big "story" of materials and experimenting with different materials from glass plates to chemicals, from selenium to coltan, from dilute sulphuric acid to shellac silk and gutta percha, to processes such as crystallization, ionization, and so forth. All of those could be approached through the non-hylomorphic idea of individuation that Simondon proposed. What is more, the materials have their aftereffects, nowadays most visible in the amount of e-waste our electronic culture leaves behind, which presents one further "materiality" for our investigation interested in tracking non-human dimensions of media culture.

This is the stuff that can contribute to one particular possibility of "new" materialism: the perspective of minerals sedimented for millions of years before being mined by cheap labor in developing countries for use in information technology factories. After that short use-period of some years, they become part of the materiality of e-waste leaking toxins into nature after river-dumping or incineration, making them into toxic vapors that attach to the nervous systems of cheap labor in China, India, Ghana, etc. De Landa wrote earlier of the "thousand years of nonlinear history" as a proposition to engage with the long durations of rocks, minerals, biomatter and language. Now we can push that into a million, billion years of non-linear history almost in the way Negarestani suggests in his work of theory-fiction concerning petroleum, dust and other material agencies. A new materialist archaeologist, excavating how the sedimented participates in the contemporary biopolitical sphere.

Such material biopolitics is embedded in a multitude of durations: A specific design solution concerning a screen or technological component has an effect on its becoming obsolescent sooner than "necessary" while the product itself is embedded in a capitalist discourse emphasizing newness as a key refrain and fetishistic value driving the purchase decisions. And, after being abandoned for another device, what is often called "recycling" is actually waste-trade, wherein old electronic media is shipped, for instance, to India, to be dismantled with very rudimentary (and dangerous) processes that attach toxins to the lungs and nervous systems of the poor workers. Hence, practices of reuse (zombie media), alternative design, an attention to components and materials used, are all tapping into the entanglement of intensity of non-human matter (dust), and the matter of abstract political economy of work and production.

Jussi Parikka, excerpt from "Dust Matter," in *Depletion Design: A Glossary of Network Ecologies*, 2012

Particular Matter(s) Jam Session

The air is restless, constantly in motion. A cubic inch of air holds 25 billion molecules, colliding and dispersing faster than the speed of sound. This perpetual movement creates a sound which is inaudible to us. What would it mean to listen to the particles?
In the installation *Particular Matter(s) Jam Session*, participants find themselves part of a rhythmic ensemble. A beam of light illuminates dust particles of domestic, earthly and cosmic origin. Cameras record the position and velocity of the particles in real time as they travel through space, transforming them into musical tones that are given voice through a set of speakers spread out across the space.
The frequencies produced by the choreographies of particles of dust resound in the threads of a spider/web. The vibratory movements produced by the spider in its web are amplified through a speaker that is positioned below the beam of light. This reverberation animates the particles, causing fluctuations and collisions. The presence of participants in the space generates new variations in this evolving ecology.
Hidden in the dust is Particulate Matter 2.5 (PM2.5), or pollution particles less than 2.5 micrometers in diameter; one prominent example is black carbon, a deadly substance created by fossil fuels. PM2.5 are the most dangerous of the particulate matters, with their danger coming from their small size: their small diameters mean they are able to pass our body's defenses, infiltrating our lungs and blood streams. The whole Anthropocene as a proposed geological epoch resonates through one particle of PM2.5, expressing the tension between the micro and the macro.
Particular Matter(s) Jam Session is an exercise in attunement to bodies and forces on air—giving voice to the multiscale, interacting agents in the room, as if it were an interspecies translator, interpreting a shared language of vibration. PM2.5, PM10, Nox, dust particles, cosmic dust, the spider/web, participants and the interplay of heat, electrostatics and air currents become the musicians of this jam session.

Particular Matter(s) Jam Session
2020
Local live spider already living in Palazzo Strozzi, spider silk, carbon fiber, light beam, cosmic, terrestrial dust, PM2.5, PM10, black carbon, stellar wind, sonic waves, 3D tracking software, computer, video camera, speakers, video projector

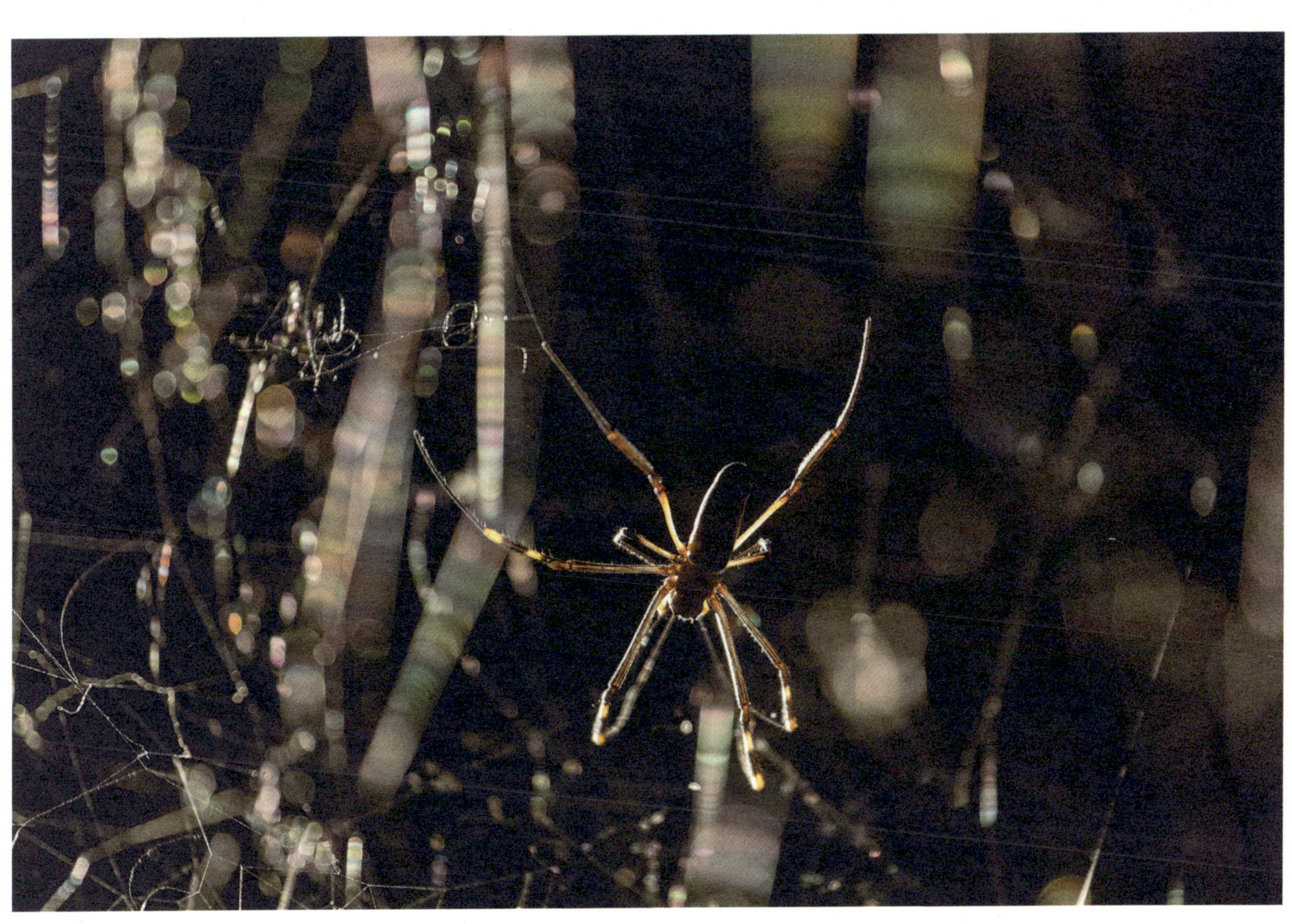

163,000 Light Years

This film lasts 163,000 years. It is the length of time needed for the light emitted by the Large
Magellanic Cloud to reach us. Located in the Mensa and Dorado constellations, this dwarf spiral
galaxy can be seen at night in the southern celestial hemisphere. However, we see it with a delay
of 163,000 years. When we observe it, we see nothing but the past.
As different temporalities appear, dimensions are projected and epochs redefined, questioning
our linear conception of time. First, because spacetime is not a fixed construction, but rather
an action that could, speculatively, warp the length of the film before its end. Then, because
the perception of time also depends on each species. Flies perceive 250 frames per second,
turtles only 15. The first will see this video in slow motion and the second accelerated. The more
perceptual frames that each second holds for an organism, the shorter its life. The question
remains which species will be able to attend the end of the video in 163,000 years.

163,000 Light Years
2016
Single channel video, sound, duration: 163,000 years, frame rate: 1 frame x year

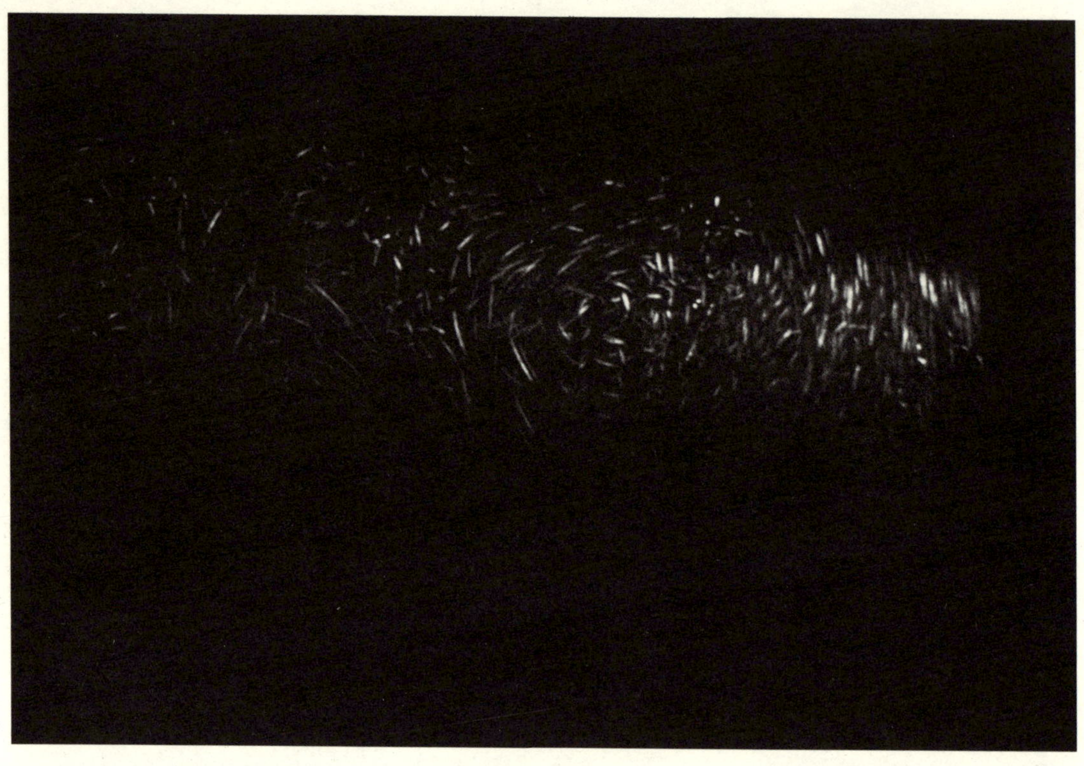

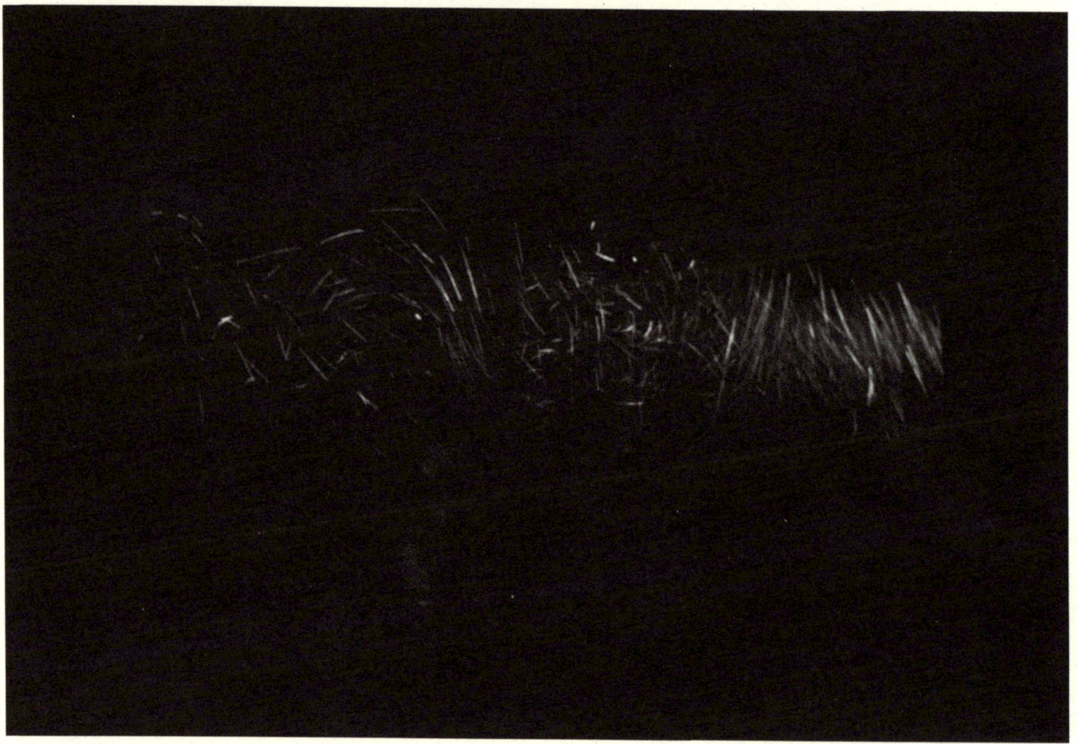

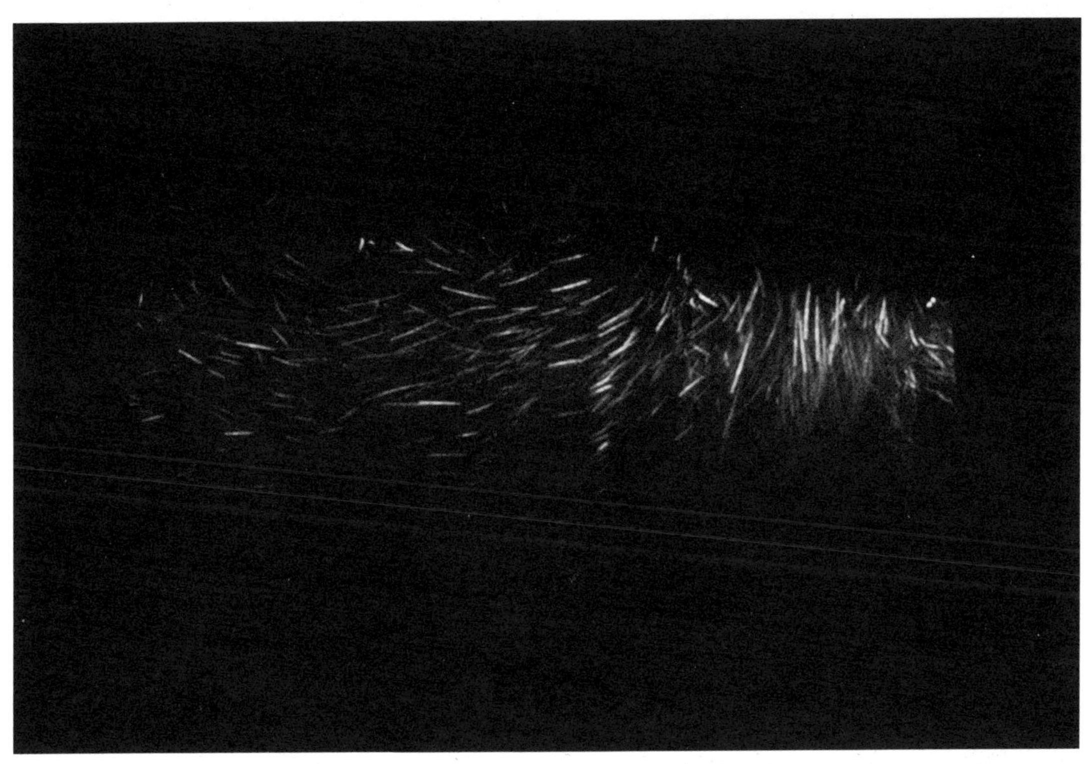

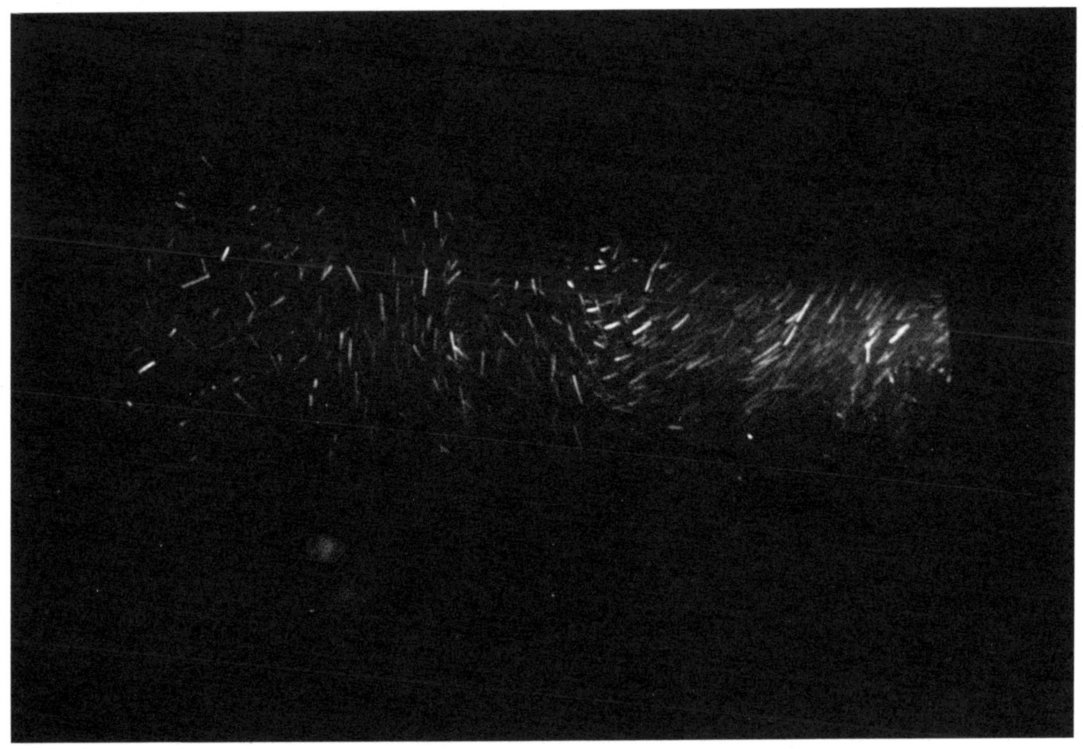

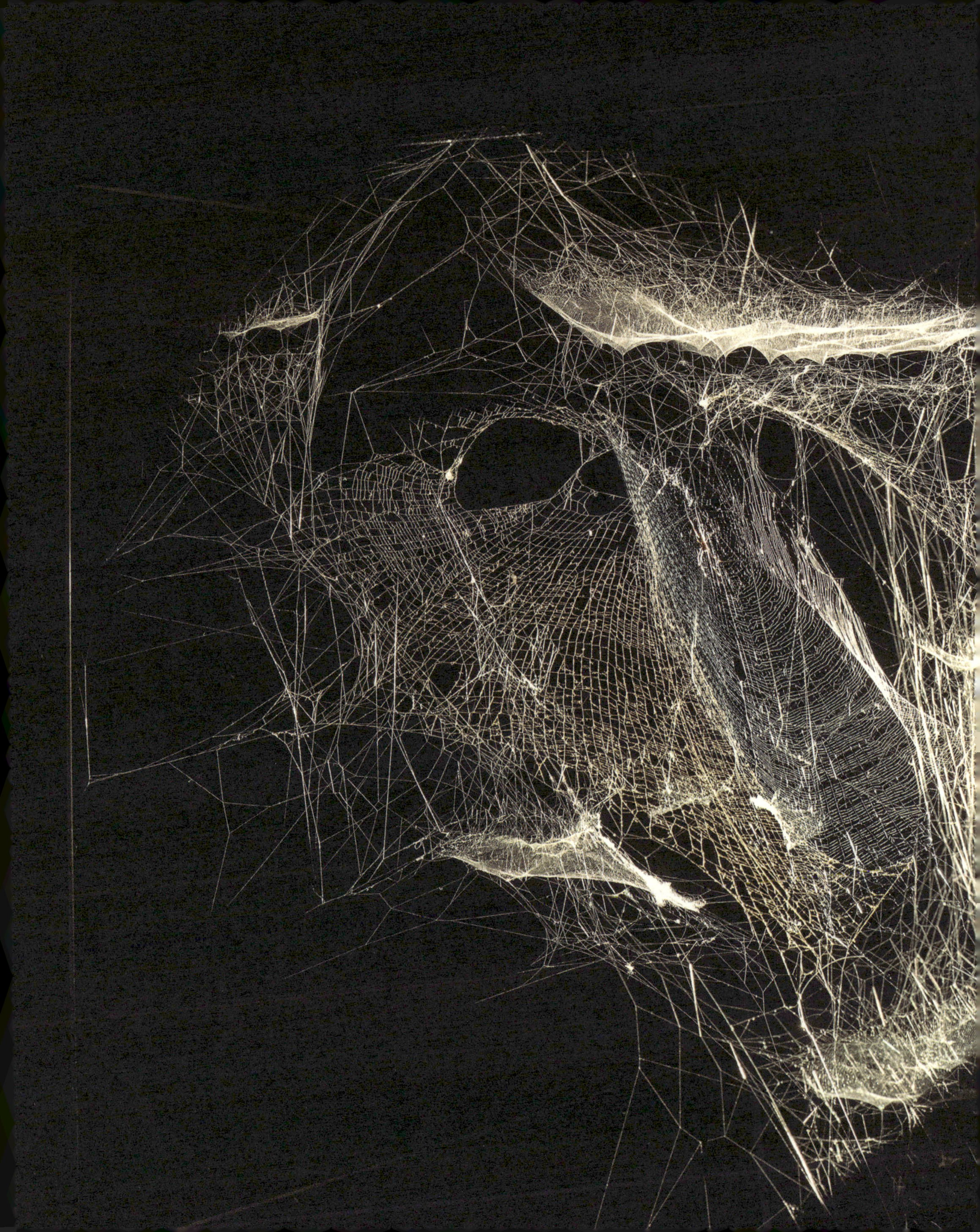

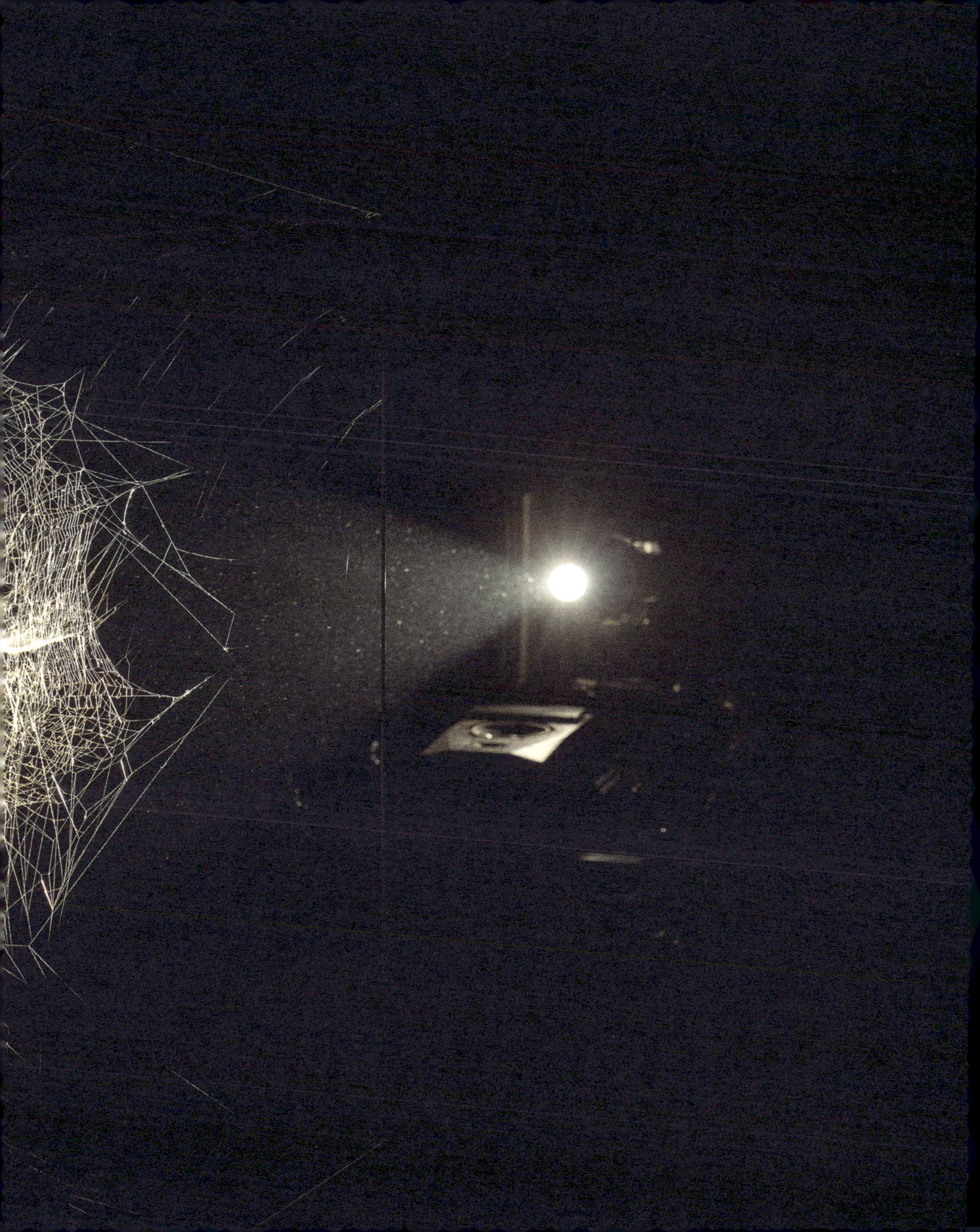

ROOM VI

Gravitational waves resounding
the cosmic web, yet to be felt.
Infinite sensing of the world,
life-forms weave constellations.
Close your eyes, cover your ears,
I will still sense your felt vibrations.

Suit: Diving Bell Spider/Web
Species: Argyroneta aquatica
Notation: D♭
Plant: Sphagnum cuspidatum

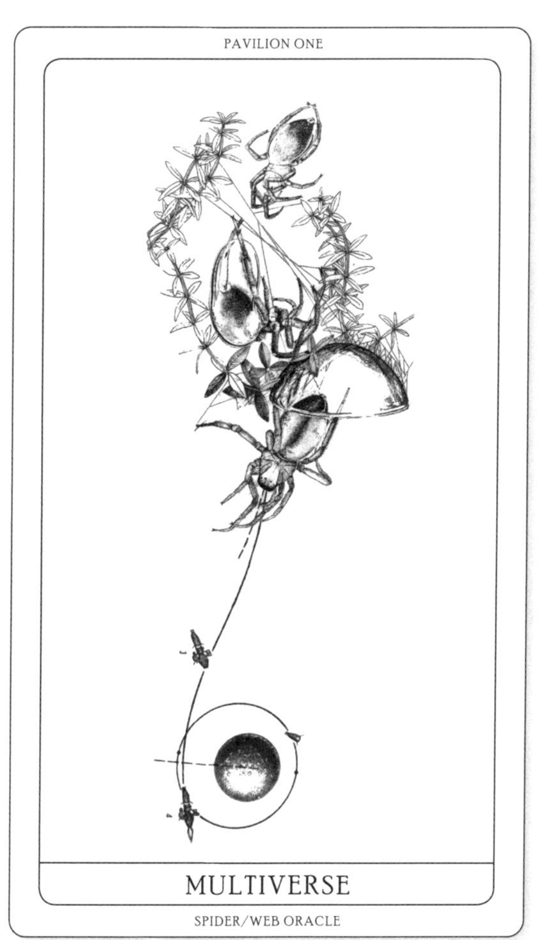
PAVILION ONE
MULTIVERSE
SPIDER/WEB ORACLE

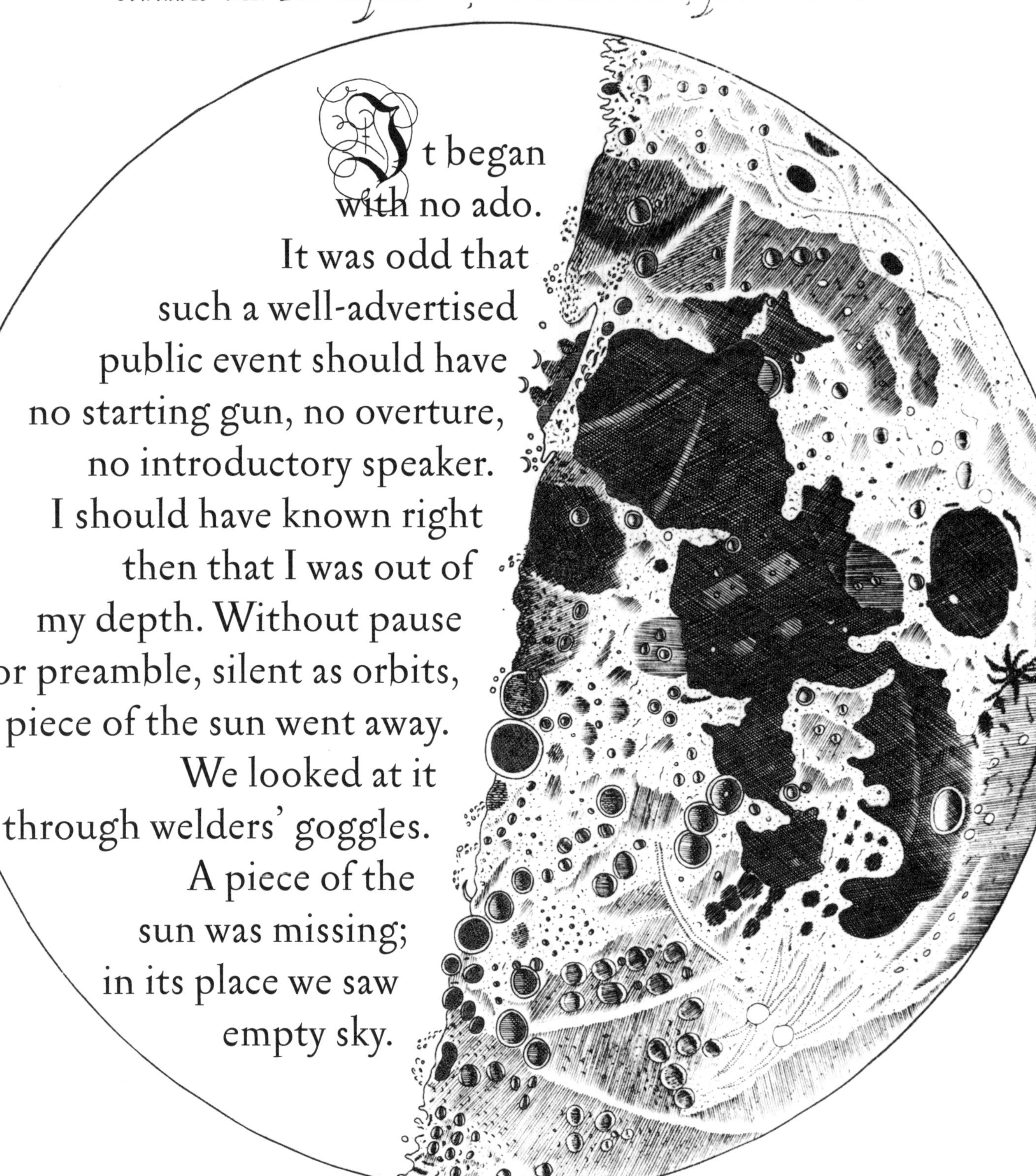

It began
with no ado.
It was odd that
such a well-advertised
public event should have
no starting gun, no overture,
no introductory speaker.
I should have known right
then that I was out of
my depth. Without pause
or preamble, silent as orbits,
a piece of the sun went away.
We looked at it
through welders' goggles.
A piece of the
sun was missing;
in its place we saw
empty sky.

I had seen a partial eclipse in 1970. A partial eclipse is very interesting. It bears almost no relation to a total eclipse. Seeing a partial eclipse bears the same relation to seeing a total eclipse as kissing a man does to marrying him, or as flying in an airplane does to falling out of an airplane. Although the one experience precedes the other, it in no way prepares you for it. During a partial eclipse the sky does not darken—not even when ninety-four percent of the sun is hidden. Nor does the sun, seen colorless through protective devices, seem terribly strange. We have all seen a sliver of light in the sky; we have all seen the crescent moon by day. However, during a partial eclipse the air does indeed get cold, precisely as if someone were standing between you and the fire. And blackbirds do fly back to their roosts. I had seen a partial eclipse before, and here was another.

What you see in an eclipse is entirely different from what you know. It is especially different for those of us whose grasp of astronomy is so frail that, given a flashlight, a grapefruit, two oranges, and fifteen years, we still could not figure out which way to set the clocks for daylight saving time. Usually it is a bit of a trick to keep your knowledge from blinding you. But during an eclipse it is easy. What you see is much more convincing than any wild-eyed theory you may know.

You may read that the moon has something to do with eclipses. I have never seen the moon yet. You do not see the moon. So near the sun, it is as completely invisible as the stars are by day. What you see before your eyes is the sun going through phases. It gets narrower and narrower, as the waning moon does, and, like the ordinary moon, it travels alone in the simple sky. The sky is of course background. It does not appear to eat the sun; it is far behind the sun. The sun simply shaves away; gradually, you see less sun and more sky.

The sky's blue was deepening, but there was no darkness. The sun was a wide crescent, like a segment of tangerine.

The towns and orchards in the valley to the south were dissolving into the blue light. Only the thin river held a trickle of sun.

Now the sky to the west deepened to indigo, a color never seen. A dark sky usually loses color. This was a saturated, deep indigo, up in the air. Stuck up into that unworldly sky was the cone of Mount Adams, and the alpenglow was upon it. The alpenglow is that red light of sunset which holds out on snowy mountaintops long after the valleys and tablelands

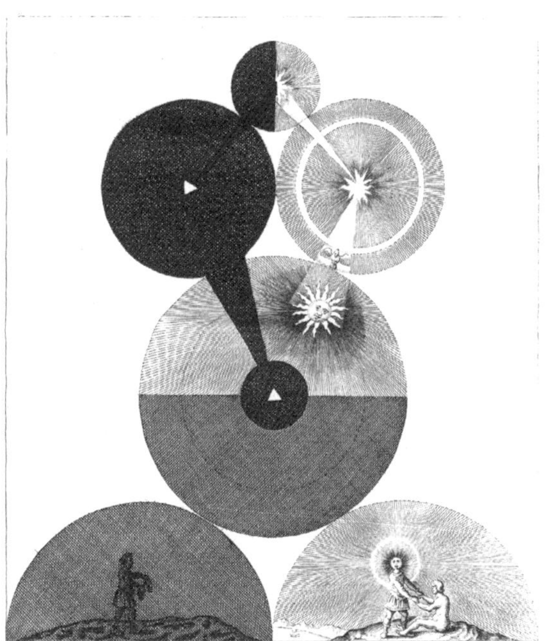

are dimmed. "Look at Mount Adams," I said, and that was the last sane moment I remember.

I turned back to the sun. It was going. The sun was going, and the world was wrong.[1] The grasses were wrong; they were platinum.

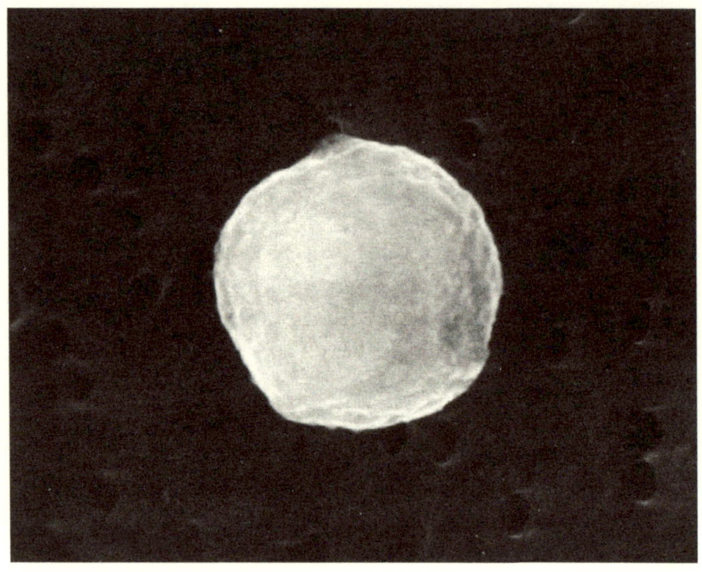

Their every detail of stem, head, and blade shone lightless and artificially distinct as an art photographer's platinum print. This color has never been seen on earth. The hues were metallic; their finish was matte. The hillside was a nineteenth-century tinted photograph from which the tints had faded. All the people you see in the photograph, distinct and detailed as their faces look, are now dead.

The sky was navy blue. My hands were silver. All the distant hills' grasses were finespun metal which the wind laid down. I was watching a faded color print of a movie filmed in the Middle Ages; I was standing in it, by some mistake. I was standing in a movie of hillside grasses filmed in the Middle Ages. I missed my own century, the people I knew, and the real light of day.

I looked at Gary. He was in the film. Everything was lost. He was a platinum print, a dead artist's version of life. I saw on his skull the darkness of night mixed with the colors of day. My mind was going out; my eyes were receding the way galaxies recede to the rim of space. Gary was light-years away, gesturing inside a circle of darkness, down the wrong end of a telescope. He smiled as if he saw me; the stringy crinkles around his eyes moved. The sight of him, familiar and wrong, was something I was remembering from centuries hence, from the other side of death:[2] yes, that is the way he used to look, when we were living. When it was our generation's turn to be alive. I could not hear him; the wind was too loud. Behind him the sun was going. We had all started down a chute of time. At first it was pleasant; now there was no stopping it. Gary was chuting away across space, moving and talking and catching my eye, chuting down the long corridor of separation. The skin on his face moved like thin bronze plating that would peel.

The grass at our feet was wild barley. It was the wild einkorn wheat which grew on the hilly flanks of the Zagros Mountains, above the Euphrates valley, above the valley of the river we called River. We harvested the grass with stone sickles, I remember. We found the grasses on the hillsides; we built our shelter beside them and cut them down. That is how he used to look then, that one, moving and living and catching my eye, with the sky so dark behind him, and the wind blowing. God save our life.

From all the hills came screams. A piece of sky beside

the crescent sun was detaching. It was a loosened circle of evening sky, suddenly lighted from the back. It was an abrupt black body out of nowhere; it was a flat disk; it was almost over the sun. That is when there were screams. At once this disk of sky slid over the sun like a lid. The sky snapped over the sun like a lens cover. The hatch in the brain slammed. Abruptly it was dark night, on the land and in the sky. In the night sky was a tiny ring of light. The hole where the sun belongs is very small. A thin ring of light marked its place. There was no sound. The eyes dried, the arteries drained, the lungs hushed. There was no world. We were the world's dead people rotating and orbiting around and around, embedded in the planet's crust, while the earth rolled down.

Our minds were light-years distant, forgetful of almost everything. Only an extraordinary act of will could recall to us our former, living selves and our contexts in matter and time. We had, it seems, loved the planet and loved our lives, but could no longer remember the way of them. We got the light wrong. In the sky was something that should not be there. In the black sky was a ring of light. It was a thin ring, an old, thin silver wedding band, an old, worn ring. It was an old wedding band in the sky, or a morsel of bone. There were stars. It was all over.

Annie Dillard, excerpt from "Total Eclipse," in *Teaching a Stone to Talk: Expeditions and Encounters*, 1982

1   "Eclipse" comes from the Greek word "ἔκλειψις" (*ékleipsis*) meaning "abandonment." Dillard describes this feeling of being deserted by reality, the relationship between ourselves, the earth, and the sun that we have come to rely on to provide stable meaning through scale collapsing into nothing, leaving only void in its wake. *Merriam-Webster*, s.v. 'eclipse (n.),' accessed December 17, 2019, https://www.merriam-webster.com/dictionary/eclipse .

2   The theme of time becoming confused, of centuries across time collapsing into single moments, recurs throughout accounts of solar eclipses. Virginia Woolf similarly wrote in a 1927 diary entry, "I thought how we were like very old people, in the birth of the world—druids on Stonehenge; (this idea came more vividly in the first pale light though)." Virginia Woolf, *A Writer's Diary*, edited by Leonard Woolf (London: Hogarth Press, 1953), 111.

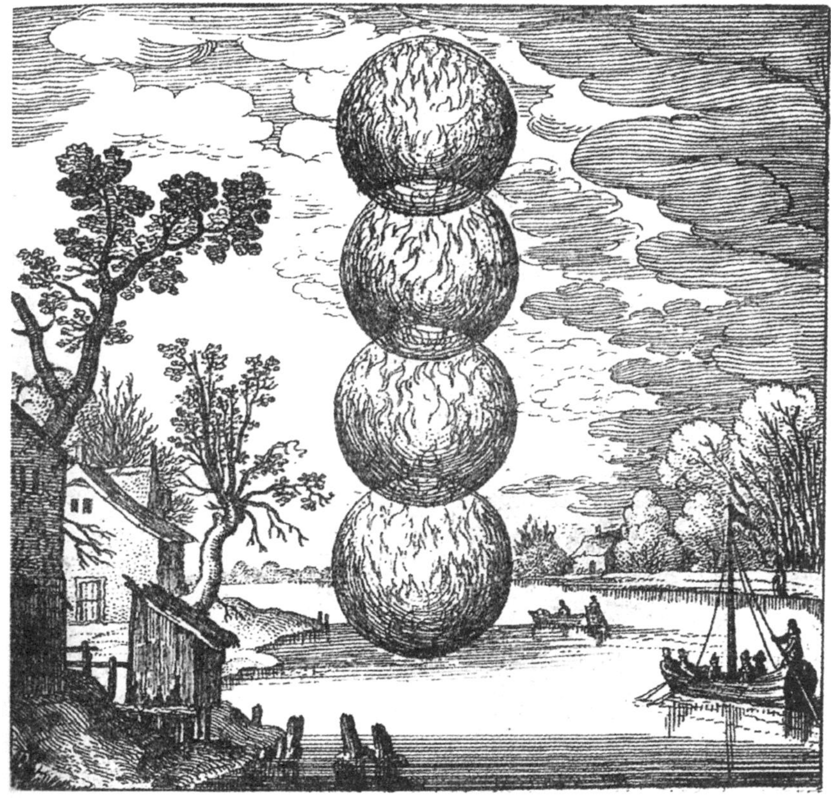

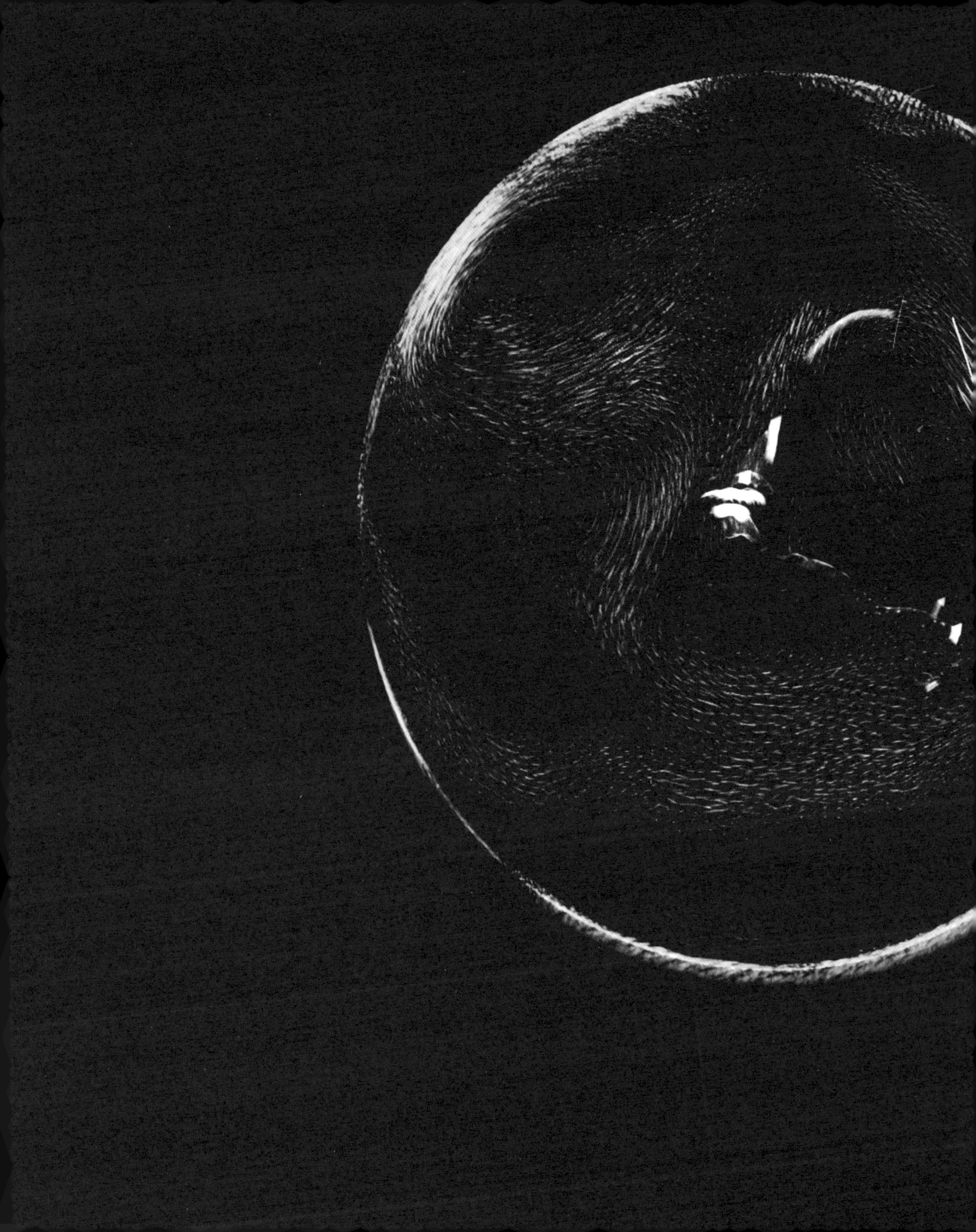

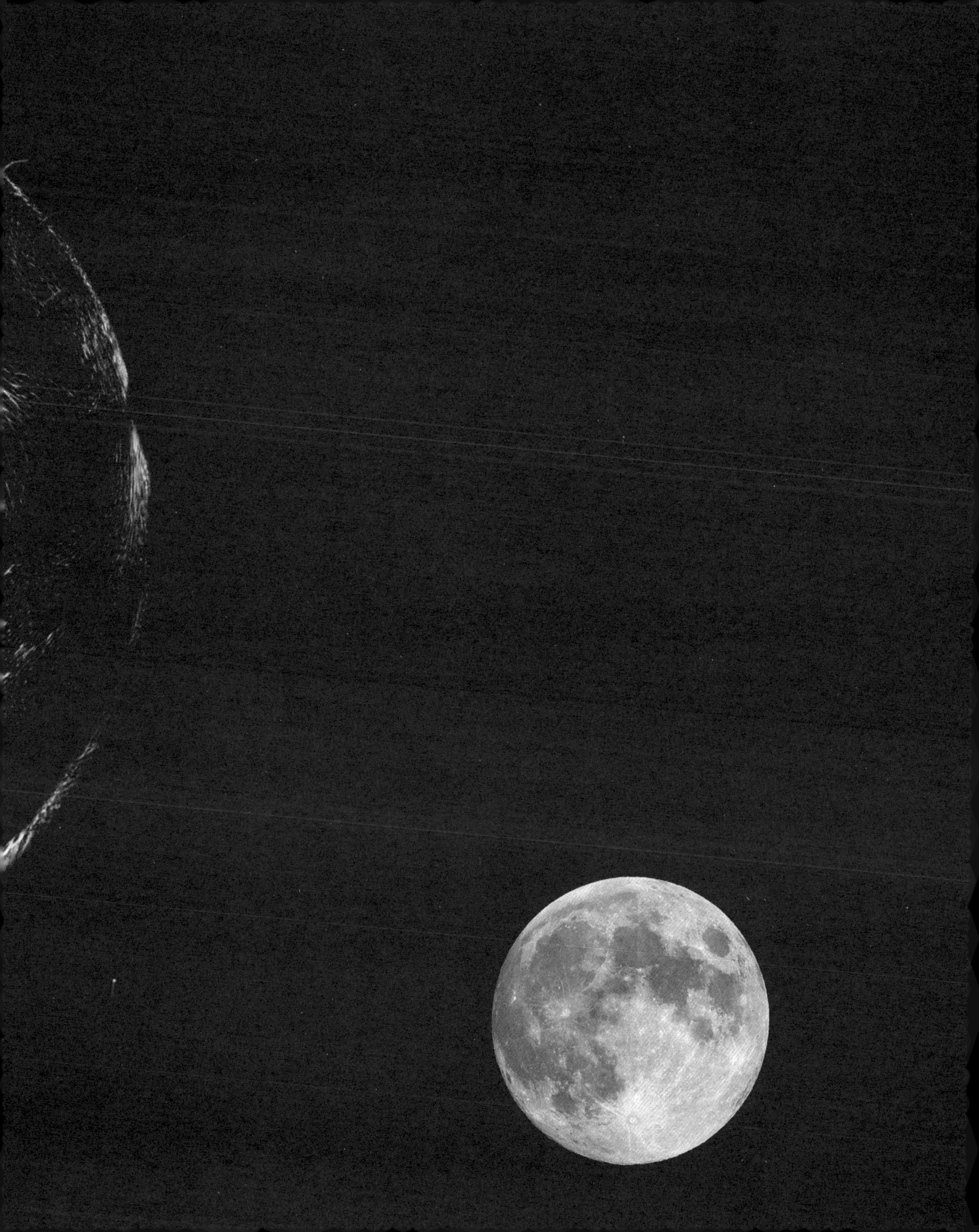

The shadow sun is bizarre, and so is everything that unfolds under it. While eyesight relies on a constant play of light and shadow to do its work properly, the vision of reason supposes a true, shadowless luminosity. When it comes to bodily sight, the shady areas of an object and its shadow define what is visible and give it perspectival depth. Shadows mark the finitude of light—a metaphor for our finite existence. Depending on the angle at which a ray falls, as well as on the variable standpoints of the object and the spectator, a shadow would dance, its length indicating the time of day based on the position of the sun *vis-à-vis* the earth. The minutest event will be, in this way, encrusted into a cosmic drama, pointing back to the alignment of our planet and its star, our senses and experiences.

In Plato's Allegory of the Cave, theater is the appearance of mere shadows, and all appearance is the shadow theater of true being. The underground realm of the cave is not, after all, qualitatively different from the cosmic theater; only the scale and extent of their respective light sources and moving shadows vary. The cold and sterile luminosity of metaphysics, in turn, is shadowless, untethered at once from shadows and the objects that cast them. Given this double separation, the play of light and shadow also ceases. One can no longer tell what time it is on the clock of existence, and for a good reason: there are no shadows, short or long, emanating from Plato's ideal objects. Does shadowlessness not account, if only in part, for Plato's designation of ideas as unchangeable and eternal?

The act of freeing shadows from objects and from light threatens to transform our world into a vast collection of phantoms. The insubstantial becomes substantial and starts leading a life of its own. Metaphysics, in effect, uses the nature of the shadows to cement its stature. Ideas are shadows unglued from, and presumed more genuine than, portions of actual existence. The intangible subject is deemed truer than mere substance. And that which appears before the senses is interpreted as an apparition, a confounding and mendacious ghost. Our fragile, ever incomplete, finite reality turns out to be a lie so long as it is illuminated by the shadow sun.

In the name of true being, unperturbed by any empirical event, philosophers have not hesitated to sacrifice the entire world. Yet, their theoretical desire has been bolstered by economics, in particular by the logic of capital. I could say that capitalism is the continuation of metaphysics by other means, because the value of anything and anyone whatsoever is a shadow that grows more significant than the valued being itself. An economic system born of and befitting two millennia of metaphysics, it finally musters enough resources to destroy the livable planet, having ushered in the geological epoch of the Anthropocene. Besides the unofficial shadow economies (that is, the black markets), capitalism is a monstrous shadow economy that keeps growing while the majority of the global population is impoverished. Detached from need, serving not its human participants but the augmentation of capital, it precisely replicates the untethering of shadows from light and from the objects in its path. In capitalism, as in philosophy, everything visible and tangible is a lie. The truth of capitalism is in the non-sensuous workings of abstract, quantitatively determined value.

The shadow sun of metaphysics, not least in its economic manifestation, has overshadowed the earth and its sun. How to emerge out of the shadow that claims for itself the status of pure light? How to come back to the physical world, woven out of an interplay of lights and shadows?

Nietzsche recommends the revaluation of all values, a project that puts in question the very value of value. It would be insufficient to invert the scale and to put the shadow sun in its rightful place below the sun of astronomy. We ought to question the hierarchy, which presumes a vertical axis with one thing above and the other below. In *Twilight of the Idols*, Nietzsche writes: "The true world is gone: which world is left? The illusory one, perhaps? But no! We got rid of the illusory world along with the true one!" The play of lights and shadows was only an illusion from the standpoint of the now-demolished static and utterly luminous conception of truth. The conclusion that both worlds disappear does not herald a wholesale destruction of real and ideal being but the inescapable necessity of learning to see and think anew, with and from the shadows.

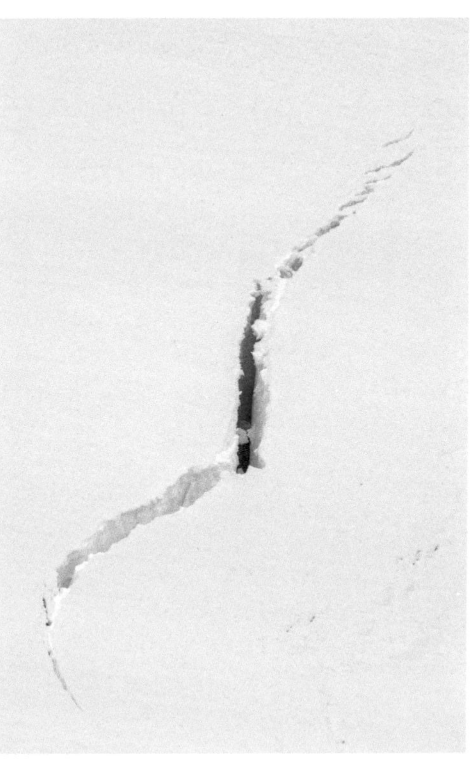

Notice that Nietzsche is reluctant to equate the moment of truth, when the "true world" is revealed as the biggest lie, with total enlightenment. However energetically a hypercritical reason smashes the old idols, however bright its light, such reason will belong together with what it destroys, unless it admits shadows—minimal, and yet irreducible—into its midst.

With his thesis, Nietzsche provides the first clue to an answer to our questions about the shadow sun of metaphysics. As long as there is meaning, as long as we make sense of the world, this meaning and this sense will be the world's shadows. The point is to live as though it is always midday, keeping semantic shadows as close as possible to the things that cast them, keeping them short. Metaphysics has not only lengthened the shadows of meaning beyond belief, nor reversed the values of these shadows and the objects that cast them. It has also lent independent existence to the double, cut off from the thing it duplicates.

Metaphysics requires dissociation from space and time: it ensures the reign of permanent daylight in one hemisphere of being (above) and a never-ending polar night in the other (below), so much so that darkness passes for non-being. Those who have moved on from metaphysics refrain from choosing between meaning and reality, thought and the world. Instead, they observe and participate in the play of lights and shadows staged in the theater of being.

Michael Marder, excerpt from "A Shadow Sun," *Wallpaper*, 2018

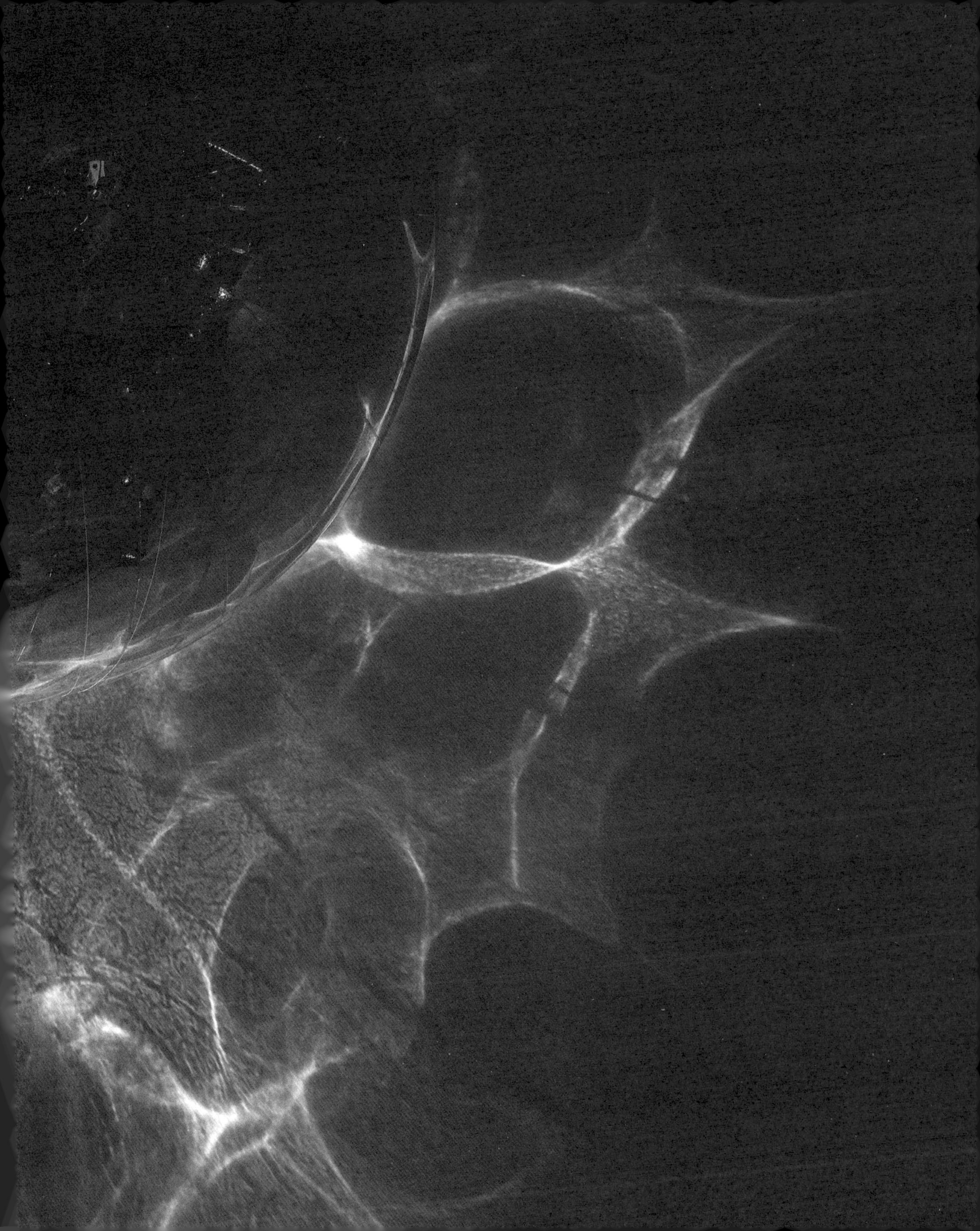

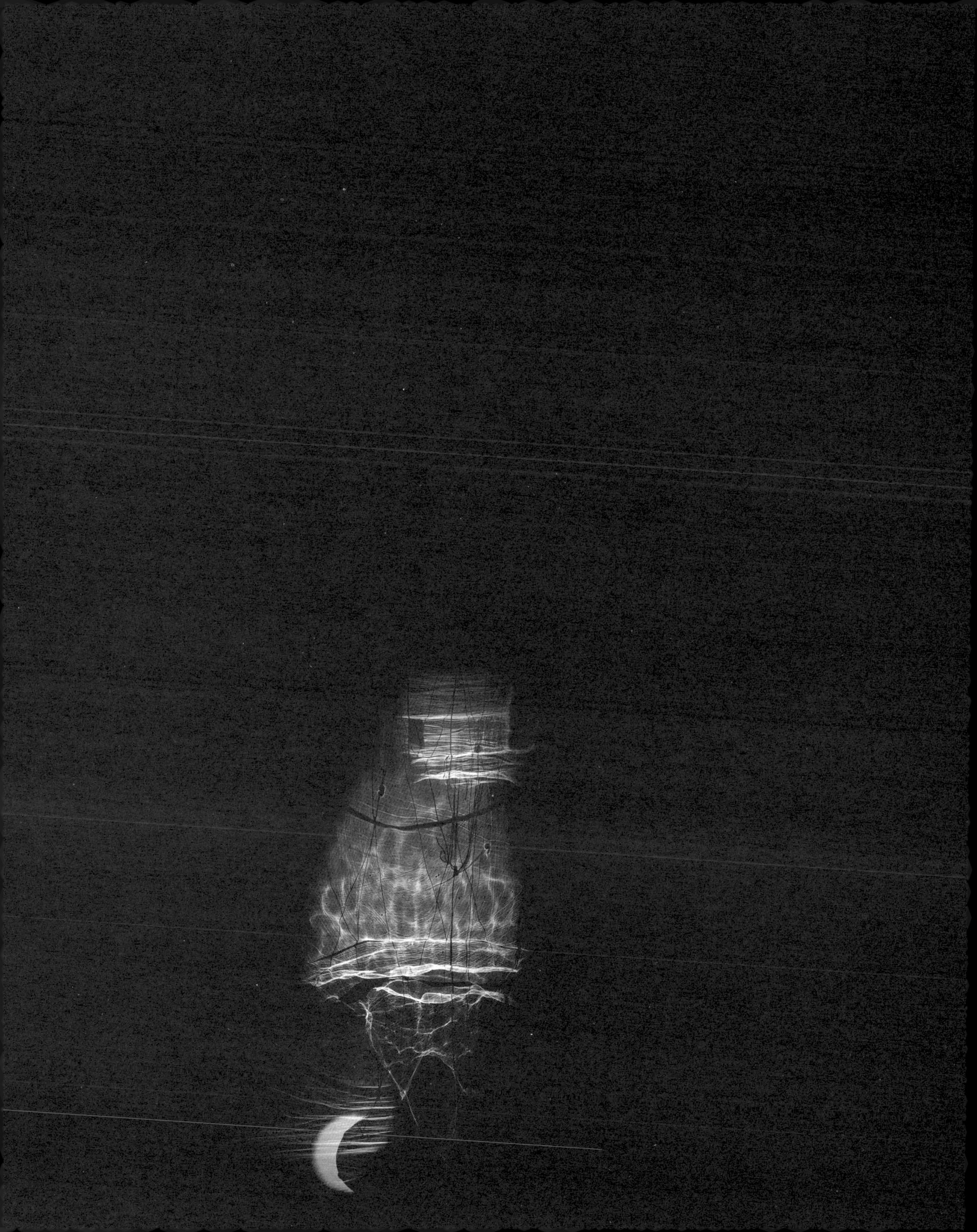

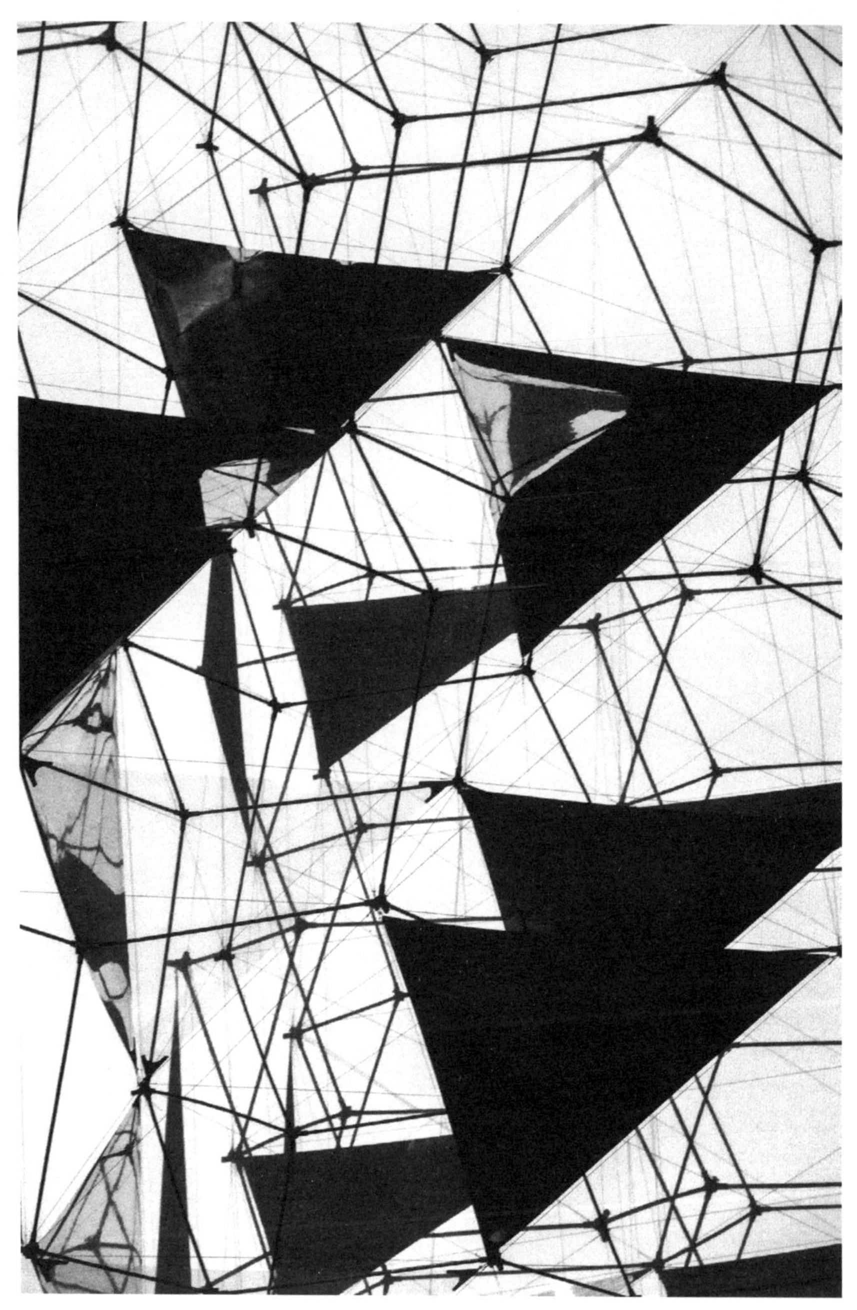

A Thermodynamic Imaginary

This installation suggests a model for a landscape that balances our relationship with, and harnesses the unlimited potential of the sun. This realization requires a thermodynamic leap of imagination, just like during an eclipse, when only in the absence of light do we become aware of our scale in the shadow of the cosmos. In that moment of alignment between Sun, Moon and Earth, we understand that we rely on a reciprocal alliance between the elements and affects, the shifting winds, the exchange of heat and momentum, and the diffusing reflection of solar radiation towards the cosmic extent. Making tangible this invisible web of relations, participants are invited to engage collectively in this exercise for planetary attunement: in the future promised by the parallel ensemble cast about the room, so extends an aerial invitation to play in the thermodynamic imaginary.
Different objects cast their shadows in an ever-changing lightscape, where all is floating, revealing, enlarging and fading away, suspended in elemental motion. You lose yourself in the dispersal of light, second-guessing your shadow as your neighbor's, as your gestures overlap, mirror and intersect, reverberating in a black and white scenography. Bodies and sculptures become diffuse, no longer limited to their physical boundaries, equally composed of matter and emptiness, light and shadow, as they merge with the other entities in the room, be they human or nonhuman, organic or constructed. The aerial sculptures, pendent geometries, clouds and soap bubbles can also be read at an atomic rather than cosmic level—as electrons and protons that exist as the building blocks of all matter. This subversive treatment of scale has pushed us to consider the imaginative potential that sees the microscopic simultaneously with the cosmic, the dark within the light and the illusory within the real.

A Thermodynamic Imaginary
2020
Various dimensions

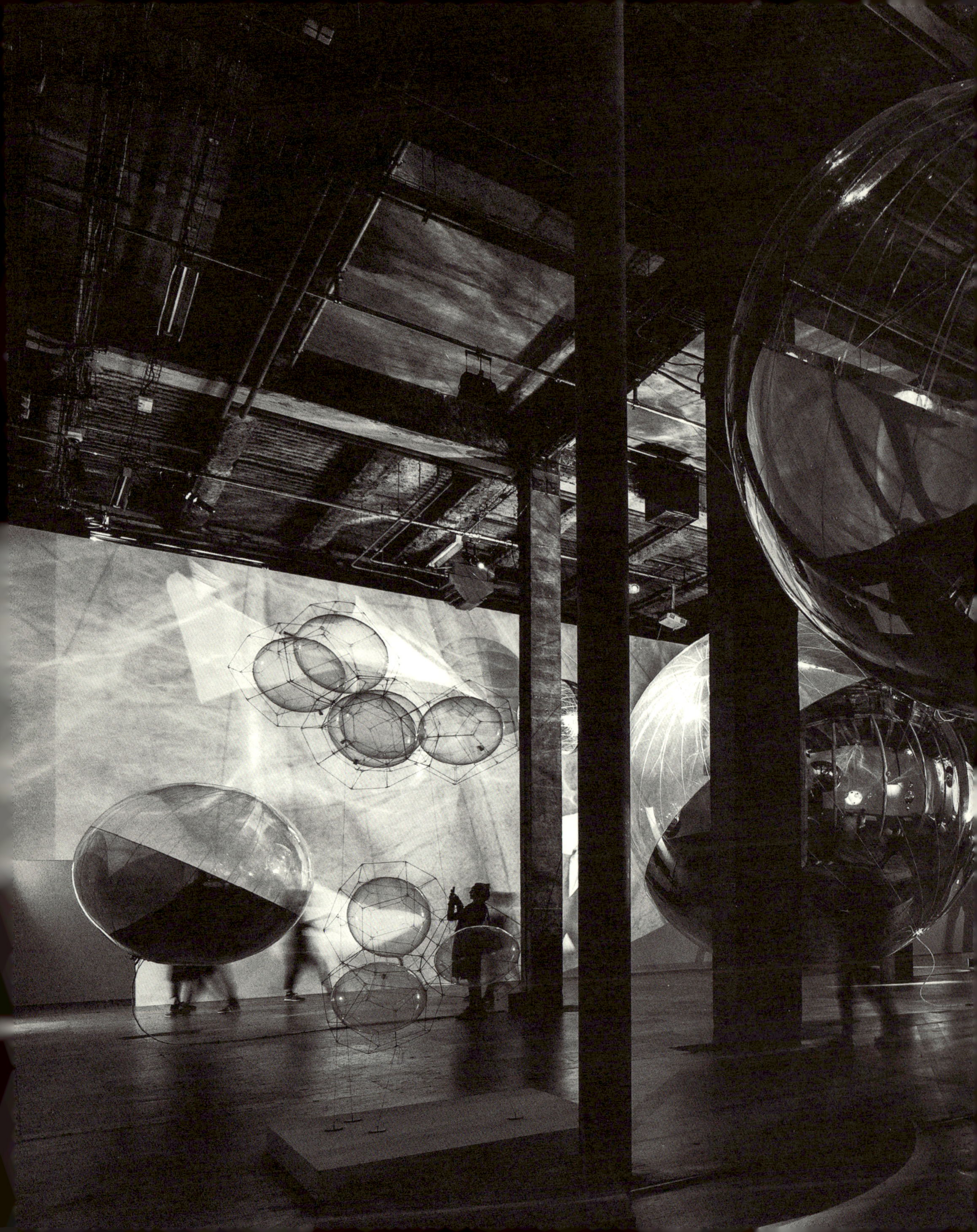

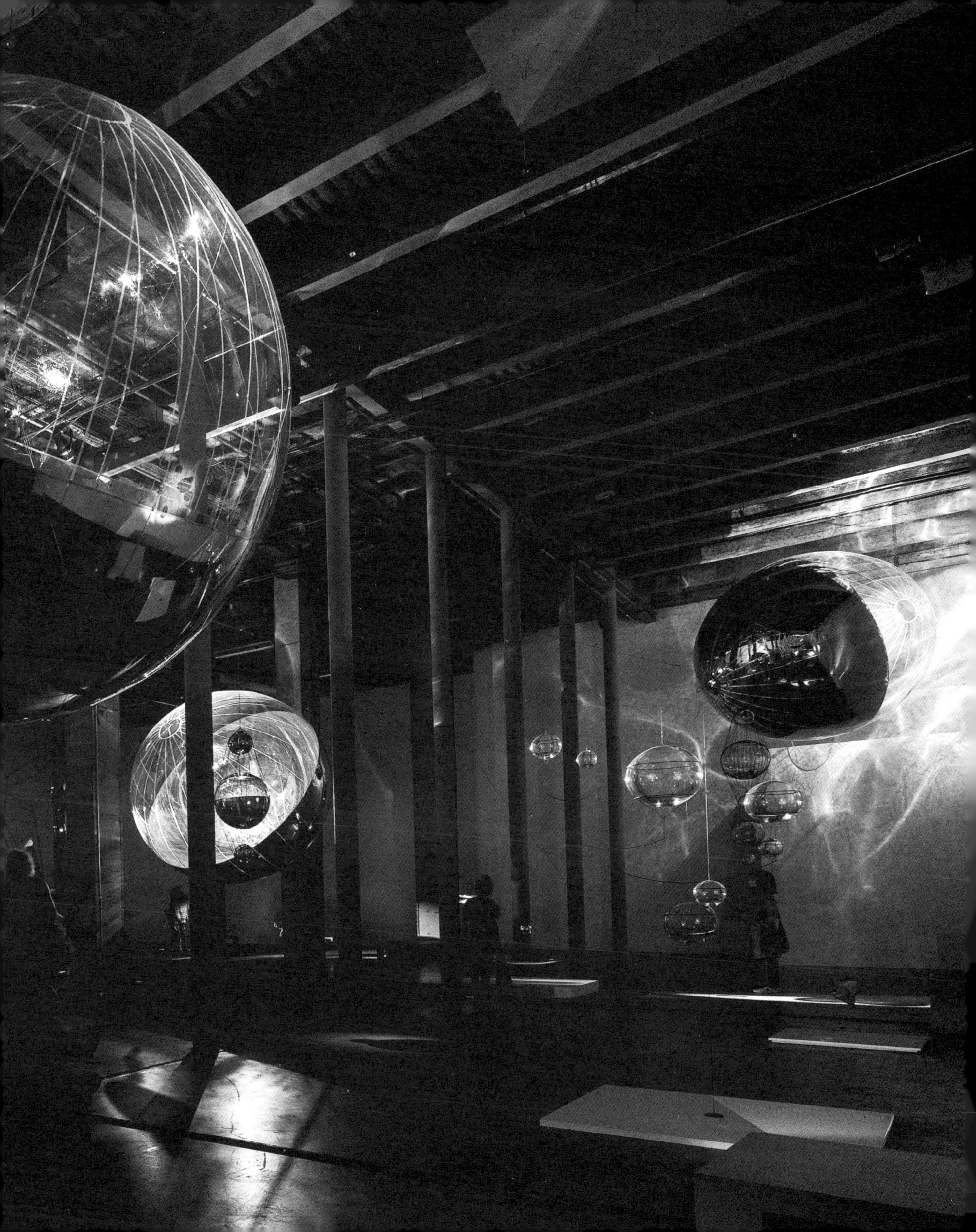

ROOM VII

Lamps and lightbulbs as allies in daily hunting,
bridging lifeways in entangled dependency.
Nature seems to elect relationships rather
than individuals, nothing makes itself alone.
Ask yourself how many multitudes you contain.

Suit: Cob Spider/Web
Species: Theridion familiare
Notation: E♭
Plant: Linum usitatissimum

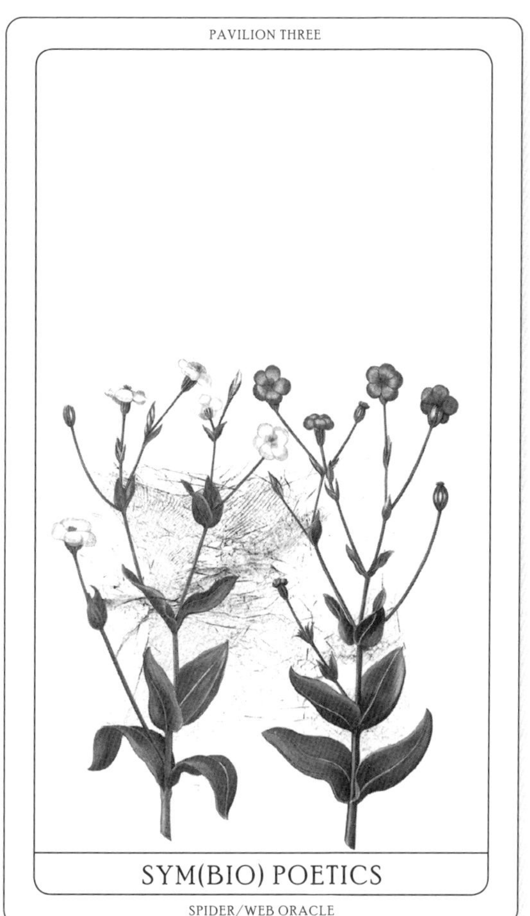

PAVILION THREE
SYM(BIO) POETICS
SPIDER/WEB ORACLE

"I . . . I thought it must be the trees," he said, and stopped.
"It's not the trees," Harfex said. "They have no
more nervous system than do plants of the Hainish
Descent on earth. None."
"You're not seeing the forest for the trees, as they say
on earth," Mannon put in, smiling elfinly; Harfex
stared at him.

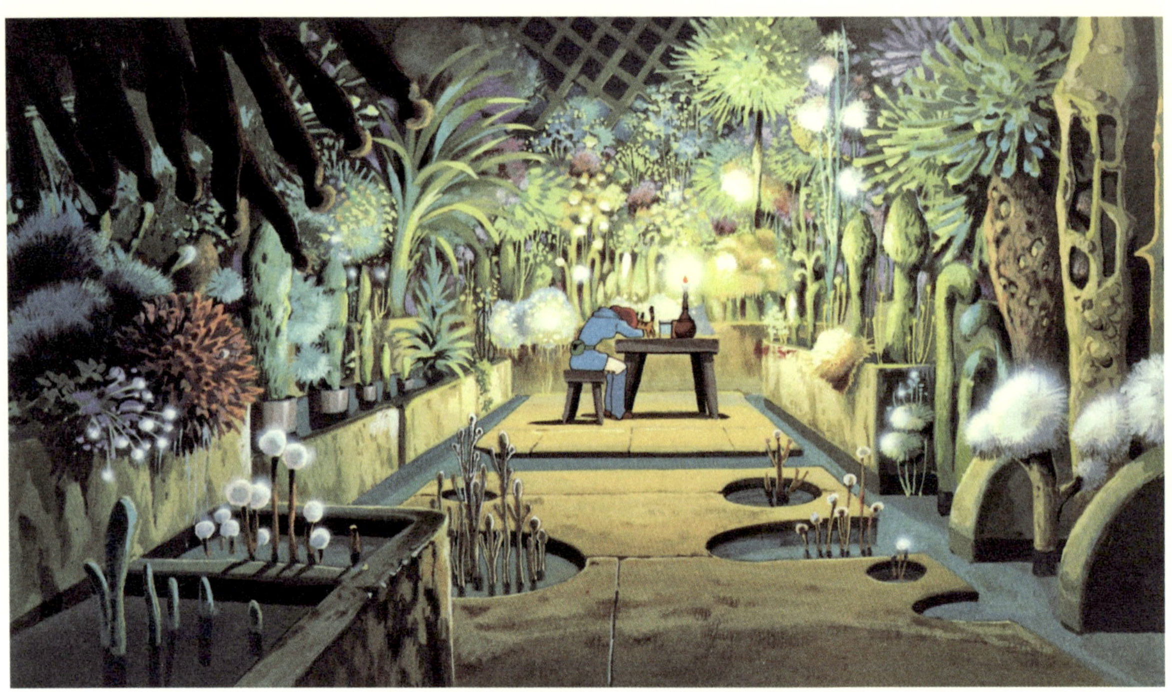

"What about those root-nodes we've been
puzzling about for twenty days—eh?"
"What about them?"
"They are, indubitably, connections.

Connections among the trees. Right? Now let's just suppose, most improbably, that you knew nothing of animal brain-structure. And you were given one axon, or one detached glial cell, to examine. Would you be likely to discover what it was? Would you see that the cell was capable of sentience?"

"No. Because it isn't. A single cell is capable of mechanical response to stimulus. No more. Are you hypothesizing that individual arboriforms are 'cells' in a kind of brain, Mannon?"

"Not exactly. I'm merely pointing out that they are all interconnected, both by the root-node linkage and by your green epiphytes in the branches.[1] A linkage of incredible complexity and physical extent. Why, even the prairie grass-forms have those root-connectors, don't they? I know that sentience or intelligence isn't a thing, you can't find it in, or analyze it out from, the cells of a brain. It's a function of the connected cells. It is, in a sense, the connection: the connectedness. It doesn't exist. I'm not trying to say it exists. I'm only guessing that Osden might be able to describe it."

And Osden took him up, speaking as if in a trance. "Sentience without senses. Blind, deaf, nerveless, moveless. Some irritability, response to touch. Response to sun, to light, to water, and chemicals in the earth around the roots. Nothing comprehensible to an animal mind. Presence without mind. Awareness of being, without object or subject. Nirvana."

"Then why do you receive fear?" Tomiko asked in a low voice.

"I don't know. I can't see how awareness of objects, of others, could arise: an unperceiving response. . . But there was an uneasiness, for days. And then when I lay between the two trees and my blood was on their roots—" Osden's face glittered with sweat. "It became fear," he said shrilly, "only fear."

"If such a function existed," Harfex said, "it would not be capable of conceiving of a self-moving, material entity, or responding to one. It could no more become aware of us than we can 'become aware' of Infinity."

"The silence of those infinite expanses terrifies me," muttered Tomiko. "Pascal was aware of Infinity. By way of fear."

"To a forest," Mannon said, "we might appear as forest fires. Hurricanes. Dangers. What moves quickly is dangerous, to a plant. The rootless would be alien, terrible. [. . .] No wonder it was afraid—" [. . .]

"Before it panicked it had a—there was a serenity. I couldn't take it in, then, I didn't realize how big it was. To know the whole daylight, after all, and the whole night. All the winds and lulls together. The winter stars and the summer stars at the same time. To have roots, and no enemies. To be entire. Do you see? No invasion. No others. To be whole. . ."[2]

Ursula K. Le Guin, excerpt from "Vaster than Empires and More Slow," in *The Wind's Twelve Quarters*, 1975

1 Epiphytes are plants that grow outside of the earth, gathering nutrients from the air. One prominent example is the tillandsia, which I use in *Flying Gardens.*

2 Le Guin is a force in speculative fiction, having entered even after being discouraged by the science fiction she read as a child, which "seemed to be all about hardware and soldiers: white men go forth and conquer the universe." In contrast to such colonial and dominating fantasies, Le Guin offers here a story that learns from what one finds— whether on a faraway planet or your own. See Gerald Jonas, "Ursula K. Le Guin, Acclaimed for Her Fantasy Fiction, Is Dead at 88," *New York Times,* January 23, 2018, https://www.nytimes. com/2018/01/23/ obituaries/ursula-k-le- guin-acclaimed-for-her- fantasy-fiction-is-dead- at-88.html.

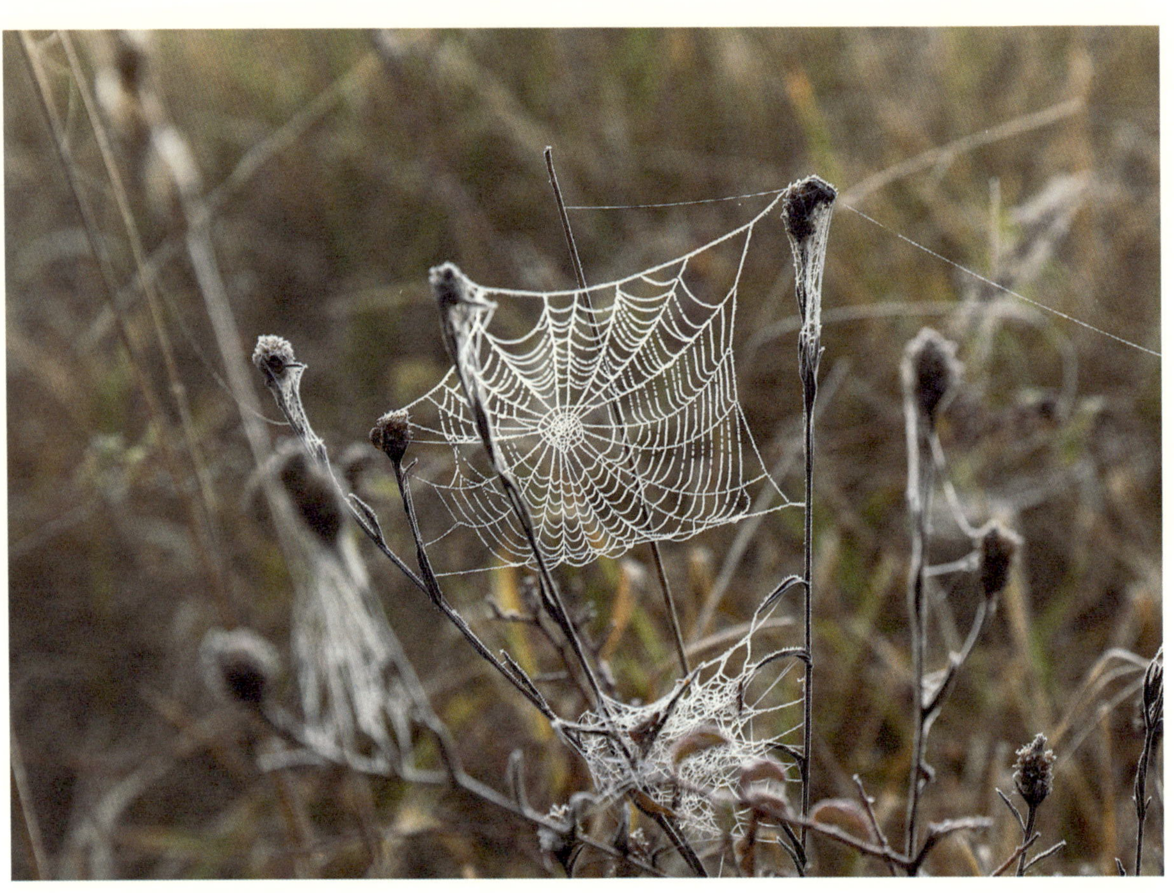

How does a gathering become a "happening," that is, greater than a sum of its parts? One answer is contamination. We are contaminated by our encounters; they change who we are as we make way for others. As contamination changes world making projects, mutual worlds—and new directions—may emerge. Everyone carries a history of contamination; purity is not an option. One value of keeping precarity in mind is that it makes us remember that changing with circumstances is the stuff of survival. But what is survival? In popular American fantasies, survival is all about saving oneself by fighting off others. The "survival" featured in U.S. television shows or alien planet stories is a synonym for conquest and expansion. I will not use the term that way. Please open yourself to another usage. [. . .] Staying alive—for every species—requires livable collaborations. Collaboration means working across difference, which leads to contamination. Without collaborations, we all die."

[. . .] Precarity is a state of acknowledgment of our vulnerability to others. In order to survive, we need help, and help is always the service of another, with or without intent. When I sprain my ankle, a stout stick may help me walk, and I enlist its assistance. I am now an encounter in motion, a woman-and-stick. It is hard for me to think of any challenge I might face without soliciting the assistance of others, human and not human. It is unselfconscious privilege that allows us to fantasize—counter-factually—that we each survive alone.

If survival always involves others, it is also necessarily subject to the indeterminacy of self-and-other transformations. We change through our collaborations both within and across species. The important stuff for life on earth happens in those transformations, not in the decision trees of self-contained individuals. Rather than seeing only the expansion-and-conquest strategies of relentless individuals, we must look for histories that develop through contamination. Thus, how might a gathering become a "happening"?

Collaboration is work across difference, yet this is not the innocent diversity of self-contained evolutionary tracks. The evolution of our "selves" is already polluted by histories of encounter; we are mixed up with others before we even begin any new collaboration. Worse yet, we are mixed up in the projects that do us the most harm. The diversity that allows us to enter collaborations emerges from histories of extermination, imperialism, and all the rest. Contamination makes diversity.

This changes the work we imagine for names, including ethnicities and species. If categories are unstable, we must watch them emerge within encounters. To use category names should be a commitment to tracing the assemblages in which these categories gain a momentary hold. [. . .] These identities entered our meeting from histories of transformative ruin, even as new collaborations changed them.

[. . .] If a rush of troubled stories is the best way to tell about contaminated diversity, then it's time to make that rush part of our knowledge practices. Perhaps, like the war survivors themselves, we need to tell and tell until all our stories of death and near-death and gratuitous life are standing with us to face the challenges of the present. It is in listening to that cacophony of troubled stories that we might encounter our best hopes for precarious survival.

[. . .] Such interwoven rhythms perform a still lively temporal alternative to the unified progress-time we still long to obey.

Anna Lowenhaupt Tsing, excerpt from
*The Mushroom at the End of the World:
On the Possibility of Life in Capitalist Ruins*, 2015

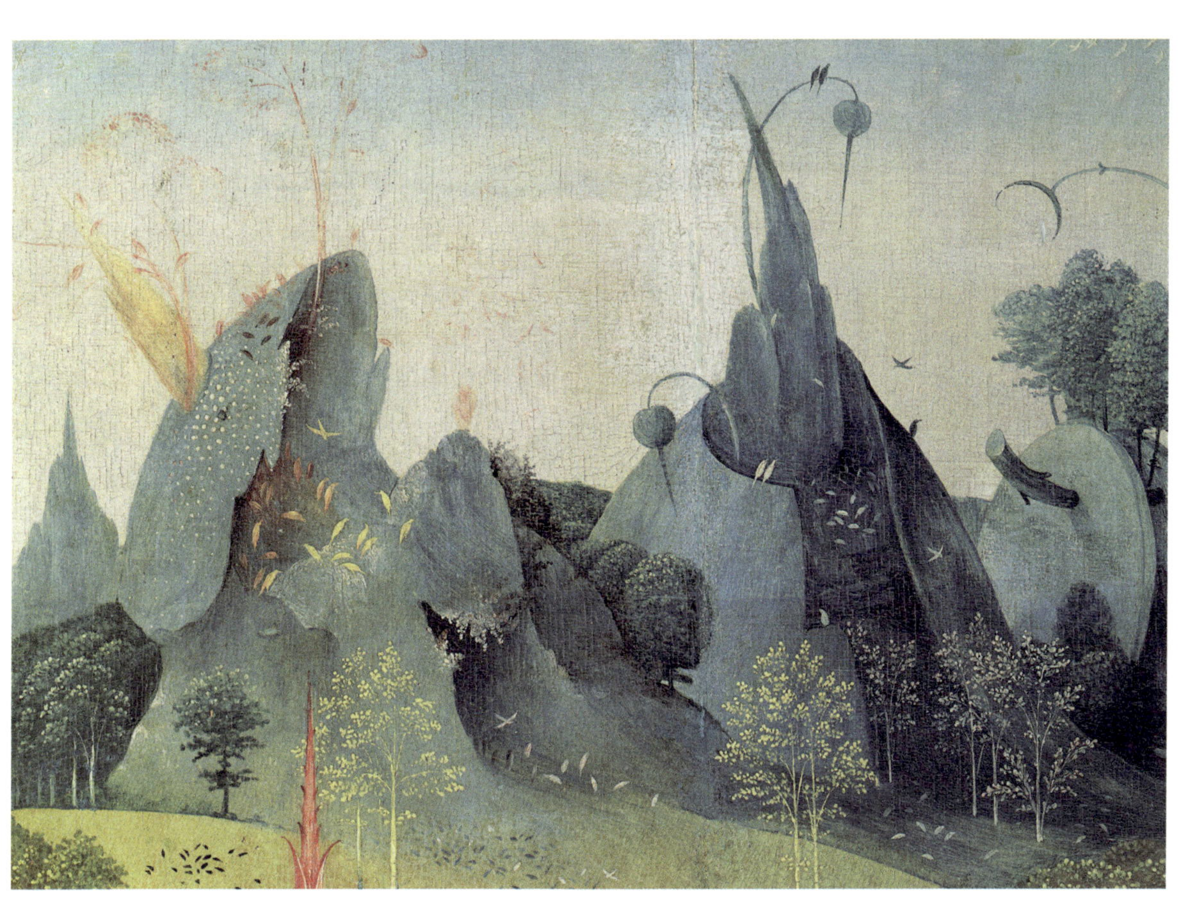

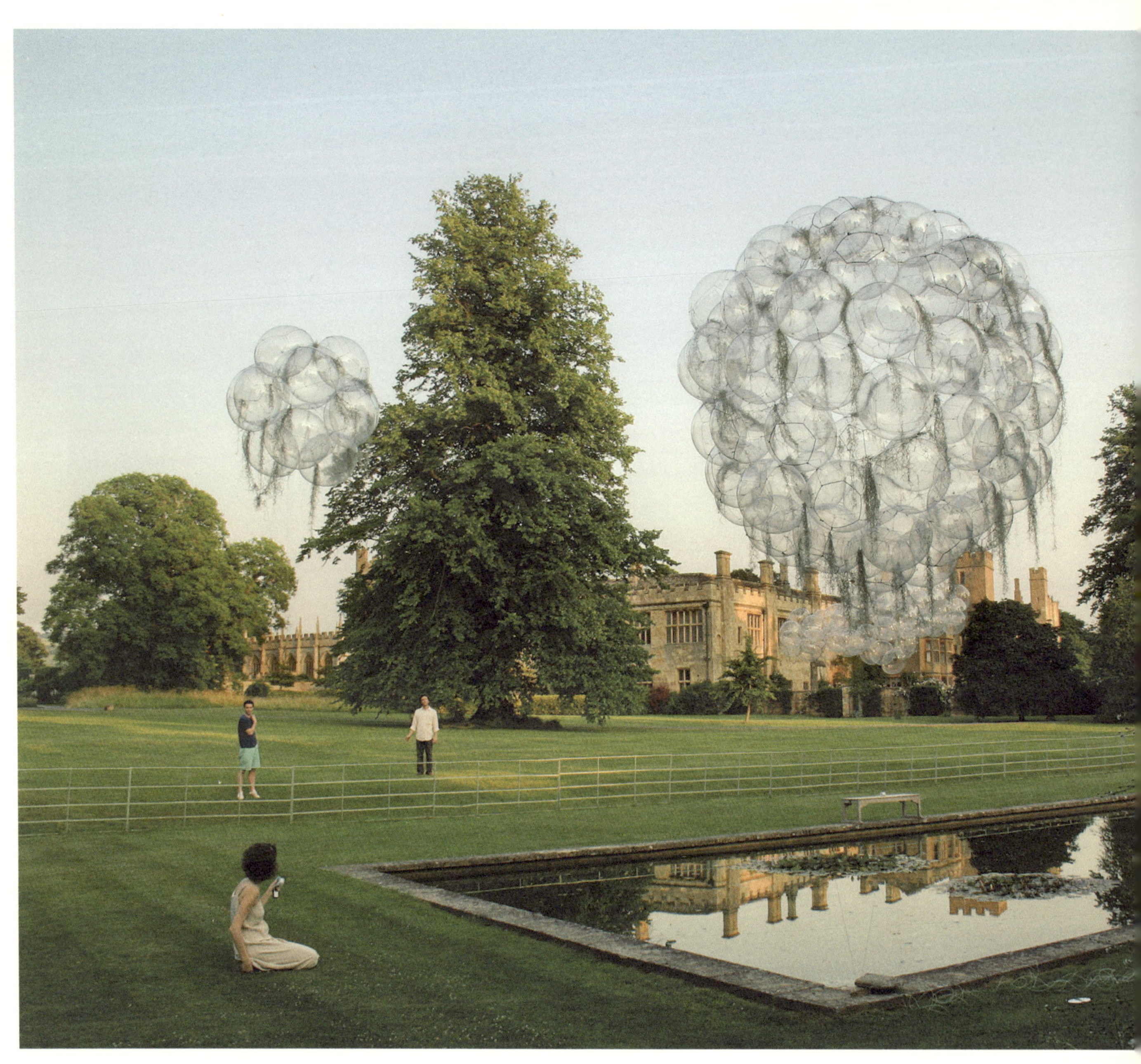

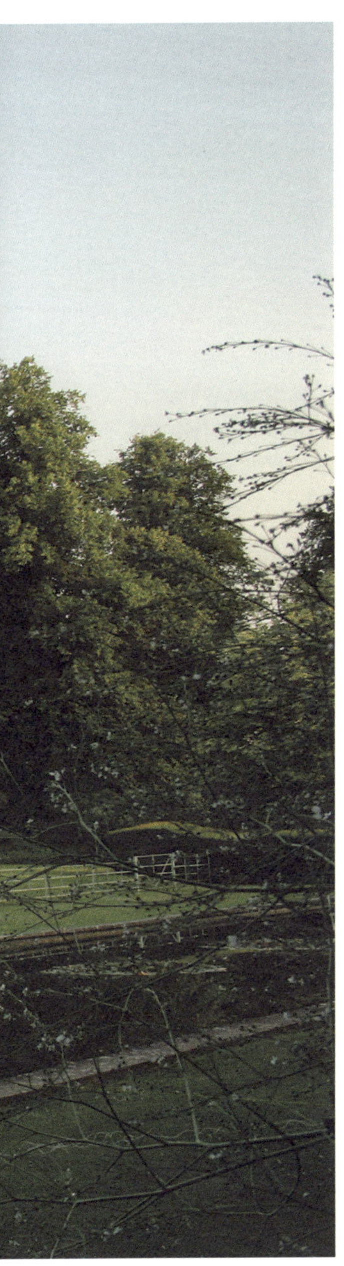

Flying Gardens

In *Flying Gardens*, Tillandsias plants, resilient aerial plants without roots that get their water and nutrients from the air, remind us that the terrestrial and the celestial are, in fact, one, not separated but united in a life cycle and shared space. Tillandsias, who grow wherever conditions allow, feeding themselves with the water, nutrients, and sunlight they find in the ocean of air, remind us that our atmosphere is teeming with life, not empty but full.

The air itself has been reminding us of this itself lately, with sky-high rates of air pollution and global warming revealing what happens when we upset its balance—not only internally, but its balance within the larger environment, with the ocean, the earth and the cosmos, as well. Fogs of pollution and capsized icebergs act as elemental warning cries linked to our delusive mastery of the environment—we must free the air from particulate matter. In his 2018 book *Down to Earth: Politics in the New Climatic Regime*, Bruno Latour speaks directly to this elemental mutiny, asking, "How are we to act if the territory itself begins to participate in history, to fight back, in short, to concern itself with us—how do we occupy a land if it is this land itself that is occupying us?" The answer is that we must recognize it as an agent, and discard a colonial framework of "occupation," seeking instead a collaboration with this actor. To create *Flying Gardens* or a *Cloud City* is not to abandon the terrestrial territory we have come to fear, not to ignore Latour's suggestion that we remain "down to earth"; instead, it is an attempt to inhabit the air differently—as we understand it to be part of one system with the other environmental elements—and in doing so reattune with the planet and air with which we live. This reattunement necessitates futures of living predicated on union. Aerial plants like the Tillandsias remind us that there are, in fact, no natural divisions— even the "distinct" elements of soil, water, and air are inexorably intertwined in reality—and that solidarity is a prerequisite for survival.

Plants exhibit this solidarity against divisions within themselves, as well; in conversations with the artist, Italian plant neurobiologist Stefano Mancuso explained that, as stationary beings, plants have had to adapt a balance with their environment—including with their predators, from whom they are not able to run—through a dispersal of organic functions throughout their entire bodies; instead of discrete organs with specialised functions—brain for thinking, lungs for breathing,

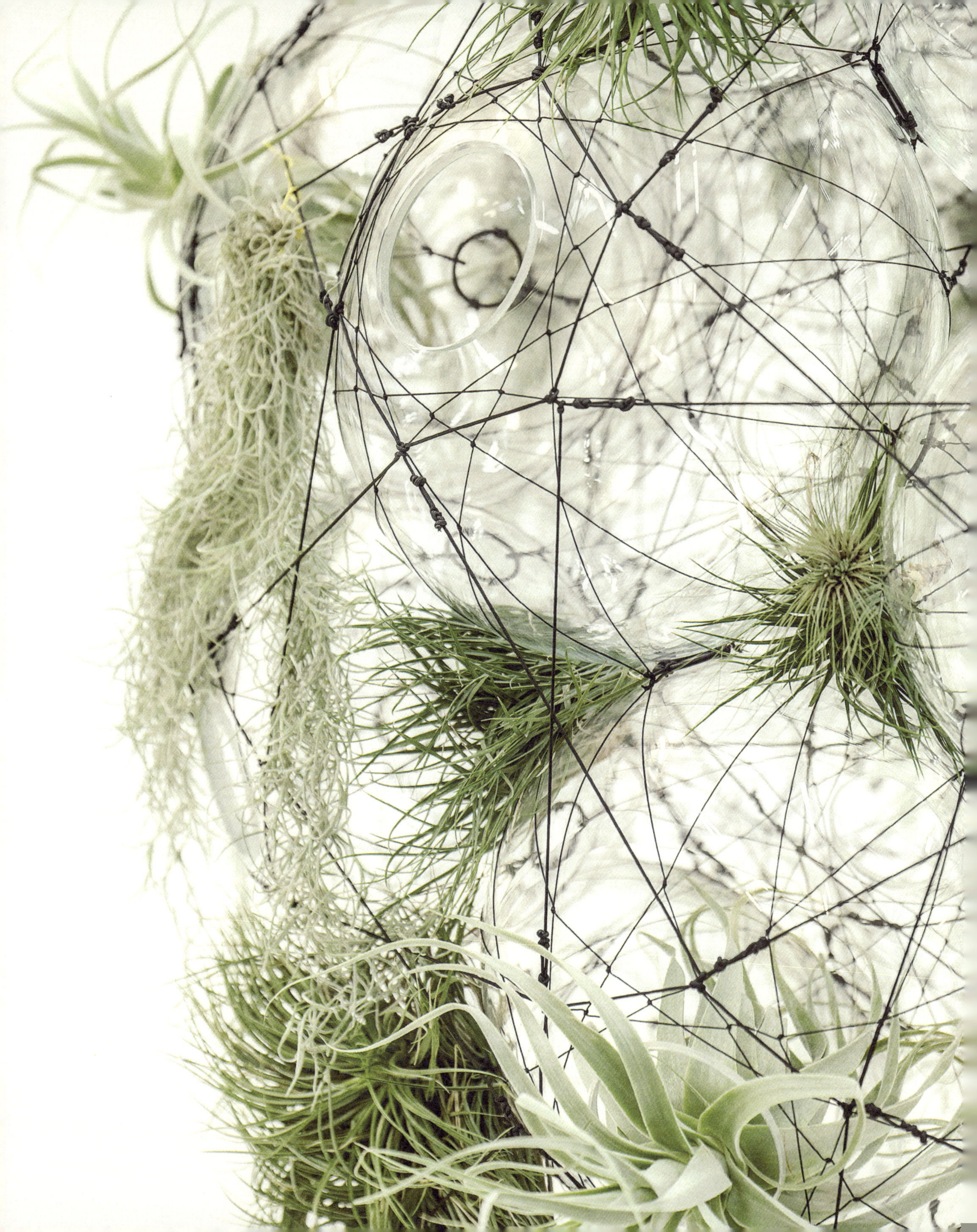

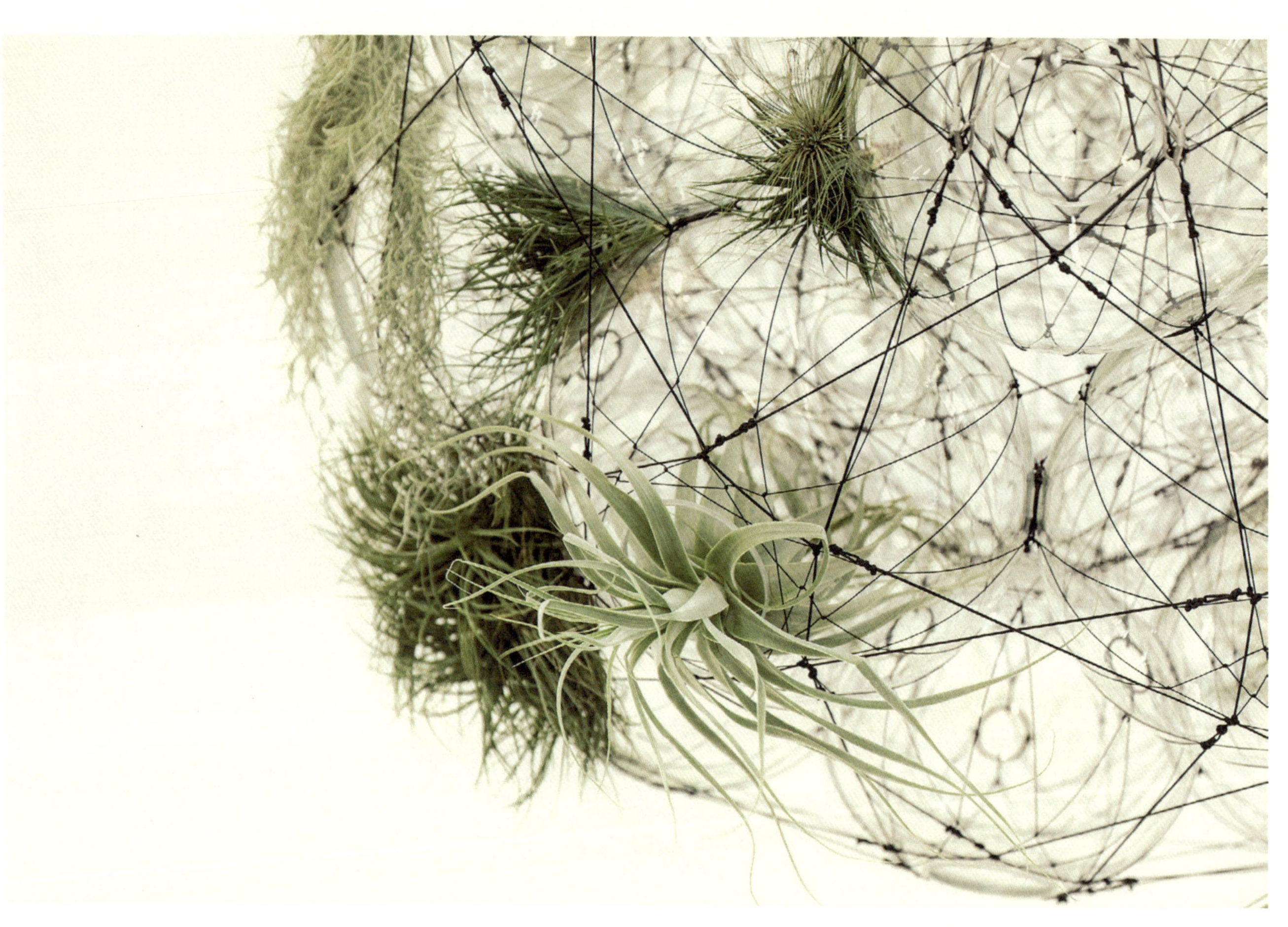

stomach for digesting, etc.—these mechanisms are made uniformly diffuse across the plant. An animal model of distinct organs would leave the plant completely vulnerable, dying as soon as the first critter came along to eat even a small portion of the plant. Survival for the plant is dependent upon decentralization, a principle it also applies outside its body into community relations; after centuries of failures stemming from hierarchy and disunion, we find our survival is dependent upon it, as well.

This dispersal of function recalls the spider/web, whose form is also evoked in the knotted cords binding *Flying Gardens*'s glass spheres: for web-building spiders, their web is an instrument for vibrational communication, the architecture of which is acutely attuned to the vibrational tremors that pass through it, and through which the spider sends signals to sense the environment. Evolutionary biologists Hilton Japyassú and Kevin Laland even propose that the web not only extends the spider's senses, but also its cognition, as it offloads cognitive tasks to its web, trusting it to "think through" the signals it receives.

It may be surprising to hear plants spoken of in terms of "community relations" and even "consciousness," terms we usually reserve for animals. But recent developments in plant neuroscience led by scientists such as Marcuso and Monica Gagliano posit that plants are thinking and even feeling beings—something that has actually been intimately known for millennia, across cultures and traditions. The same is true for the agential capacities of non-living beings: we need look no further than the Roman gods of classical antiquity here in Italy to see a belief system that understands the power of the elements. But we must not anthropomorphize as we move forward; it is enough—and better—to acknowledge the existential being of these entities on their own terms, in their own forms.

The political and affective possibilities this opens up for us are endless. As Latour notes, "A world composed of objects does not have the same type of resistance as a world composed of agents." To this, Gagliano has added, when asked of how her life has changed through her scientific study, "The main difference is that I used to live in a world of objects, and now I live in a world of subjects. And so, I am never alone."

Flying Gardens
2020
Tillandsia plants, hand blown glass, monofilament, polyester rope, velvet rope, carbon fiber
Various dimensions

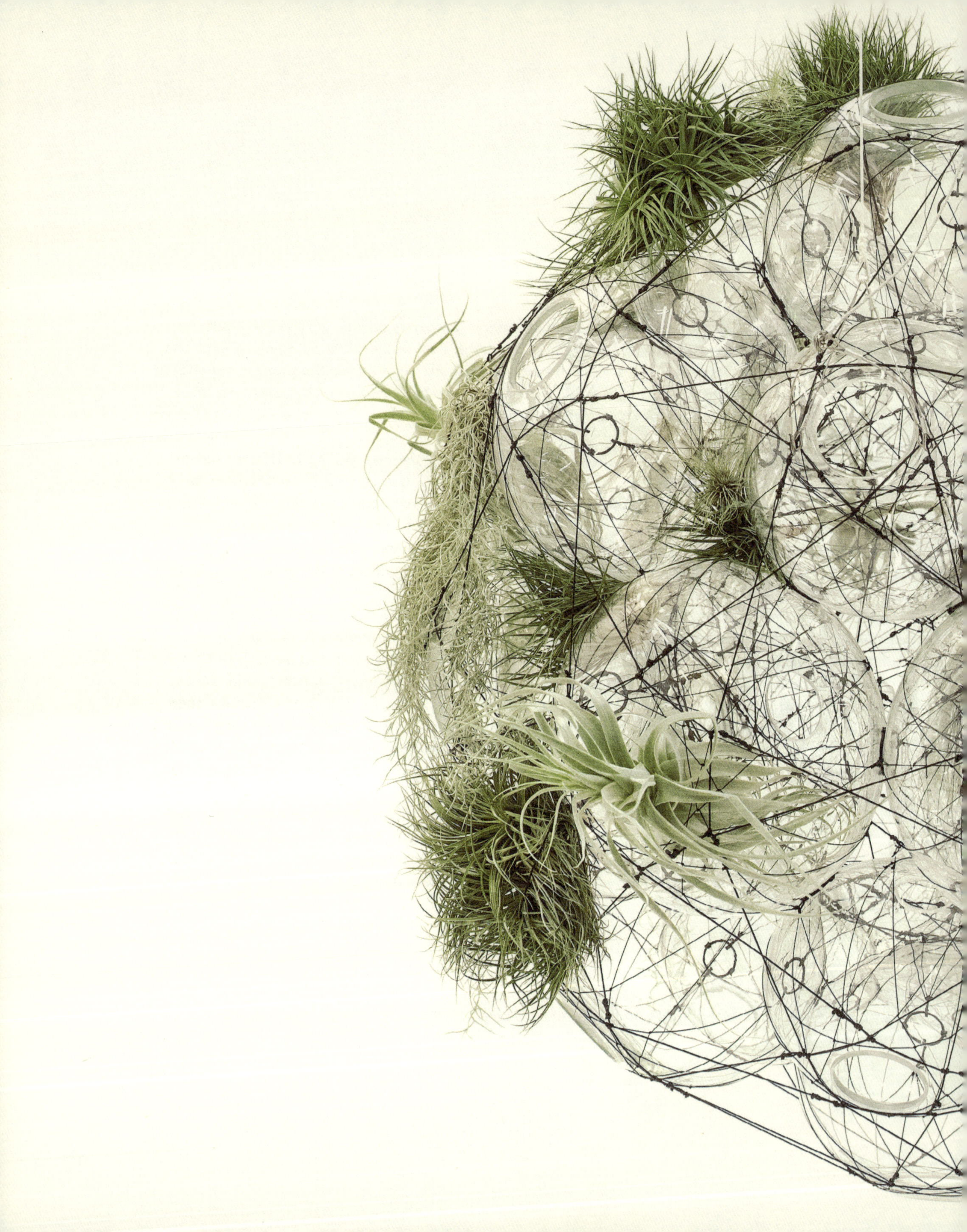

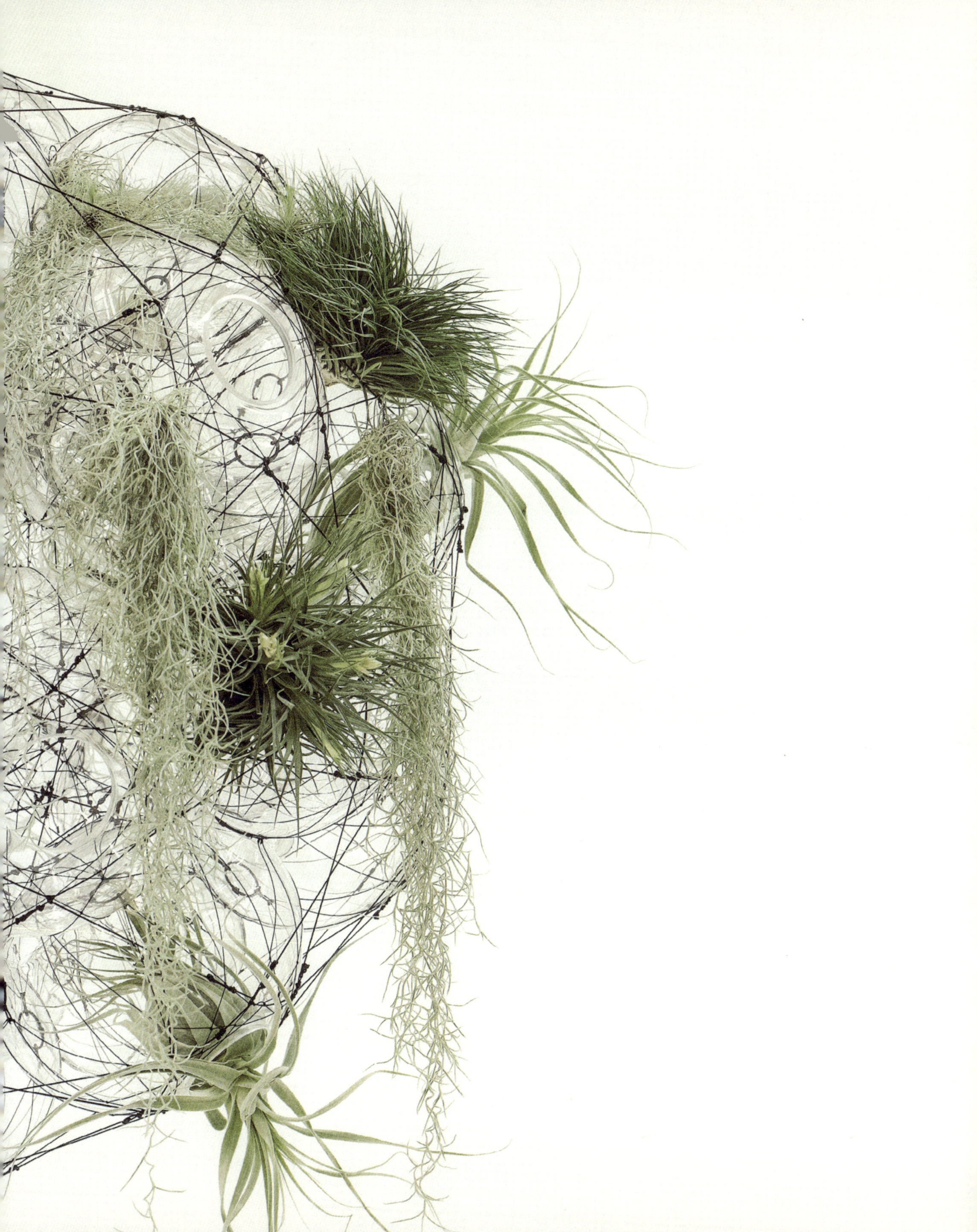

ROOM VIII

Amid the hills and galaxies, starlight exposure,
she sews together earth and sky to illuminate the
night and help wandering beings find their paths.
Please remember that baser passions could
interrupt her balance of ecosystemic forces
when asking your question.

Suit: Orb Spider/Web
Species: Araneus diadematus
Notation: F#
Plant: Betula pendula

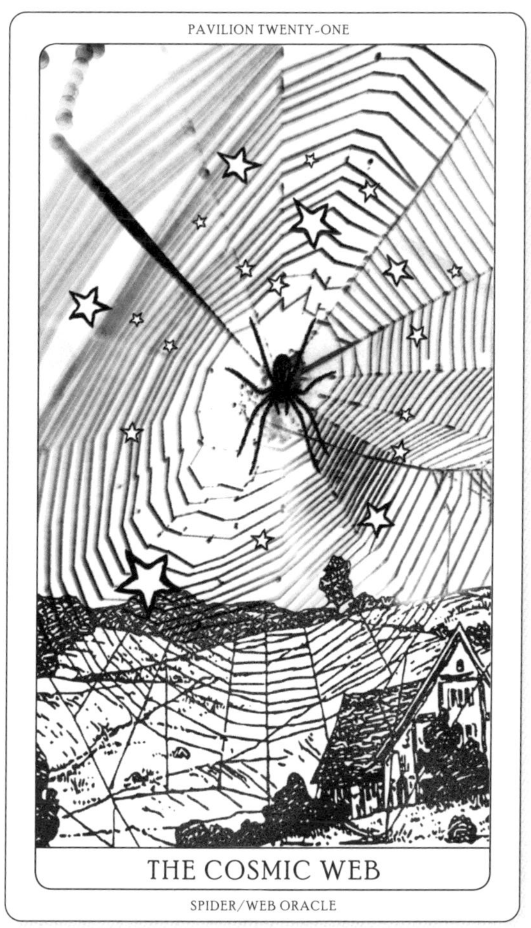

PAVILION TWENTY-ONE
THE COSMIC WEB
SPIDER/WEB ORACLE

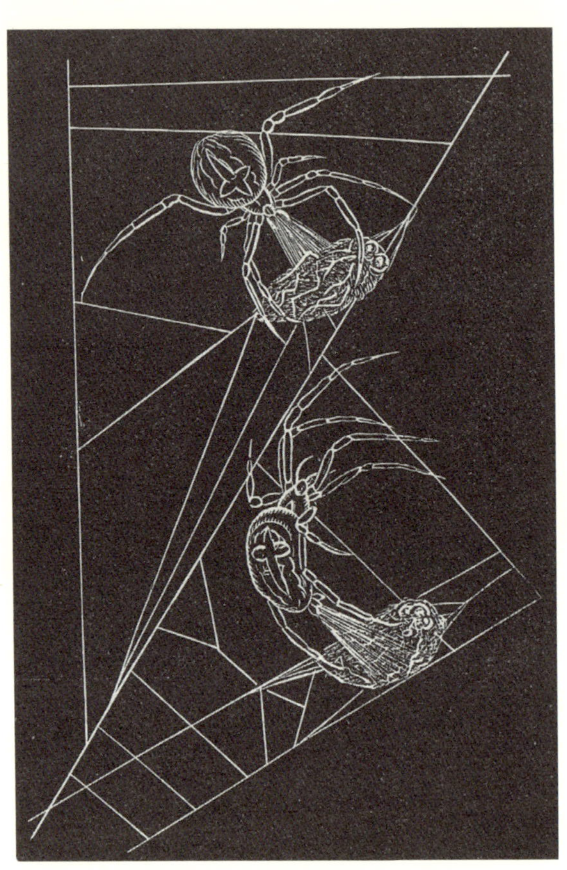

Now I will tell how Octavia, the spiderweb city,
is made. There is a precipice between two steep
mountains: the city is over the void, bound to the
two crests with ropes and chains and catwalks. You
walk on the little wooden ties, careful not to set your
foot in the open spaces, or you cling to the hempen
strands. Below there is nothing for hundreds and
hundreds of feet: a few clouds glide past; farther
down you can glimpse the chasm's bed.
This is the foundation of the city: a net which serves
as passage and as support. All the rest, instead of
rising up, is hung below: rope ladders, hammocks,
houses made like sacks, clothes hangers, terraces like
gondolas, skins of water, gas jets, spits, baskets on
strings, dumb-waiters, showers, trapezes and rings
for children's games, cable cars, chandeliers, pots
with trailing plants.
Suspended over the abyss, the life of Octavia's
inhabitants is less uncertain than in other cities.
They know the net will last only so long.

Italo Calvino, excerpt from *Invisible Cities*, 1972

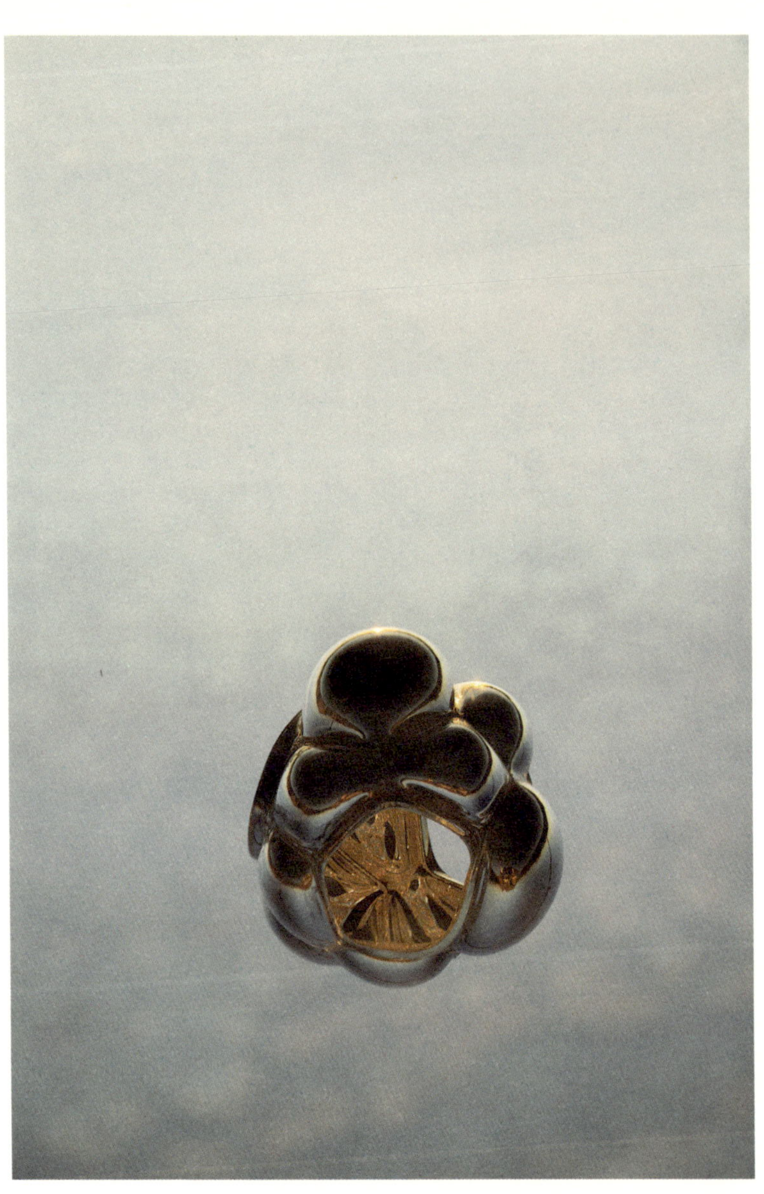

Vidal de la Blache wrote early in the twentieth century that "it is obvious that [Man], through his breathing, feeding and secretory organs, remains, just like the animals, impregnated with the influences of his environment" (cited in Mercier 1995, n.p.; and Vidal de la Blache 1922, 108).[1] His distinctive Human Geography linked geological and geophysical attributes from the environment with cultures, identities and ideas from the social world. The result was not an environmental form of determinism but a holistic understanding of the entangled relationality between social processes and environmental dynamics. For Vidal de la Blache (1922, 7), the answer to the question of where these two worlds meet was not a terrestrial issue or one of the ground on which social relations are often unconsciously assumed to take place, but "essentially" one of a "composite milieu, which is capable of grouping and consolidating different beings in reciprocal and vital interrelationships."[2] "Milieu" was a term that Vidal frequently used to refer to a place of cultural and environmental entanglement, calling into question the dualism that places nature on one side and culture on the other (Barad 2012).[3] The geographer's task was, according to Vidal, meant "to understand the dynamics of the natural environment and show its varying manifestations in different world milieus" (cited in Buttimer 1971, 45).[4] It is clear that the emphasis on milieu was not lost on Foucault (2009, 65–66)for whom it would come to constitute a crucial element in his biopolitics which, he explains, is the "control over relations between the human race, or human beings insofar as they are a species, insofar as they are living beings, and their environment, the milieu in which they live."[5]

The idea of milieu as a relational composite of social-political and material realities makes possible an exploration into "the material and meaningful ways in which air enters into human and geographic life as such" (Choy 2010, 22).[6] A materialization of air makes clear, to paraphrase Lefebvre's (in Elden 2007)famous dictum, that "there is a politics of the air because air is political."[7] This first section explores this theme not by accepting the air as an abstraction, but by focusing on its physicality and the way it materially enters and changes society through the practice of breathing. Many contemporary analyses, some of which are discussed in the next paragraphs, on the question of what the air is either underplay the issue, rephrasing it with a focus on what is located in it, or confront the air as an abstraction of thought. The air is in this article instead argued to be a pervasive materiality which is intimately and deeply entangled with breathing bodies. Such an understanding of the air as a relational respiratory materiality complements and "floats" somewhere in-between existing analyses that focus either on its phenomenology or on things moving in its verticality.

[. . .]

Breathing today is no longer understood as mere respiration, but is in record-breaking pace becoming recognized as evidence of our ecological embeddedness. Awareness of this very material process of immergence in the world, or being in and part of "aerial milieu" [*Luftmilieu*] requires a way of thinking akin to Vidal's commitment to a holistic ecological epistemology in which humans consider themselves not separate but part of the air. If the air changes, so do humans. Aerial materiality is, in other words, not inert but relational. The material composition of "air" has an immediate effect on social realities which respond by mirroring, adopting and resisting to either harmful or beneficial "changes in the winds." Such changes unfold in a geographically differentiated manner, as particles erratically and freely swerve around, ignoring political lines of division drawn in the earth, affecting some places and bodies differently than others (see especially Graham 2015).[8] The result is a moving mosaic aerial geography in which certain bodies are psychometrically forced to suffer from "saturated air" and "dry air," while others delight in more hospitable milieus of "clean air." Adey (2013, 293)writes about how "atmospheres carry us away in their buoyancy

and lightness, or, conversely, they may sink us, drowning us with heaviness, lethargy or exhaustion."[9] An exploration into the materiality of the air does not limit itself to a figurative politics, but reveals whose lives matter and whose do not, "who belongs and who does not, who is deserving and who is not" (2013, 294).[10] Jackson and Fannin (2011)explain in new materialist language how a process of "thinking through air" as matter can help us to make visible existing politics otherwise thought to be invisible.[11]

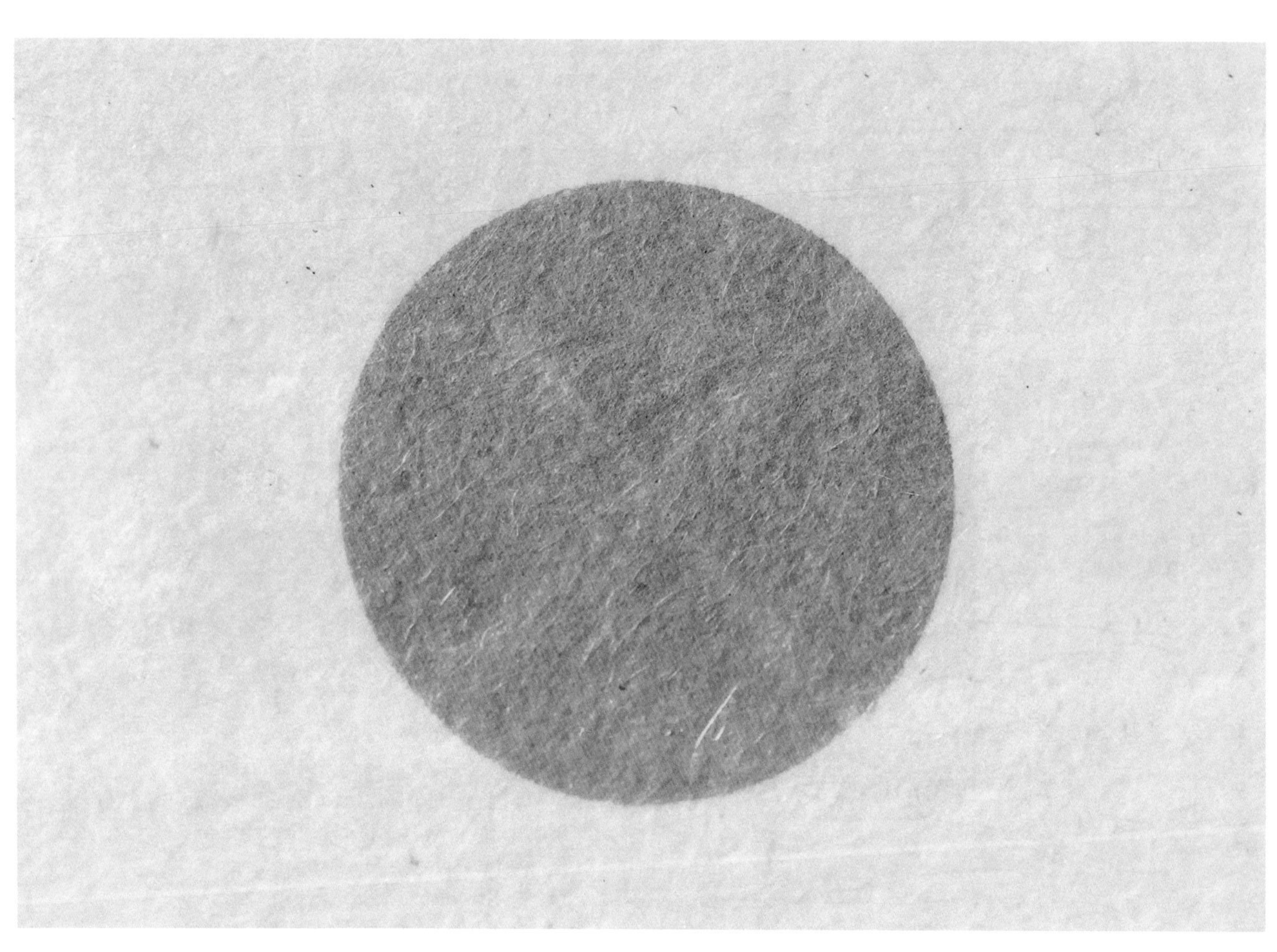

Obvious examples of the hidden politics in the air are the unevenly distributed seven million deaths as a result of airborne particle pollution (WHO 2014),[12] which besides its medical and biological effects also leads to psychological diseases and neurological traumas (see, for example, Genc et al. 2012).[13] One could also think of the politics of air-conditioning during heat waves or the social economics of access to heating in periods of cold. It is particularly the places inhabited by temperatured bodies of the urban poor, the disabled and the elderly which are affected most dramatically by warm and cold airs (Gasparrini et al. 2015).[14] On the other end of the spectrum, we are witness to indoor places with air filtering technologies designed to protect bodies from harmful materialities, while providing them an optimum balance somewhere between hot and cold. Koolhaas (2002, 176) famously remarked that "air conditioning has launched the endless building. If architecture separates buildings, air conditioning unites them. . . A single shopping center now is the work of generations of space planners, repairmen and fixers, like in the Middle Ages; air-conditioning sustains our cathedrals."[15] Indeed, as Bakke (2006, 18) writes, "[a] griculture, urban planning, architecture, interior design, electronic technologies, and the like all condition air according to human politics and economics."[16] Air has increasingly become differentiated by its engineered conditioning or, for that matter, the lack thereof.

Marijn Nieuwenhuis, excerpt from "Breathing materiality: aerial violence at a time of atmospheric politics," *Critical Studies on Terrorism*, 2015

1. Guy Mercier, "La région et l'État selon Friedrich Ratzel et Paul Vidal de la Blache," *Annales de géographie* 104, no. 583 (1995): 211–235; and Paul Vidal de la Blache, *Principes de Géographie Humaine* (Paris: Armand Colin, 1922).

2. Paul Vidal de la Blache, *Principes de Géographie Humaine* (Paris: Armand Colin, 1922).

3. "Interview with Karen Barad," in *New Materialism: Interviews & Cartographies*, edited by Rick Dolphijn and Iris van der Tuin (Ann Harbor: Open Humanity Press, 2012): 48–70.

4. Anne Buttimer, *Society and Milieu in the French Geographic Tradition* (Chicago: Rand McNally, 1971).

5. Michel Foucault, *Security, Territory, Population: Lectures at the College de France 1977-1978* (New York: Palgrave Macmillan, 2009).

6. Tim Choy, "Air's Substantiations," paper for Berkeley Environmental Politics Colloquium (Berkeley, 2010), http://globetrotter.berkeley.edu/bwep/colloquium/papers/ChoyAirEP.pdf.

7. Stuart Elden, "There is a Politics of Space because Space is Political: Henri Lefebvre and the Production of Space," *Radical Philosophy Review* 10, no. 2 (2007): 101–116.

8. Stephen Graham, "Life Support: The Political Ecology of Urban Air," *City* 19 no. 2–3 (2015): 192–215.

9. Peter Adey, "Air/Atmospheres of the Megacity," *Theory, Culture & Society* 30, no. 7–8 (2013): 291–308.

10. Ibid.

11. Mark Jackson, Maria Fannin, "Letting Geography Fall Where it May—Aerographies Address the Elemental," *Environment and Planning D: Society and Space* 29, no. 3 (2011): 435–444.

12. World Health Statistics 2014.

13. Sermin Genc et al., "The adverse effects of air pollution on the nervous system," *Journal of Toxicology* 4 (2012).

14. A. Gasparrini et al., "Mortality risk attributable to high and low ambient temperature: a multicountry observational study," *The Lancet* 386, no. 9991 (2015).

15. Rem Koolhaas, "Junkspace," *October* 100 (2002): 175–190.

16. Monika Bakke, *Going Aerial: Air, Art, Architecture* (Maastricht: Jan van Eyck Academie, 2006).

Aerographies

This room puts into perspective the different ways in which the movements of people, heat, animals and spider/webs affect and are affected by the air. Every gesture leaves a trace: the movements of persons, sounds, and spider/webs translate as the potential language of earthly phenomena, an emergent cartography of the air. Spider/webs laid out on paper produce strange new spider maps of invisible cities; alongside, the trajectories of aerosolar sculptures that float freely in the air without the help of fossil fuels trace out *Aeroglyphs*, plotting a path forward out of the extractive ideology of the Capitalocene. Pens suspended from balloons act as utensils for the wind to draw its trajectories; filled with ink made from black carbon pollution from Mumbai's air, these pens answer the question of what the air would write with—the material with which we have poisoned the air becomes a tool of its communication, reminding us of its ever-present agency even in the face of our destruction. Together these *Aerographies* are letters, characters and signatures of a new language for the Aerocene era. A three-dimensional web connects floor and the air above, challenging the idea of a hierarchical tree of life and its linear convictions, instead proposing a rhizomatic web of life, highlighting the hybridities between and among species and worlds.
The participatory *Aeroglyphs* series manifests the everyday movements and air currents that exist otherwise outside visibility. Acting out alternative modes of collective map-making, the series is inspired by the Situationist International's affective explorations of the urban environment. Coined by the Marxist theorist Guy Debord in 1955, the term "psychogeography" focuses on our psychological experiences of the city, revealing its discarded and oftentimes marginalized aspects. The *Aeroglyphs* series extends this critical and affective effort upwards, off the surface of the street into the sky, drawing the contours of today's globalizing trajectories. They unravel our obscured imprint on this planet and speak to the many agents who affect it alongside us.
Yet to be interpreted, they also resemble the maps of past courses and future routes drawn by spider/webs, actual psychogeographical charts of their environments. A spider/web begins with a single thread of silk cast out into the air, loose and undulating until pulled taut by the wind. Each thread of spider silk is a web-in-becoming containing an infinite multitude of futures, adrift on air until it meets a surface, bridging the spider/webs' ability to write their passage, their drifting and ways forward. Spider/webs therefore become the real-life maps of suspended cities inhabited by spider/webs.
Mapping was utilized in the past to prove our knowledge; these alternative cartographies highlight instead its limits.

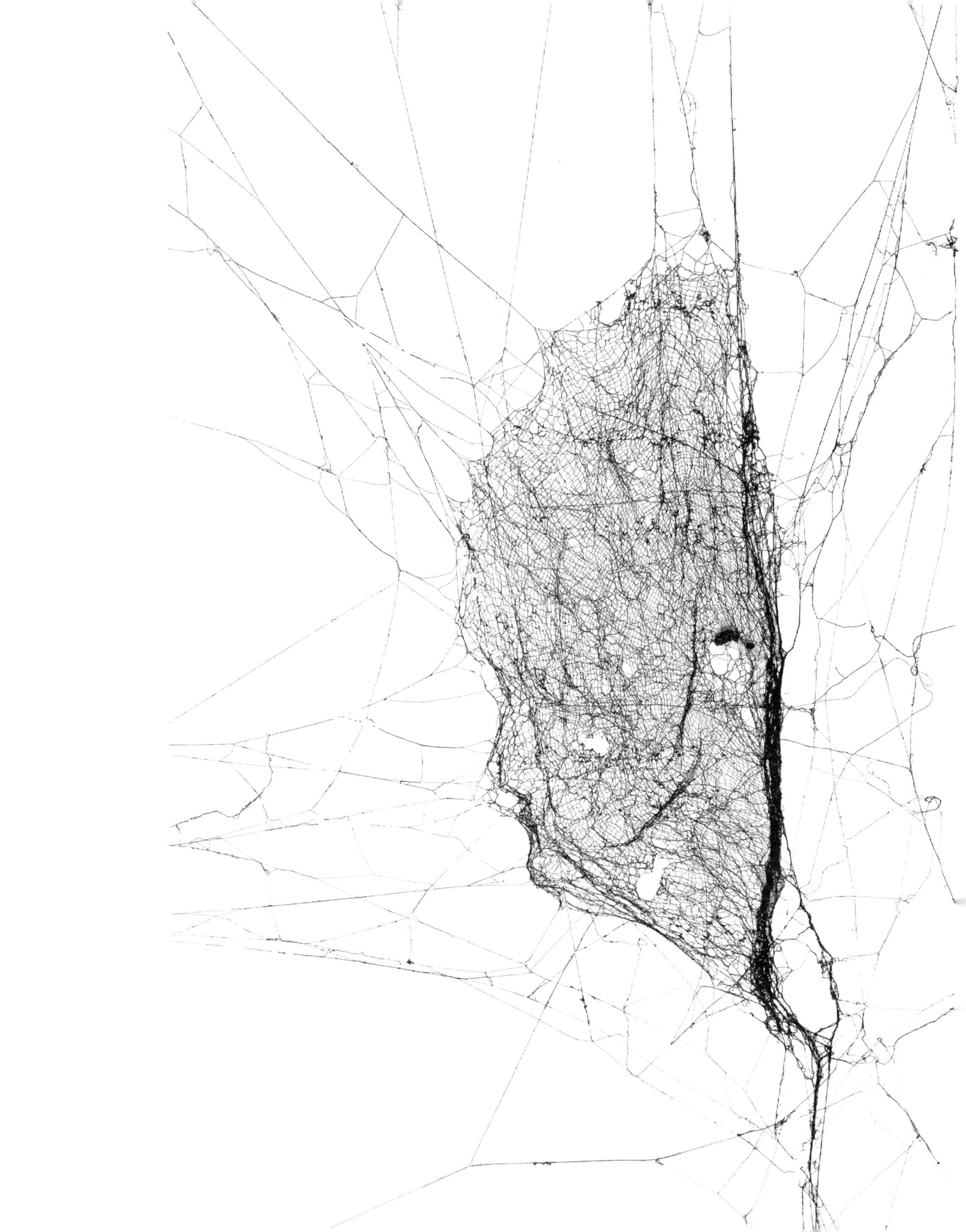

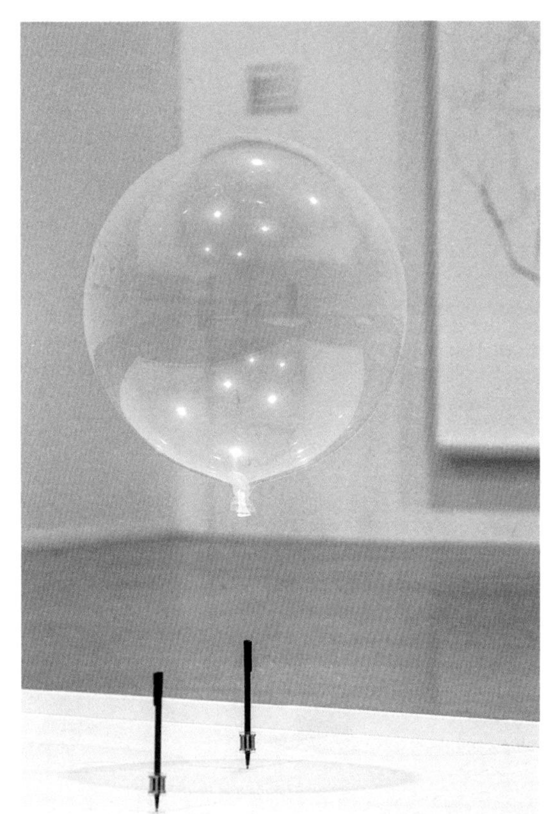

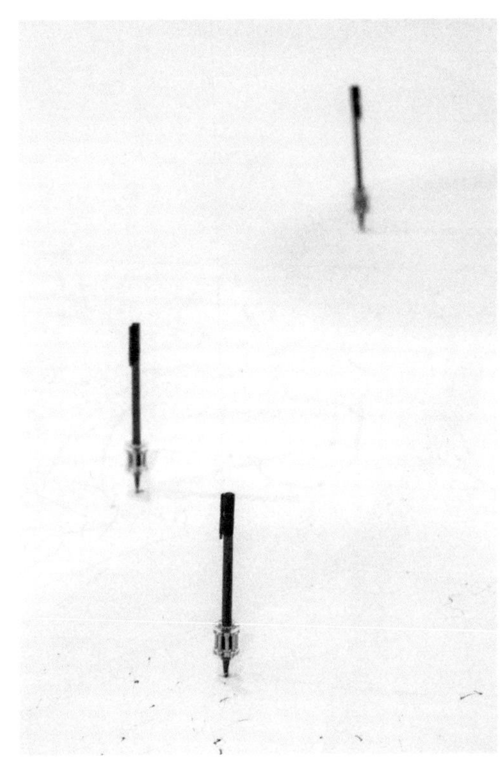

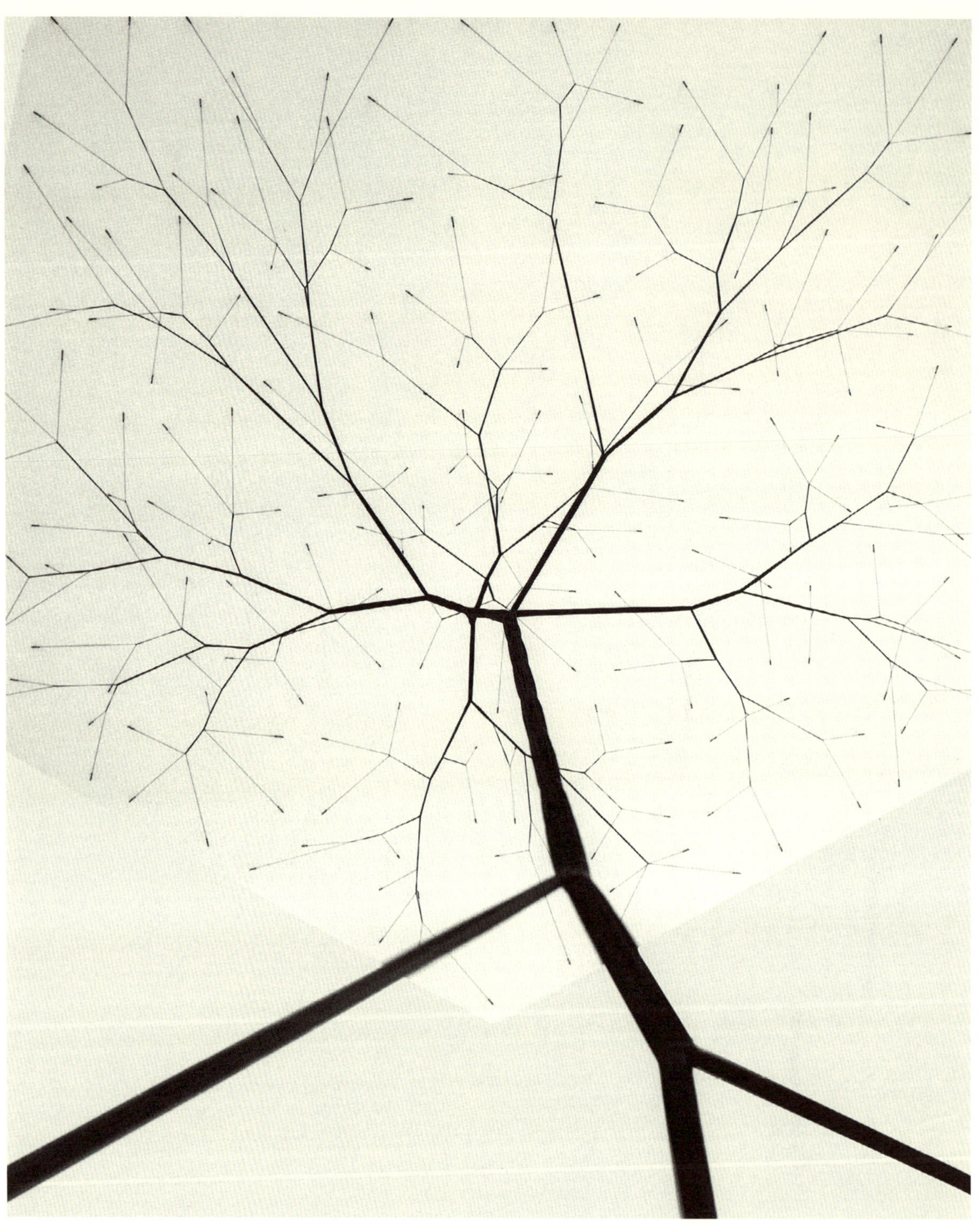

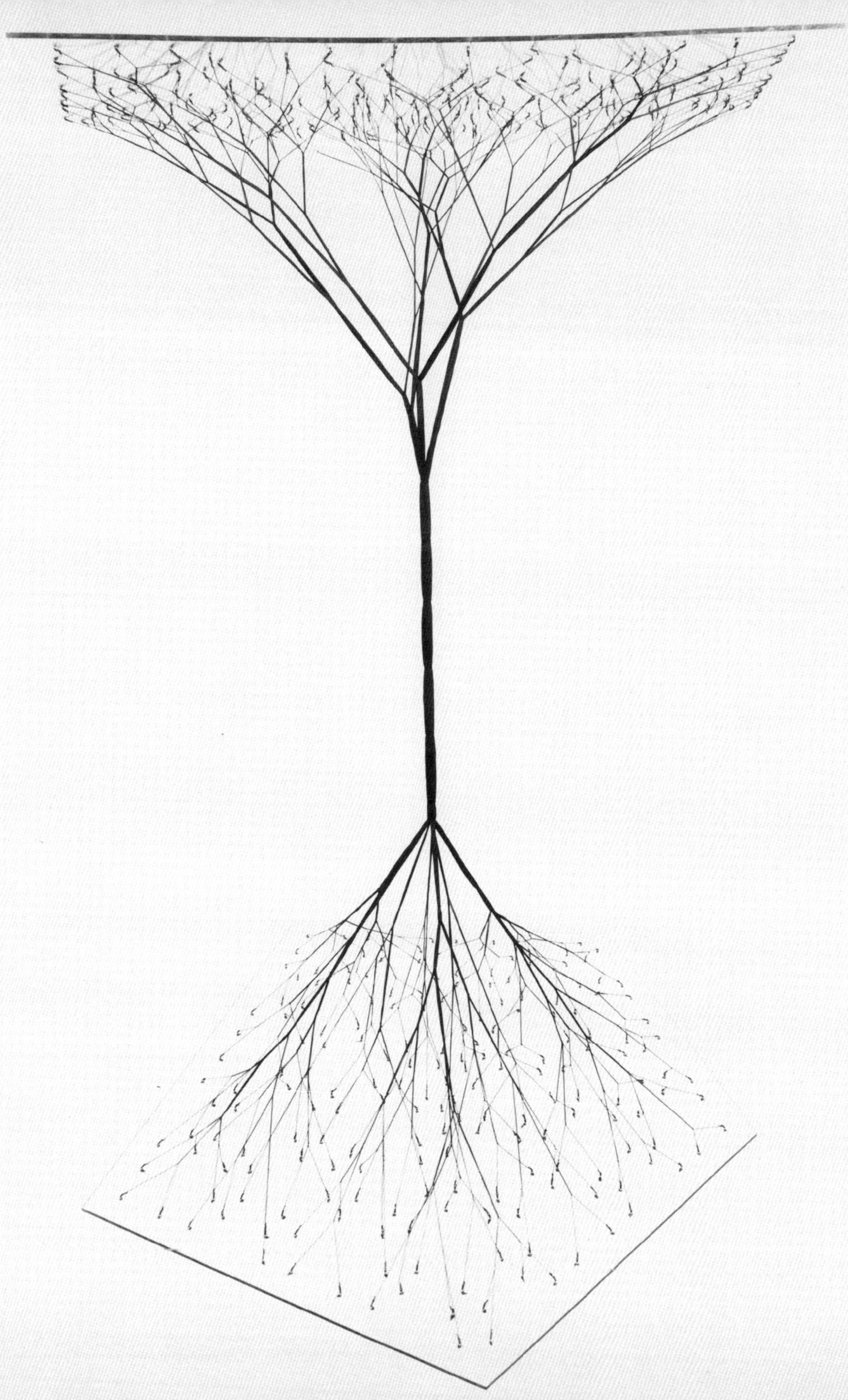

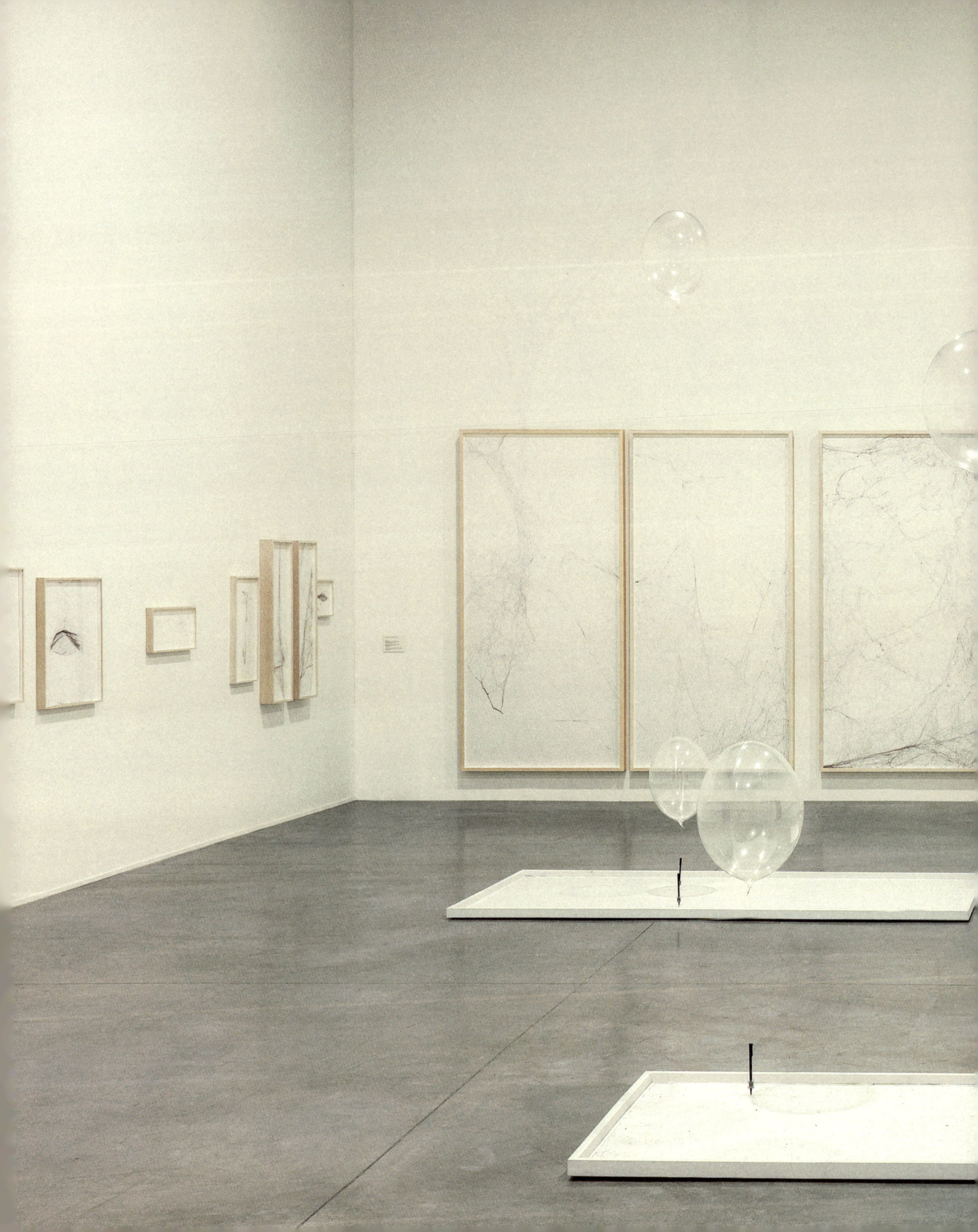

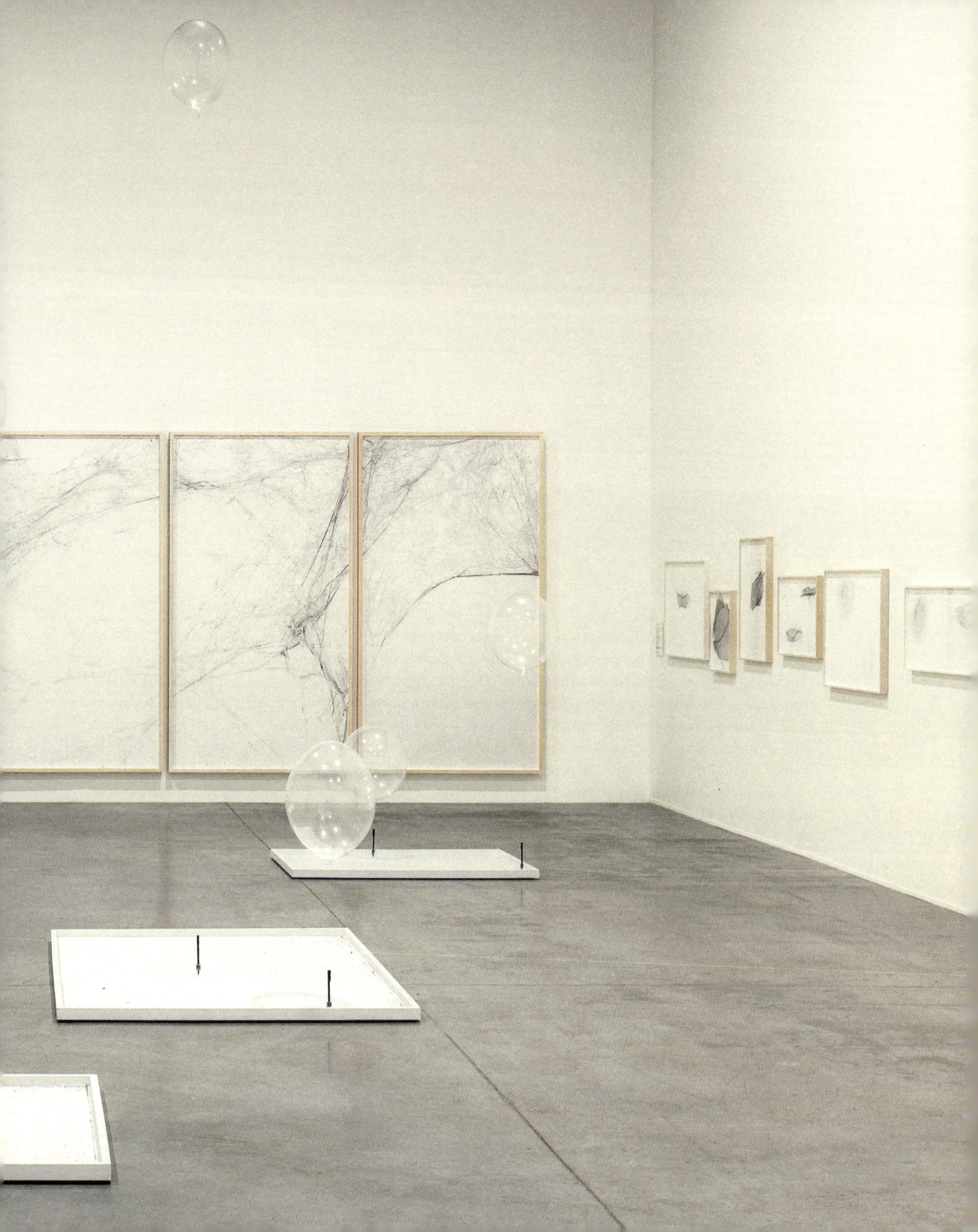

AEROCENE

Aerocene is an interdisciplinary artistic community that seeks to devise new modes of ecological sensitivity, reactivating a common imaginary towards an ethical collaboration with the atmosphere and the environment, in an era free from borders, free from fossil fuels. Aerocene's activities manifest in the testing and circulation of aerosolar sculptures that become buoyant only by the heat of the Sun and infrared radiation from the surface of Earth. As an ever growing research and experimental practice, Aerocene is open-source and collaborative. It consists of a dedicated and diverse global community of practitioners who collaborate to promote environmental awareness and atmospheric sensing experiments. Imagining new infrastructures of planetary mobility and ethics, Aerocene aims to build a new ecology of practice with a DIT (Do-It-Together) spirit, attempting to overcome the extractive approach certain humans have developed towards planetary landscapes, ecosystems and nonhuman species.

These aims are achieved and complemented through a bottom-up, participatory approach to environmental policy-making and citizen science, encouraged through the international community-building carried out by the Aerocene Foundation, initiated by artist Tomás Saraceno in 2015.

Tomás Saraceno's exhibition *Aria* at Palazzo Strozzi has been accompanied by an extensive public program featuring Aerocene events and activities, including *Museo Aero Solar* and Aerocene Flights to Florence and Tuscany—aerosolar performances of the Aerocene epoch that move us from carbon-powered flights to moments of drift, as we float at the bottom of an ocean of air.

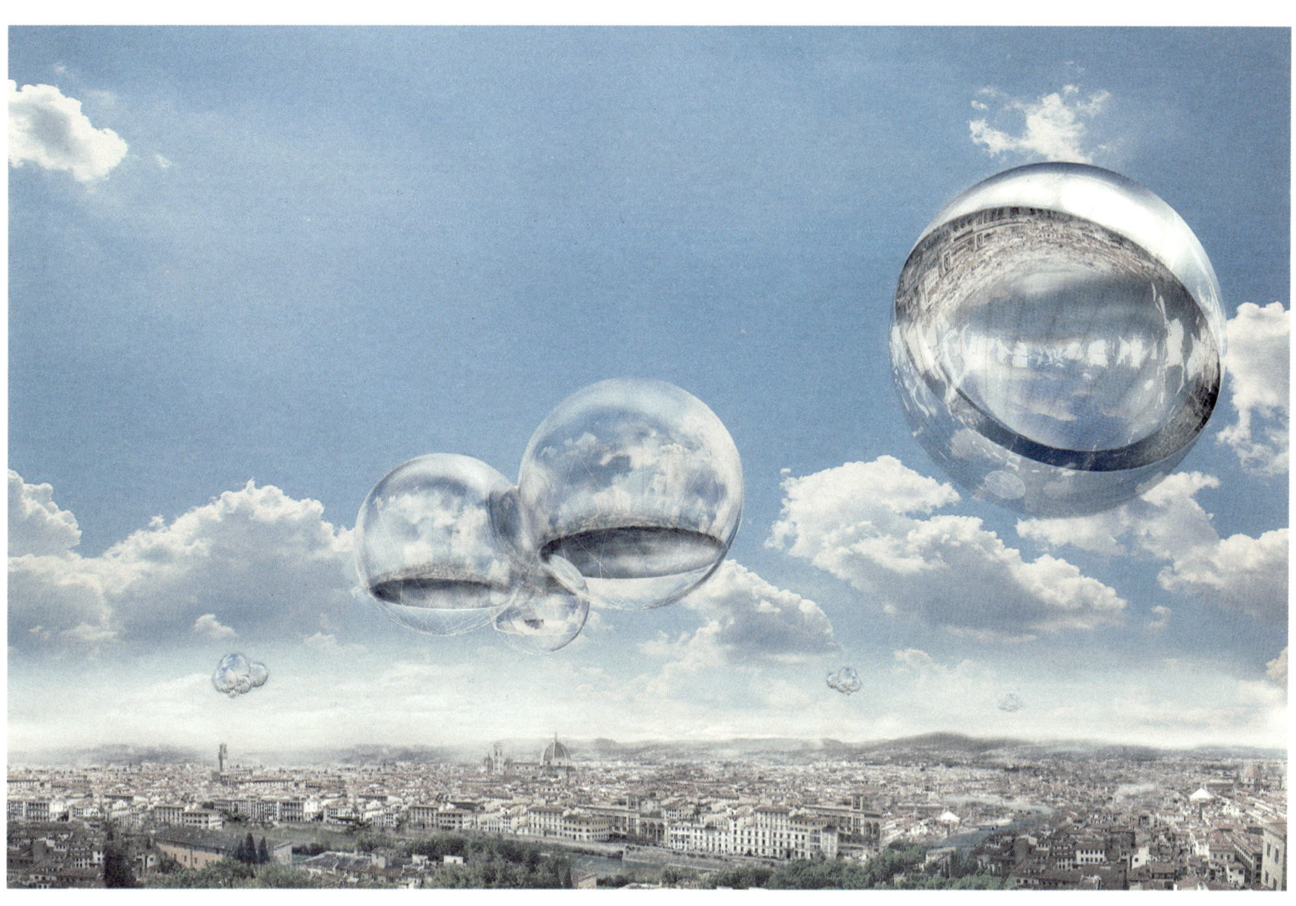

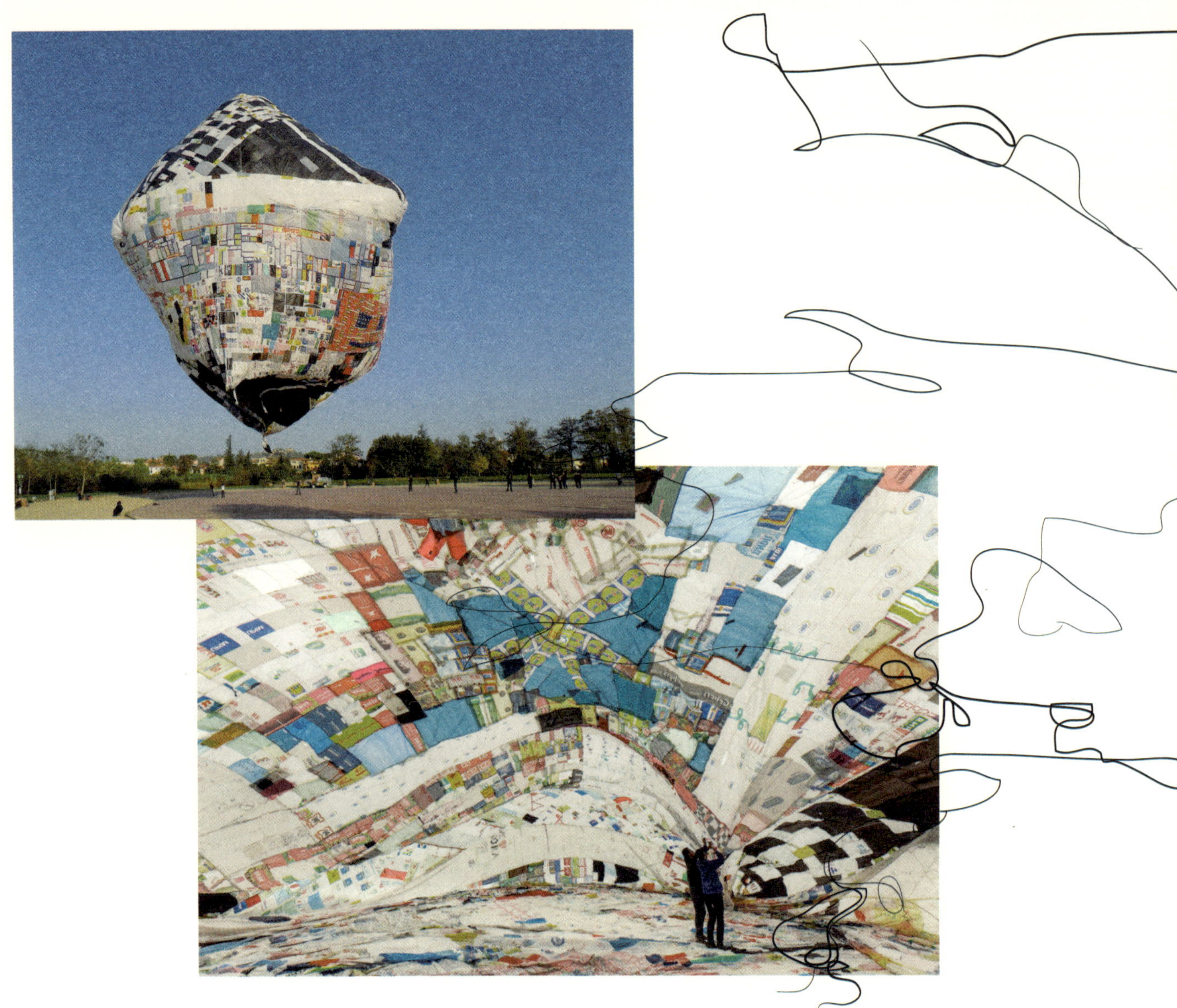

01.07.17 | GBR Exhibition Rd, London | Tethered flight | Hans Martin | Garmin tracker | 2017

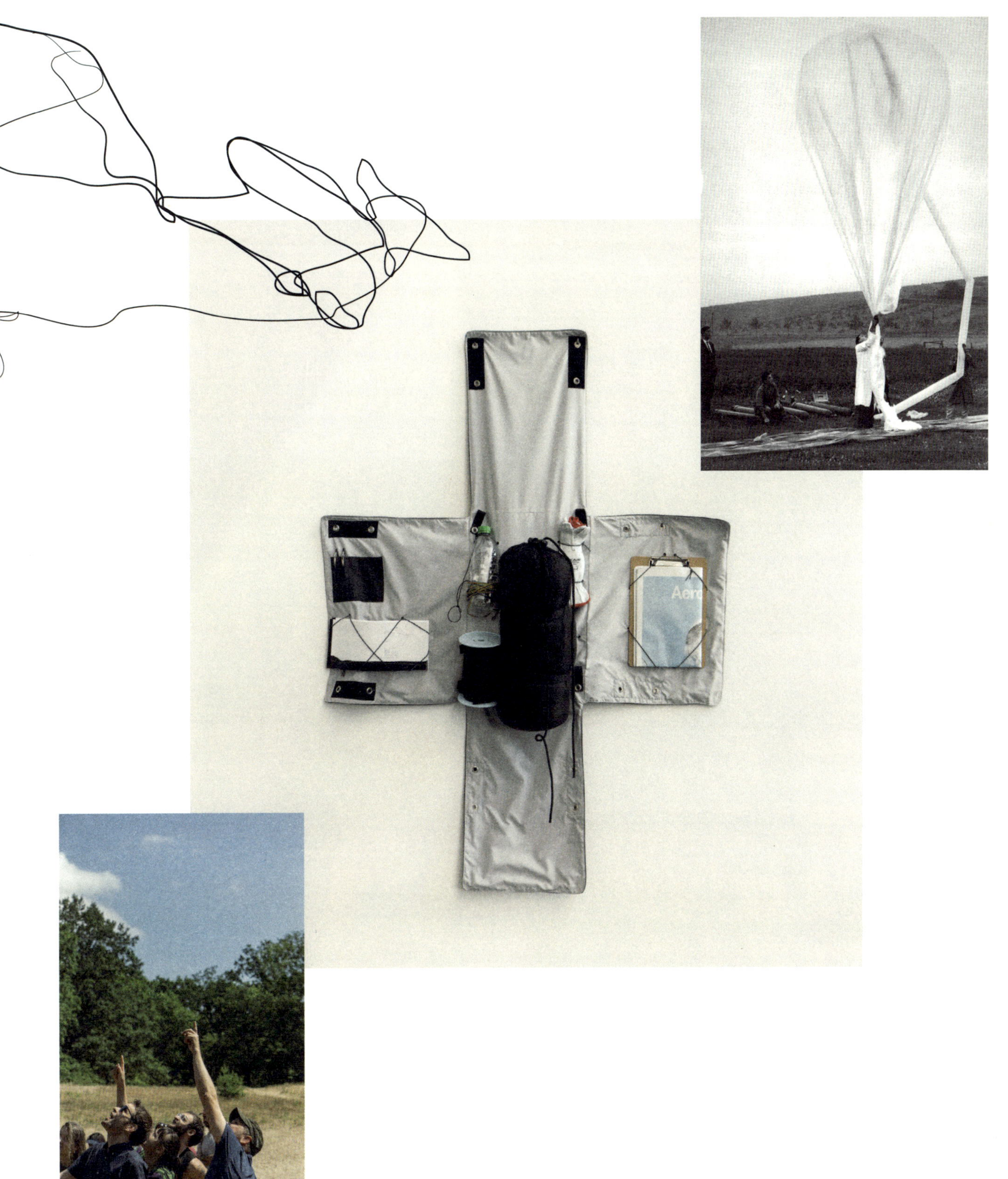

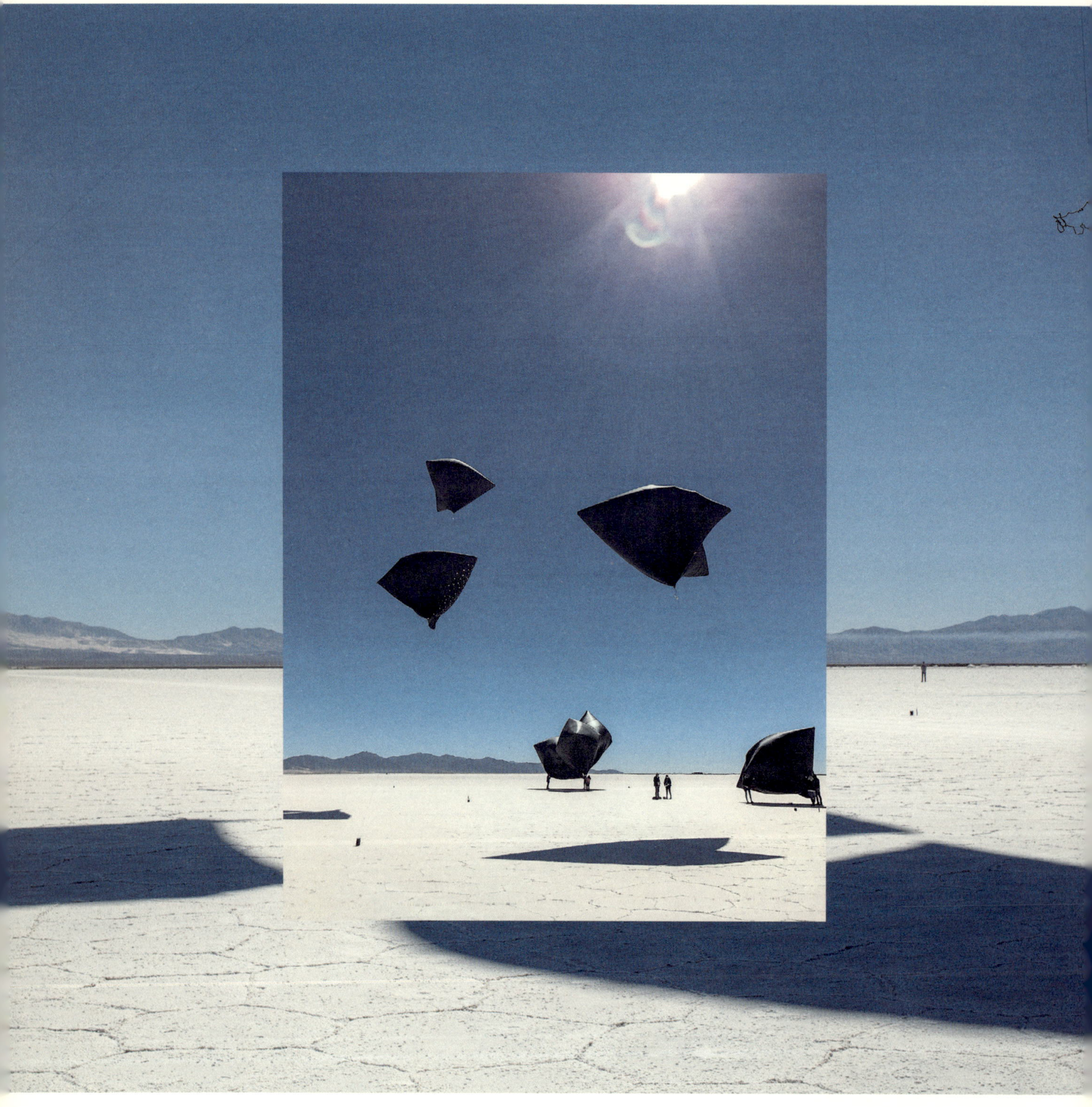

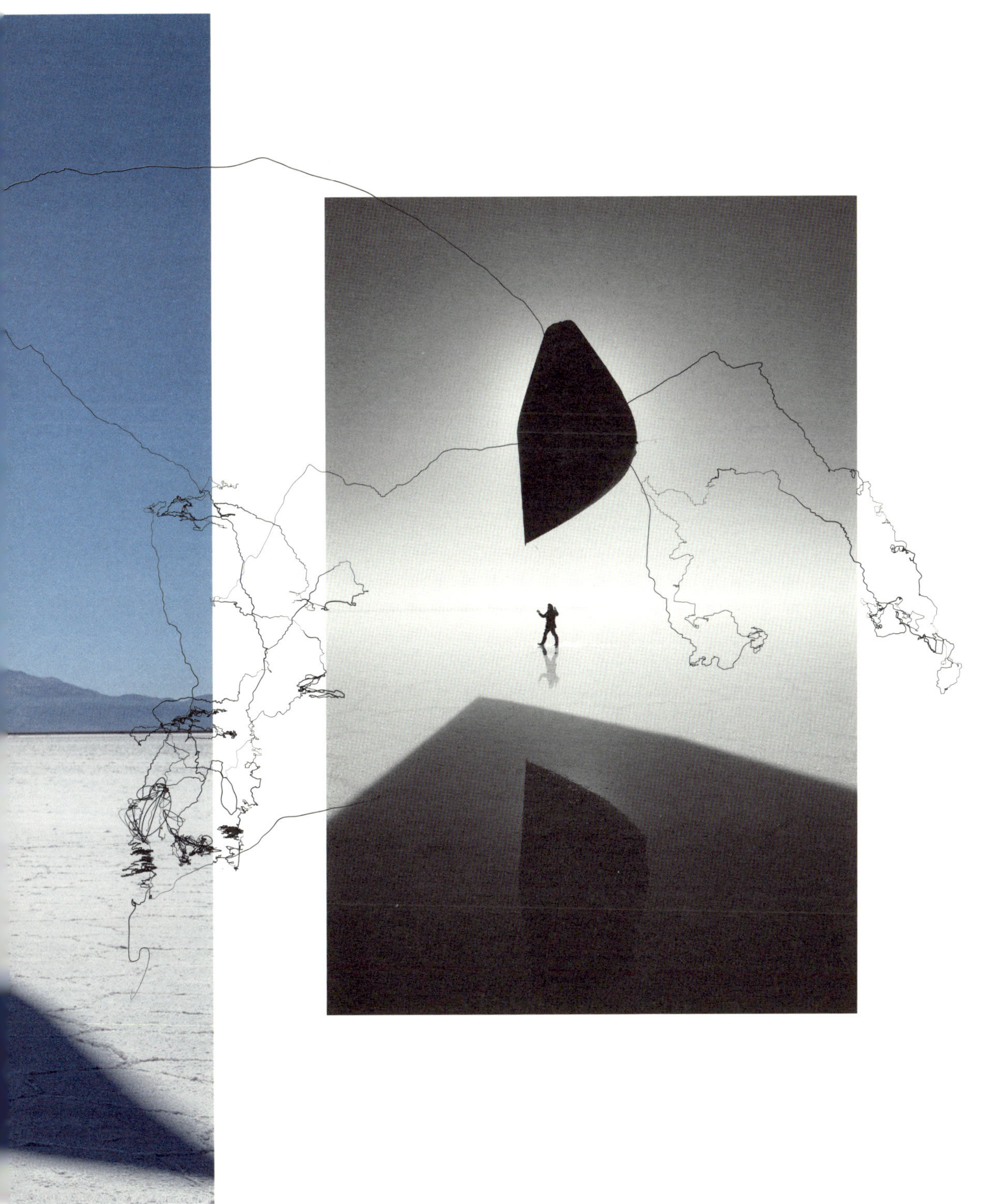

Aeroglyph 07.08.17 | ARG | Jujuy | Explorer flight | Joaquin, Tomas | Garmin tracker | 2018

COURTYARD
Thermodynamic Constellation
2020
Mylar transparent and metalized, mirrored acrylic plate, membrane pump with pressure control, overpressure release valve, PE tube, PES rope
Dimensions: 2.5m / 5m / 4m diameter

ups And c/M+M, 2019

HR 5183 b/M+M, 2019

Metal, monofilament, metal wire, polyester rope, mirror panels

Courtesy the artist; Andersen's, Copenhagen; Ruth Benzacar, Buenos Aires; Tanya Bonakdar Gallery, New York/Los Angeles; Pinksummer Contemporary Art, Genoa; Esther Schipper, Berlin

ROOM I
Connectome
2020
Metal, polyester rope, nylon rope, mirror panels, monofilament
Various dimensions

Stillness in Motion – 35.02, 2017
Metal, polyester rope, black nylon rope, mirror panels

21/Borisov/M+M, 2019
Metal, steel thread, polyester rope, monofilament, metal wire, mirror panels

beta Pic c/M+M, 2019
Metal, polyester rope, monofilament, metal wire, mirror panels

Courtesy the artist; Andersen's, Copenhagen; Ruth Benzacar, Buenos Aires; Tanya Bonakdar Gallery, New York/Los Angeles; Pinksummer Contemporary Art, Genoa; Esther Schipper, Berlin

ROOM II
Sounding the Air
2020
Spider silk, carbon fiber, microphone, transducer, speakers, lights, computer, camera

Courtesy the artist; Andersen's, Copenhagen; Ruth Benzacar, Buenos Aires; Tanya Bonakdar Gallery, New York/Los Angeles; Pinksummer Contemporary Art, Genoa; Esther Schipper, Berlin

ROOM III
Webs of At-tent(s)ion
2020
Spider silk, glass, carbon fiber, metal, lights, silicone
Various dimensions

Hybrid semi-social solitary solitary Instrument Azmidi built by: an ensemble of Cyrtophora citricola – *eight weeks, a solo* Nephila inaurata – *eight weeks, a solo* Holocnemus pluchei – *four weeks*, 2019

Hybrid solitary solitary semi-social Instrument HD 206936 built by: a solo Nephila inaurata – *two weeks, a solo* Larinioides sclopetarius – *two weeks, a sextet of* Cyrtophora citricola – *two weeks*, 2019

Hybrid solitary solitary solitary Instrument 8 Scorpii built by: a solo Nephila inaurata – *one week, a solo* Nephila edulis – *two weeks, and a triplet of* Agelena labyrinthica – *three weeks, rotated 90°*, 2019

Hybrid solitary semi-social solitary Instrument HD 178524 built by: a solo Nephila senegalensis – *four weeks, a quartet of* Cyrtophora citricola – *eight weeks, a solo* Holocnemus pluchei – *one week*, 2019

Hybrid semi-social solitary solitary Instrument SAO 66943 built by: a quintet of Cyrtophora citricola – *three weeks, a solo* Nephila senegalensis – *eight weeks, a sextet of* Holocnemus pluchei – *three weeks, rotated 90°*, 2020

Hybrid solitary semi-social BD+10° 4321 built by: a triplet of Nephila inaurata – *eight weeks, a septet of* Cyrtophora citricola – *four weeks, rotated 90°*, 2019

Spider silk, carbon fiber, glass, metal, silicone

Courtesy the artist; Andersen's, Copenhagen; Ruth Benzacar, Buenos Aires; Tanya Bonakdar Gallery, New York/Los Angeles; Pinksummer Contemporary Art, Genoa; Esther Schipper, Berlin

ROOM IV
How to Entangle the Universe in a Spider/Web?
2020
Spider silk, carbon fiber, laser

Courtesy the artist; Andersen's, Copenhagen; Ruth Benzacar, Buenos Aires; Tanya Bonakdar Gallery, New York/Los Angeles; Pinksummer Contemporary Art, Genoa; Esther Schipper, Berlin

Gravitational solitary semi-social Choreography built by: a solo Nephila senegalensis – *two weeks, a septet of* Cyrtophora citricola – *one week, rotated 180°*, 2018

Gravitational semi-social semi-social Choreography Kabdhilinan built by: a triplet of Nephila senegalensis – *three weeks, nineteen* Cyrtophora citricola – *four weeks, twenty* Holocnemus pulchei – *two weeks*, 2018

Gravitational solitary semi-social Choreography HR 1577 built by: a solo Nephila inaurata – *one week, a septet of* Cyrtophora citricola – *two weeks, rotated 180°*, 2018

Spider silk, carbon fiber

Courtesy the artist

ROOM V
Particular Matter(s) Jam Session
2020
Local live spider already living in Palazzo Strozzi, spider silk, carbon fiber, light beam, cosmic dust, terrestrial dust, PM2.5, PM10, black carbon, stellar wind, sonic waves, 3D tracking software, computer, video camera, speakers, video projector

Courtesy the artist; Andersen's, Copenhagen; Ruth Benzacar,
Buenos Aires; Tanya Bonakdar Gallery, New York/Los Angeles;
Pinksummer Contemporary Art, Genoa; Esther Schipper, Berlin

*Gravitational solitary semi-social Choreography 34 Aurigae built
by: a duet of* Nephila senegalensis – *eight weeks, a quintet of*
Cyrtophora citricola – *three weeks, rotated 180°,* 2017
Spider silk, carbon fiber, glass, metal, silicone

Courtesy the artist

Passages of Time
2020
Double projection of

163,000 Light Years, 2016
Single channel video, sound, duration: 163,000 years, frame
rate: 1 frame x year
Commissioned by MARCO, Museum of Contemporary Art
of Monterrey

Untitled, 2019
Livestream of dust circulating in *Particular Matter(s) Jam
Session*
Light beam, cosmic dust, terrestrial dust, pollen, soot, smoke,
PM 2.5, stellar wind, sonic waves, video camera, loud speakers,
video projector, processor, dust tracking software frame rate:
70 frames x second

Courtesy the artist; Andersen's, Copenhagen; Ruth Benzacar,
Buenos Aires; Tanya Bonakdar Gallery, New York/Los Angeles;
Pinksummer Contemporary Art, Genoa; Esther Schipper, Berlin

ROOM VI
A Thermodynamic Imaginary
2020
Various dimensions

Courtesy the artist; Andersen's, Copenhagen; Ruth Benzacar,
Buenos Aires; Tanya Bonakdar Gallery, New York/Los Angeles;
Pinksummer Contemporary Art, Genoa; Esther Schipper, Berlin

Aeroke, 2019
Mylar transparent and metalized, tape, pump with
overpressure release valve, polyester rope, microphone,
headphones

Aquarius Dwarf/M+N, 2019
Metal, polyester rope, monofilament

Aerosolar Constellation 22.5/55/19.5/36/15.5, 2018

Aerosolar Pisces, 2019

Hand blown glass, polyester rope, velvet rope

RAY 19.819, 2018
Hand blown glass, metal, polyester rope, velvet rope,
monofilament

Calder Upside Down 28/10/8
Hand blown glass, metal, polyester rope, velvet rope

Aeroscale 170, 2018
Hand blown glass, glass disks, polyester rope, velvet rope,
monofilament

Solar eclipse 1.100, 2018
Hand blown glass sphere, glass disks, metal, polyester rope,
velvet rope, monofilament

RAY 30.058, 2018
Hand blown glass sphere, metal, polyester rope, velvet rope,
monofilament

Courtesy the artist; Andersen's, Copenhagen; Ruth Benzacar,
Buenos Aires; Tanya Bonakdar Gallery, New York/Los Angeles;
Pinksummer Contemporary Art, Genoa; Esther Schipper, Berlin

ROOM VII
Flying Gardens
2020
Tillandsia plants, hand blown glass, monofilament, polyester
rope, velvet rope, carbon fiber

Courtesy the artist; Andersen's, Copenhagen; Ruth Benzacar,
Buenos Aires; Tanya Bonakdar Gallery, New York/Los Angeles;
Pinksummer Contemporary Art, Genoa; Esther Schipper, Berlin

Pneuma 20.95, 2020

Pneuma 15.999 HM, 2019

Pneuma 78.09, 2020

Hand blown glass, polyester rope, velvet rope, monofilament

Pneuma 420, 2020
Hand blown glass, polyester rope, velvet rope

Haboob, 2018

Haboob HM, 2019

Hand blown glass, polyester rope, velvet rope

Callisto 13, 2019
Glass disk, carbon fiber, polyester rope, velvet rope,
monofilament

Aeolus 15.759, 2019

Aeolus 36.184, 2019

Aeolus 8.79, 2019

Aeolus 4.67, 2019

Aeolus 7.5, 2019

Hand blown glass, metal

Aeolus 19.2, 2019
Hand blown glass, nylon

Aeolus 8.80, 2019
Hand blown glass, monofilament, Tillandsia plants

Aeolus 9.7, 2019
Hand blown glass

Courtesy the artist; Andersen's, Copenhagen; Ruth Benzacar, Buenos Aires; Tanya Bonakdar Gallery, New York/Los Angeles; Pinksummer Contemporary Art, Genoa; Esther Schipper, Berlin

ARACHNOMANCY ROOM
Arachnomancy Cards
2019
Deck of 33 cards printed on carbon footprint neutral paper. Card's drawings and reinterpretation based on Winifred Duncan (1949), *Webs In The Wind*. New York: The Ronald Press Company; W. S. Bristowe (1958), *The World of Spiders*. London: Collins; Curtis, William, 1746–1799; Marbury, Elizabeth, 1856–1933, donor; F. Vollrath (1988), "Untangling the spider's web," *Trends in Ecology & Evolution* 3 (1988): 331–5, with the Arachnophilia archives and Studio Tomás Saraceno

Courtesy the artist, with thanks to the Arachnophilia archives; Andersen's, Copenhagen; Ruth Benzacar, Buenos Aires; Tanya Bonakdar Gallery, New York/Los Angeles; Pinksummer Contemporary Art, Genoa; Esther Schipper, Berlin

Hybrid solitary solitary Instrument WDS J12266-6306 built by: a solo Nephila senegalensis – *six weeks, a solo* Parasteatoda tepidariorum – *three weeks, rotated 180°*, 2020
Spider silk, carbon fiber, glass, metal, silicone

Courtesy the artist; Andersen's, Copenhagen; Ruth Benzacar, Buenos Aires; Tanya Bonakdar Gallery, New York/Los Angeles; Pinksummer Contemporary Art, Genoa; Esther Schipper, Berlin

ROOM VIII
Aerographies
2020
Various dimensions

Courtesy the artist; Andersen's, Copenhagen; Ruth Benzacar, Buenos Aires; Tanya Bonakdar Gallery, New York/Los Angeles; Pinksummer Contemporary Art, Genoa; Esther Schipper, Berlin

Aeroglyph 17-20.04.18 / BEL / Market & Burg Square, Bruges / Explorer flight / Erik, Gwilym, Hannah / Garmin tracker /, 2018

Aeroglyph 07.08.17 / ARG / Jujuy / Explorer flight / Joaquin, Tomas / Garmin tracker /, 2018

Aeroglyph 12.04.17 / ANT / Antarctica Biennale – Ushuaia / Explorer flight / Nick & Liz / Unknown tracker /, 2018

Print on adhesive paper

Solitary semi-social mapping of Erakis by a solo Nephila senegalensis – *one week, a duet of* Cyrtophora citricola – *one week, rotated 90°*, 2019

Solitary semi-social solitary mapping of HD 28305 by a solo Nephila inaurata – *four weeks, a quintet of* Cyrtophora citricola – *three weeks, a solo* Linyphiidae sp. – *one week*, 2019

Semi-social solitary mapping of Ursae Majoris by a solo Cyrtophora citricola – *six weeks, and a quintet of* Nephila edulis juvenile – *two weeks, rotated 180°*, 2019

Solitary semi-social mapping of FK5 337 by a solo Nephila inaurata – *six weeks, a duet of* Cyrtophora citricola – *five weeks*, 2019

Solitary semi-social mapping of CCDM J08585+1151A by a solo Nephila inaurata – *three weeks, a quartet of* Cyrtophora citricola – *five weeks*, 2019

Solitary semi-social mapping of Alioth by a solo Nephila edulis juvenile – *one week, a triplet of* Cyrtophora citricola juvenile – *one week*, 2019

Expanse NGC 1579 by a Tegenaria domestica, 2017

Solitary semi-social mapping of GJ 4095 by a triplet of Nephila inaurata – *five weeks, an ensemble of* Cyrtophora citricola – *seven weeks*, 2019

Spider silk, archival paper, ink, fixative

Thermodynamic Suite, 2020
Paper, ink, balloon

Resine Tree Connectome, 2020
Wood, polyester rope, monofilament

Courtesy the artist; Andersen's, Copenhagen; Ruth Benzacar, Buenos Aires; Tanya Bonakdar Gallery, New York/Los Angeles; Pinksummer Contemporary Art, Genoa; Esther Schipper, Berlin

PAGE 1
Tomás Saraceno
FORTUNATE WEBBING
Card 7 out of a deck of 33 Arachnomancy Cards, 2019-ongoing
Card's drawings and reinterpretation based on Winifred Duncan
(1949), *Webs In The Wind*. New York: The Ronald Press Company;
W. S. Bristowe (1958), *The World of Spiders*. London: Collins; Curtis,
William, 1746–1799; Marbury, Elizabeth, 1856–1933, donor; F. Vollrath
(1988), "Untangling the spider's web," *Trends Ecol. Evol.* 3(12): 331–5
Courtesy the artist, with thanks to the Arachnophilia archives
Let your future be read by a spider/web and download the
Arachnomancy App, joining an exercise mapping against extinction
For more information visit Arachnophilia.net
© Studio Tomás Saraceno, 2019

PAGE 14
Giuliano D'Arrigo Pesello, *The Northern Hemisphere at Florence
Latitude on July 4, 1442*, c. 1442, basilica of San Lorenzo,
Old Sacristy of San Lorenzo, Florence. © Raffaello Bencini /
Bridgeman Images

Master of the Mantegna Tarots, *Moon* (no. 41), 1465–75.
© Fine Art Images / Bridgeman Images

Leonardo da Vinci, *Vitruvian Man*, c. 1490. Venice, Gallerie
dell'Accademia, inv. 228. © Archivio fotografico G.A.VE, courtesy
of the Ministero dei beni e delle attività culturali – Gallerie
dell'Accademia di Venezia

Andrea Mantegna, *Saint Sebastian* (detail), c. 1459,
Kunsthistorisches Museum, Vienna. © Fine Art Images /
Bridgeman Images

Thomas Cole, *View of Florence*, 1837, Cleveland Museum of Art,
Cleveland. © Bridgeman Images

PAGE 16
Tomás Saraceno
Calendrier Lun-AIR (detail), 2018
Installation view at ON AIR, *carte blanche* exhibition
to Tomás Saraceno, Palais de Tokyo, Paris, 2018
Curated by Rebecca Lamarche-Vadel
Courtesy the artist; Andersen's, Copenhagen; Ruth Benzacar,
Buenos Aires; Tanya Bonakdar Gallery, New York/Los Angeles;
Pinksummer Contemporary Art, Genoa; Esther Schipper, Berlin
© Photography by Studio Tomás Saraceno, 2018

Galileo Galilei, *Sidereus Nuncius* (Starry Messenger), c. 28r,
Drawings of phases and surface of the Moon, 1609, Biblioteca
Nazionale Centrale, Florence, Italy. © De Agostini Picture
Library / Bridgeman Images

PAGE 17
Leonardo da Vinci, *Codex Atlanticus* (Atlantic Codex), f. 1058v,
Studies on aerodynamics and studies on artificial flight;
a parachute (detail). © Veneranda Biblioteca Ambrosiana /
Mondadori Portfolio

Aerocene Launch. August 7, 2017, Salinas Grandes, Jujuy,
Argentina. With the support of CCK Buenos Aires. Courtesy

the Aerocene Foundation and CCK Agency. Photography by
Studio Tomás Saraceno, 2017, Licensed under CC by Aerocene
Foundation 4.0

PAGE 18
View from below from the Palazzo Strozzi Courtyard
Photo Alessandro Moggi

PAGE 19
Rendering of *Thermodynamic Costellation*. Fernweh Architettura

PAGE 20
Superstudio, *Rescuing Historical Italian Landmarks*, 1972
Photo Cristiano Toraldo di Francia

Palazzo Strozzi during the 1966 flood. Alluvione n. 20
© Archivio Foto Locchi, Florence

PAGE 21
Tomás Saraceno
Collage for *Aria*, 2019
Courtesy the artist
© Studio Tomás Saraceno, 2019

PAGE 22
Tomás Saraceno
Flying Garden (detail), 2020
Courtesy the artist; Andersen's, Copenhagen; Ruth Benzacar,
Buenos Aires; Tanya Bonakdar Gallery, New York/Los Angeles;
Pinksummer Contemporary Art, Genoa; Esther Schipper, Berlin
© Photography by Studio Tomas Saraceno, 2019

PAGE 28–29
Argyroneta aquatica in its diving bell: the bubble of air in which
the spider lives, secured underwater with threads of silk,
Oldenburg, Germany, Berlin, 2017
Courtesy the artist; Andersen's, Copenhagen; Ruth Benzacar,
Buenos Aires; Tanya Bonakdar Gallery, New York/Los Angeles;
Pinksummer Contemporary Art, Genoa; Esther Schipper, Berlin
© Photography by Studio Tomas Saraceno, 2017

PAGE 30
Tomás Saraceno
*Spider/Web Pavilion 7: Oracle Readings, Weaving Arachnomancy,
Synanthropic Futures: At-ten(t)sion to invertebrate rights!*, 2019
Installation view at the 58th International Art Exhibition –
La Biennale di Venezia, titled *May You Live in Interesting Times*
Curated by Ralph Rugoff
Courtesy the artist; Andersen's, Copenhagen; Ruth Benzacar,
Buenos Aires; Tanya Bonakdar Gallery, New York/Los Angeles;
Pinksummer Contemporary Art, Genoa; Esther Schipper, Berlin
With thanks to Arachnophilia
© Photography by Studio Tomás Saraceno, 2019

PAGE 33
Tomás Saraceno
ANARCHIST
Card 29 out of a deck of 33 Arachnomancy Cards, 2019-ongoing
Card's drawings and reinterpretation based on Winifred Duncan
(1949), *Webs in the Wind, The Habits of Web-Weaving Spiders*,
New York, The Ronald Press Company.
Courtesy the artist, with thanks to the Arachnophilia archives
Let your future be read by a spider/web and download the
Arachnomancy App, joining an exercise mapping against extinction

For more information visit Arachnophilia.net
© Studio Tomás Saraceno, 2019

PAGE 34
Michael Maier, *Atalanta fugiens*, Oppenheim 1618

Johannes de Sacrobosco, *De Sphaera*, c. 1230

PAGE 35
Tomás Saraceno
W7029EI6, 2018
From the series Printed Matter, printed with black carbon PM 2.5
pollution, extracted from the air on 8-gram hand-made paper
Image from a special issue of NASA Cosmic Dust Catalogue,
April 1982, p. 85
Courtesy the artist; Andersen's, Copenhagen; Ruth Benzacar,
Buenos Aires; Tanya Bonakdar Gallery, New York/Los Angeles;
Pinksummer Contemporary Art, Genoa; Esther Schipper, Berlin
© Studio Tomás Saraceno, 2018

PAGE 36
Soap bubbles flying across Jujuy Argentina, 2018
Courtesy the artist; Andersen's, Copenhagen: Ruth Benzacar,
Buenos Aires; Tanya Bonakdar Gallery, New York/Los Angeles;
Pinksummer Contemporary Art, Genoa; Esther Schipper, Berlin
© Tomás Saraceno, 2018

PAGE 37
Tomás Saraceno
Aerocene 5,2m, 2015
Courtesy the artist; Andersen's, Copenhagen: Ruth Benzacar,
Buenos Aires; Tanya Bonakdar Gallery, New York/Los Angeles;
Pinksummer Contemporary Art, Genoa; Esther Schipper, Berlin
© Photography by Studio Tomás Saraceno, 2015

PAGE 39
Argyroneta aquatica in its diving bell: the bubble of air in which
the spider lives, secured underwater with threads of silk,
Oldenburg, Germany, Berlin, 2017
Courtesy the artist; Aerocene Foundation; Andersen's,
Copenhagen; Ruth Benzacar, Buenos Aires; Tanya Bonakdar
Gallery, New York/Los Angeles; Pinksummer Contemporary Art,
Genoa; Esther Schipper, Berlin
© Photography by Studio Tomas Saraceno, 2017

PAGE 40
Tomás Saraceno
Aerocene 5,2m, 2015
Courtesy the artist; Andersen's, Copenhagen: Ruth Benzacar,
Buenos Aires; Tanya Bonakdar Gallery, New York/Los Angeles;
Pinksummer Contemporary Art, Genoa; Esther Schipper, Berlin
© Photography by Studio Tomás Saraceno, 2015

PAGE 41
Tomás Saraceno
Aerocene 5,2m, 2015
Courtesy the artist; Andersen's, Copenhagen: Ruth Benzacar,
Buenos Aires; Tanya Bonakdar Gallery, New York/Los Angeles;
Pinksummer Contemporary Art, Genoa; Esther Schipper, Berlin
© Photography by Studio Tomás Saraceno, 2015

PAGE 44–45
Tomás Saraceno
Tryout for *Thermodynamic Constellation*, 2019

On the occasion of *Aria* solo exhibition of Tomás Saraceno
at Palazzo Strozzi, Florence, Italy, 2020
Curated by Arturo Galansino
Courtesy the artist; Aerocene Foundation; Andersen's,
Copenhagen; Ruth Benzacar, Buenos Aires; Tanya Bonakdar
Gallery, New York/Los Angeles; Pinksummer Contemporary Art,
Genoa; Esther Schipper, Berlin
© Photography by Studio Tomas Saraceno, 2017

PAGE 47
Tomás Saraceno
LOST SECRET
Card 15 out of a deck of 33 Arachnomancy Cards, 2019-ongoing
Card's drawings and reinterpretation based on Winifred Duncan
(1949), *Webs in The Wind*. New York: The Ronald Press Company;
W. S. Bristowe (1958), *The World of Spiders*. London: Collins; Curtis,
William, 1746–1799; Marbury, Elizabeth, 1856–1933, donor; F. Vollrath
(1988), "Untangling the spider's web," *Trends Ecol. Evol.* 3 (12): 331–35
Courtesy the artist, with thanks to the Arachnophilia archives
Let your future be read by a spider/web and download
the Arachnomancy App, joining an exercise mapping against
extinction
For more information visit Arachnophilia.net
© Studio Tomás Saraceno, 2019

PAGE 48
Nicolas Flamel (attr.), *The Fair Flower on the Mountain*, allegorical
illustration showing *chimerae* representing alchemical processes,
f. 20-21, Bibliothèque Nationale de France © Bridgeman Images

Stacker-reclaimer at coal terminal in Port of Gdansk. Shutterstock

PAGE 49
Tomás Saraceno
*Aero(s)cene: When breath becomes air, when atmospheres
become the movement for a post fossil fuel era against carbon-
capitalist clouds*, 2019
Installation view of *On the Disappearance of Clouds*, 2019
at the 58th International Art Exhibition – La Biennale di Venezia,
titled *May You Live in Interesting Times*
Curated by Ralph Rugoff
Courtesy the artist; Aerocene Foundation; Andersen's,
Copenhagen; Ruth Benzacar, Buenos Aires; Tanya Bonakdar
Gallery, New York/Los Angeles; Pinksummer Contemporary Art,
Genoa; Esther Schipper, Berlin
© Photography by Studio Tomás Saraceno, 2019

Open-pit coal mining. Shutterstock

Coal. Shutterstock

PAGE 50
Rudolf von Ems, Weltchronik, *The First Rain in Paradise*, 1400–10
Digital image courtesy of the Getty's Open Content Program

PAGE 52
Étienne Léopold Trouvelot, *The November Meteors. As Observed
Between Midnight and 5 O'Clock A.M. on the Night of November
13–14 1868*, plate XII from *The Trouvelot Astronomical Drawings*,
1881–82. The New York Public Library Digital collections

PAGE 53
Bernard Picart, *The Fall of Icarus*, 1731. The Print Collector / Alamy
Photo Stock

PAGE 54
Altimetric image of Saint Marc's Square, Venice. Courtesy SMU
Insula

PAGE 55
Tomás Saraceno
*Aero(s)cene: When breath becomes air, when atmospheres
become the movement for a post fossil fuel era against carbon-
capitalist clouds*, 2019
Installation view of *On the Disappearance of Clouds*, 2019
at the 58th International Art Exhibition – La Biennale di Venezia,
titled *May You Live in Interesting Times*
Curated by Ralph Rugoff
Courtesy the artist; Aerocene Foundation; Andersen's,
Copenhagen; Ruth Benzacar, Buenos Aires; Tanya Bonakdar
Gallery, New York/Los Angeles; Pinksummer Contemporary Art,
Genoa; Esther Schipper, Berlin
© Photography by Studio Tomás Saraceno, 2019

PAGE 59
Tomás Saraceno
*Aero(s)cene: When breath becomes air, when atmospheres
become the movement for a post fossil fuel era against carbon-
capitalist clouds*, 2019
Installation view of *On the Disappearance of Clouds*, 2019
at the 58th International Art Exhibition – La Biennale di Venezia,
titled *May You Live in Interesting Times*
Curated by Ralph Rugoff
Courtesy the artist; Aerocene Foundation; Andersen's,
Copenhagen; Ruth Benzacar, Buenos Aires; Tanya Bonakdar
Gallery, New York/Los Angeles; Pinksummer Contemporary Art,
Genoa; Esther Schipper, Berlin
© Photography by Studio Tomás Saraceno, 2019

PAGE 61
Tomás Saraceno
Sundial for Spatial Echoes, 2019
Installation view at Bauhaus-Museum Weimar, Germany
Courtesy the artist; Andersen's, Copenhagen; Ruth Benzacar,
Buenos Aires; Tanya Bonakdar Gallery, New York/Los Angeles;
Pinksummer Contemporary Art, Genoa; Esther Schipper, Berlin
Bauhaus-Museum Weimar, courtesy of Heike Hanada_laboratory
of art and architecture. With thanks to Klassik Stiftung Weimar
© Photography by Studio Tomás Saraceno, 2019

PAGE 62–63
Tomás Saraceno
Sundial for Spatial Echoes, 2019
Installation view at Bauhaus-Museum Weimar, Germany
Courtesy the artist; Andersen's, Copenhagen; Ruth Benzacar,
Buenos Aires; Tanya Bonakdar Gallery, New York/Los Angeles;
Pinksummer Contemporary Art, Genoa; Esther Schipper, Berlin.
Bauhaus-Museum Weimar, courtesy of Heike Hanada_laboratory
of art and architecture. With thanks to Klassik Stiftung Weimar
© Photography by Studio Tomás Saraceno, 2019

PAGE 65
ON AIR
Card 9 out of a deck of 33 Arachnomancy Cards, 2019-ongoing
Card's drawings and reinterpretation based on Winifred Duncan
(1949), *Webs in the Wind*, *The Habits of Web-Weaving Spiders*.
New York, The Ronald Press Company
Courtesy the artist, with thanks to the Arachnophilia archives
Let your future be read by a spider/web and download

the Arachnomancy App, joining an exercise mapping against
extinction
For more information visit Arachnophilia.net
© Studio Tomás Saraceno, 2019

PAGE 66
Unknown British artist, *The Spider and the Fly*, detail, 19th century
© Liszt Collection / Bridgeman Images

PAGE 67
Balthasar Walther, Jakob Böhme, *Viertzig Fragen von der
Seelen Urstand, Essentz, Wesen, Natur und Eigenschafft, was
sie von Ewigkeit in Ewigkeit sey: darbey am Ende beygefüget ist
das umgewandte Auge von der Seelen und ihrer Bildnüss*. Zu
Amsterdam: [s. n.], 1682. Stiftung der Werke von C.G. Jung, Zürich

PAGE 69
Tomás Saraceno
Semiallas voladoras, 2005
Courtesy the artist; Andersen's, Copenhagen; Ruth Benzacar,
Buenos Aires; Tanya Bonakdar Gallery, New York/Los Angeles;
Pinksummer Contemporary Art, Genoa; Esther Schipper,
Berlin
© Studio Tomás Saraceno, 2005

PAGE 70
Henry Christopher McCook, *American Spiders and their Spinning
Work: A Natural History of the Orbweaving Spiders of the United
States, with Special Regard to Their Industry and Habits*, 1889,
vol. II, p. 266. © Cornell University Library

PAGE 72
Tomás Saraceno
Semiallas voladoras, 2005
Courtesy the artist; Andersen's, Copenhagen; Ruth Benzacar,
Buenos Aires; Tanya Bonakdar Gallery, New York/Los Angeles;
Pinksummer Contemporary Art, Genoa; Esther Schipper, Berlin
© Studio Tomás Saraceno, 2005

PAGE 73
Tomás Saraceno
Semiallas voladoras, 2005
Courtesy the artist; Andersen's, Copenhagen; Ruth Benzacar,
Buenos Aires; Tanya Bonakdar Gallery, New York/Los Angeles;
Pinksummer Contemporary Art, Genoa; Esther Schipper, Berlin
© Studio Tomás Saraceno, 2005

PAGE 74
Tomás Saraceno
Sounding the Air, 2018
Installation view at ON AIR, *carte blanche* exhibition
to Tomás Saraceno, Palais de Tokyo, Paris, 2018
Curated by Rebecca Lamarche-Vadel
Courtesy the artist; Andersen's, Copenhagen; Ruth Benzacar,
Buenos Aires; Tanya Bonakdar Gallery, New York/Los Angeles;
Pinksummer Contemporary Art, Genoa; Esther Schipper, Berlin
© Photography by Studio Tomás Saraceno, 2018

PAGE 76–77
Tomás Saraceno
Sounding the Air, 2018
Installation view at ON AIR, *carte blanche* exhibition
to Tomás Saraceno, Palais de Tokyo, Paris, 2018
Curated by Rebecca Lamarche-Vadel

Courtesy the artist; Andersen's, Copenhagen; Ruth Benzacar, Buenos Aires; Tanya Bonakdar Gallery, New York/Los Angeles; Pinksummer Contemporary Art, Genoa; Esther Schipper, Berlin
© Photography by Andrea Rossetti, 2018

PAGE 79
SPIDER/WEB INTELLIGENCE
Card 2 out of a deck of 33 Arachnomancy Cards, 2019-ongoing
Courtesy the artist, with thanks to the Arachnophilia archives
Let your future be read by a spider/web and download the Arachnomancy App, joining an exercise mapping against extinction
For more information visit Arachnophilia.net
© Studio Tomás Saraceno, 2019

PAGES 80–81
Caspar David Friedrich, *The Woman with a Spider's Web in the Middle of Leafless Trees*, Hamburger Kunsthalle, Hamburg
© Bridgeman Images

PAGE 83
Athanasius Kircher, *Ars magna sciendi, in XII libros digesta: qua nova & universali methodo per Artificiosum Combinationum contextum de omni re proposita plurimis & prope infinitis rationibus disputari, omniumque […]*. Amstelodami: apud Ioannem Ianssonium a Waesberge, 1669. ETH-Bibliothek Zürich, Rar 894 GF

PAGE 85
Tomás Saraceno
Spider/Web Pavilions, 2019
Installation view at the 58th International Art Exhibition – La Biennale di Venezia, titled *May You Live in Interesting Times*
Curated by Ralph Rugoff
With thanks to Arachnophilia
© Photography by Studio Tomás Saraceno, 2019

PAGE 86, 89
Johannes C. Andersen, "Māori String Games" (part III), with illustrations by J. McDonald, *The New Zealand Journal of Science and Technology*, vol. III, no. 4, Wellington, November, 1920, p. 199, 202, 204

PAGE 90
Tomás Saraceno
Spider/Web Pavilions, 2019
Installation view at the 58th International Art Exhibition – La Biennale di Venezia, titled *May You Live in Interesting Times*
Curated by Ralph Rugoff
With thanks to Arachnophilia
© Photography by Studio Tomás Saraceno, 2019

Depiction of retorts and stills used in alchemy from a Greek manuscript, 15th Century, Bibliothèque Nationale De France, Paris. © De Agostini Picture Library / Bridgeman Images

PAGE 91
Tomás Saraceno
Spider/Web Pavilions, 2019
Installation view at the 58th International Art Exhibition – La Biennale di Venezia, titled *May You Live in Interesting Times*
Curated by Ralph Rugoff
With thanks to Arachnophilia
© Photography by Studio Tomás Saraceno, 2019

Tomás Saraceno
Spider/Web Pavilion 7: Oracle Readings, *Weaving Arachnomancy*, *Synanthropic Futures: At-ten(t)sion to invertebrate rights!*, 2019
Installation view at the 58th International Art Exhibition – La Biennale di Venezia, titled *May You Live in Interesting Times*
Curated by Ralph Rugoff
Courtesy the artist; Andersen's, Copenhagen; Ruth Benzacar, Buenos Aires; Tanya Bonakdar Gallery, New York/Los Angeles; Pinksummer Contemporary Art, Genoa; Esther Schipper, Berlin
With thanks to Arachnophilia
© Photography by Studio Tomás Saraceno, 2019

PAGE 93
Tomás Saraceno
Webs of At-tent(s)ion (detail), 2018
Installation view at ON AIR, *carte blanche* exhibition to Tomás Saraceno, Palais de Tokyo, Paris, 2018
Curated by Rebecca Lamarche-Vadel
Courtesy the artist; Andersen's, Copenhagen; Ruth Benzacar, Buenos Aires; Tanya Bonakdar Gallery, New York/Los Angeles; Pinksummer Contemporary Art, Genoa; Esther Schipper, Berlin
© Photography by Studio Tomás Saraceno, 2018

PAGE 94–95
Tomás Saraceno
Webs of At-tent(s)ion, 2018
Installation view at ON AIR, *carte blanche* exhibition to Tomás Saraceno, Palais de Tokyo, Paris, 2018
Curated by Rebecca Lamarche-Vadel
Courtesy the artist; Andersen's, Copenhagen; Ruth Benzacar, Buenos Aires; Tanya Bonakdar Gallery, New York/Los Angeles; Pinksummer Contemporary Art, Genoa; Esther Schipper, Berlin
© Photography by Andrea Rossetti, 2018

PAGE 97
HIDDEN PATHS
Card 20 out of a deck of 33 Arachnomancy Cards, 2019-ongoing
Courtesy the artist, with thanks to the Arachnophilia archives
Let your future be read by a spider/web and download the Arachnomancy App, joining an exercise mapping against extinction
For more information visit Arachnophilia.net
© Studio Tomás Saraceno, 2019

PAGE 98–99
List of Internet Phenomena. Map of Neural Pathways. Pngkey

PAGE 100
Michael Cukr, *Spider*, California 2016. ©Michael Cukr

PAGE 102
Hugo Heikenwaelder, *Universum*, 2020. © Hugo Heikenwaelder
www.heikenwaelder.at

Tomás Saraceno
Cosmic Filaments, 2013
Courtesy the artist; Aerocene Foundation; Andersen's, Copenhagen; Ruth Benzacar, Buenos Aires; Tanya Bonakdar Gallery, New York/Los Angeles; Pinksummer Contemporary Art, Genoa; Esther Schipper, Berlin
© Studio Tomás Saraceno, 2013

Tomás Saraceno
Cosmic Filaments, 2013
Courtesy the artist; Aerocene Foundation; Andersen's,

Copenhagen; Ruth Benzacar, Buenos Aires; Tanya Bonakdar
Gallery, New York/Los Angeles; Pinksummer Contemporary Art,
Genoa; Esther Schipper, Berlin
© Studio Tomás Saraceno, 2013

PAGE 103
Herbert List, *Bomarzo Holy Wood: Monster in the Garden
of Pier Francesco Orsini*, 1952
© Herbert List / Magnumphotos / Contrasto

*Thesaurus of Alchemy, Symbolic Alchemical Watercolour
Drawings*, c. 1725, f. 74. © Wellcome Trust 2019

Bomarzo Holy Wood: Etruscan Bench. Shutterstock

PAGES 104–5
Tomás Saraceno
How to Entangle the Universe in a Spider/Web?, 2018
Installation view at ON AIR, *carte blanche* exhibition
to Tomás Saraceno, Palais de Tokyo, Paris, 2018
Curated by Rebecca Lamarche-Vadel
Courtesy the artist; Aerocene Foundation; Andersen's,
Copenhagen; Ruth Benzacar, Buenos Aires; Tanya Bonakdar
Gallery, New York/Los Angeles; Pinksummer Contemporary Art,
Genoa; Esther Schipper, Berlin
© Photography by Studio Tomás Saraceno, 2018

PAGE 107
Athanasius Kircher, *Ars magna lucis et umbrae, in decem libros
digesta: quibus admirandae lucis et umbrae in mundo, atque adeò
universa natura, vires effectusque uti nova, ita varia novorum
reconditiorumque speciminum exhibitione, [...]. Romae i.e. Rom:
Sumptibus Scheus*; ex Typographia Grignani, 1646. ETH-Bibliothek
Zürich, Rar 8883 q

PAGE 109
Tomás Saraceno
How to Entangle the Universe in a Spider/Web?, 2018
Installation view at ON AIR, *carte blanche* exhibition
to Tomás Saraceno, Palais de Tokyo, Paris, 2018
Curated by Rebecca Lamarche-Vadel
Courtesy the artist; Aerocene Foundation; Andersen's,
Copenhagen; Ruth Benzacar, Buenos Aires; Tanya Bonakdar
Gallery, New York/Los Angeles; Pinksummer Contemporary Art,
Genoa; Esther Schipper, Berlin
© Photography by Studio Tomás Saraceno, 2018

PAGE 110–11
Tomás Saraceno
Tryout for *How to Entangle the Universe in a Spider/Web?*, 2019
On the occasion of *Aria* solo exhibition of Tomás Saraceno
at Palazzo Strozzi, Florence, Italy, 2020.
Curated by Arturo Galansino
Courtesy the artist; Aerocene Foundation; Andersen's,
Copenhagen; Ruth Benzacar, Buenos Aires; Tanya Bonakdar
Gallery, New York/Los Angeles; Pinksummer Contemporary Art,
Genoa; Esther Schipper, Berlin
© Photography by Studio Tomás Saraceno, 2019

PAGE 113
Tomás Saraceno
TREMOR
Card 14 out of a deck of 33 Arachnomancy Cards, 2019-ongoing
Card's drawings and reinterpretation based on Peter Apian,

The Ptolemaic Solar System, Cosmographia (1539). Reprinted in
Alexandre Koyre, *From the Closed World to the Infinite Universe*.
Baltimore; Johns Jopkins, 1957.
Courtesy the artist, with thanks to the Arachnophilia archives
Let your future be read by a spider/web and download the
Arachnomancy App, joining an exercise mapping against
extinction
For more information visit Arachnophilia.net
© Studio Tomás Saraceno, 2019

PAGE 114
Jugend: Münchner illustrierte Wochenschrift für Kunst und Leben,
11.1906, Band 2 (Nr. 52). © Universitätsbibliothek Heidelberg

PAGE 116–17
Tomás Saraceno
Particular Matter(s) Jam Session, 2018
Installation view at ON AIR, *carte blanche* exhibition
to Tomás Saraceno, Palais de Tokyo, Paris, 2018
Curated by Rebecca Lamarche-Vadel
Courtesy the artist; Aerocene Foundation; Andersen's,
Copenhagen; Ruth Benzacar, Buenos Aires; Tanya Bonakdar
Gallery, New York/Los Angeles; Pinksummer Contemporary Art,
Genoa; Esther Schipper, Berlin
© Photography by Studio Tomás Saraceno, 2018

PAGE 118
The surface mine storage place, mining minerals and brown coal
in diferent colours. View from above. Industrial background
Photo by Curioso Photography, Poland on Unsplash

PAGE 121
Tomás Saraceno
Webs of At-tent(s)ion (detail), 2018
Installation view at ON AIR, *carte blanche* exhibition
to Tomás Saraceno, Palais de Tokyo, Paris, 2018
Curated by Rebecca Lamarche-Vadel
Courtesy the artist; Aerocene Foundation; Andersen's,
Copenhagen; Ruth Benzacar, Buenos Aires; Tanya Bonakdar
Gallery, New York/Los Angeles; Pinksummer Contemporary Art,
Genoa; Esther Schipper, Berlin
© Photography by Studio Tomás Saraceno, 2018

PAGE 122–23
Tomás Saraceno
163,000 Light Years, 2016
Commissioned by MARCO, Museum of Contemporary Art
of Monterrey
Courtesy the artist; Andersen's, Copenhagen: Ruth Benzacar,
Buenos Aires; Tanya Bonakdar Gallery, New York/Los Angeles;
Pinksummer Contemporary Art, Genoa; Esther Schipper, Berlin
© Photography by Studio Tomás Saraceno, 2016

PAGE 124–25
Tomás Saraceno
Passages of Time, 2018
Installation view at ON AIR, *carte blanche* exhibition
to Tomás Saraceno, Palais de Tokyo, Paris, 2018
Curated by Rebecca Lamarche-Vadel
Courtesy the artist; Andersen's, Copenhagen; Ruth Benzacar,
Buenos Aires; Tanya Bonakdar Gallery, New York/Los Angeles;
Pinksummer Contemporary Art, Genoa; Esther Schipper, Berlin
© Photography by Studio Tomás Saraceno, 2018

Tomás Saraceno
Passages of Time, 2018
Installation view at ON AIR, *carte blanche* exhibition
to Tomás Saraceno, Palais de Tokyo, Paris, 2018
Curated by Rebecca Lamarche-Vadel
Courtesy the artist; Andersen's, Copenhagen; Ruth Benzacar,
Buenos Aires; Tanya Bonakdar Gallery, New York/Los Angeles;
Pinksummer Contemporary Art, Genoa; Esther Schipper, Berlin
© Photography by Studio Tomás Saraceno, 2018

Tomás Saraceno
Passages of Time, 2018
Installation view at ON AIR, *carte blanche* exhibition
to Tomás Saraceno, Palais de Tokyo, Paris, 2018
Curated by Rebecca Lamarche-Vadel
Courtesy the artist; Andersen's, Copenhagen; Ruth Benzacar,
Buenos Aires; Tanya Bonakdar Gallery, New York/Los Angeles;
Pinksummer Contemporary Art, Genoa; Esther Schipper, Berlin
© Photography by Studio Tomás Saraceno, 2018

Tomás Saraceno
Passages of Time, 2018
Installation view at ON AIR, *carte blanche* exhibition
to Tomás Saraceno, Palais de Tokyo, Paris, 2018
Curated by Rebecca Lamarche-Vadel
Courtesy the artist; Andersen's, Copenhagen; Ruth Benzacar,
Buenos Aires; Tanya Bonakdar Gallery, New York/Los Angeles;
Pinksummer Contemporary Art, Genoa; Esther Schipper, Berlin
© Photography by Studio Tomás Saraceno, 2018

PAGE 126–27
Tomás Saraceno
Particular Matter(s) Jam Session, 2018
Installation view at ON AIR, *carte blanche* exhibition
to Tomás Saraceno, Palais de Tokyo, Paris, 2018
Curated by Rebecca Lamarche-Vadel
Courtesy the artist; Andersen's, Copenhagen; Ruth Benzacar,
Buenos Aires; Tanya Bonakdar Gallery, New York/Los Angeles;
Pinksummer Contemporary Art, Genoa; Esther Schipper, Berlin
© Photography by Studio Tomás Saraceno, 2018

PAGE 129
Tomás Saraceno
MULTIVERSE
Card 1 out of a deck of 33 Arachnomancy Cards, 2019-ongoing
Card's drawings and reinterpretation based on Winifred Duncan
(1949), *Webs In The Wind*. New York: The Ronald Press Company;
W. S. Bristowe (1958), *The World of Spiders*. London: Collins;
Curtis, William, 1746–1799; Marbury, Elizabeth, 1856–1933, donor;
F. Vollrath (1988), "Untangling the spider's web," *Trends Ecol. Evol.*
3 (12): 331–35
Courtesy the artist, with thanks to the Arachnophilia archives
Let your future be read by a spider/web and download the
Arachnomancy App, joining an exercise mapping against extinction
For more information visit Arachnophilia.net
© Studio Tomás Saraceno, 2019

PAGE 130
Johannes Hevelius, *Selenographia sive lunae descriptio: atque
accurata, tam macularum ejus, … delineatio, …; addita est,
lentes expoliendi nova ratio, ut et telescopia diversa construendi,
et experiendi*, […]. Gedani: Hünefeld, 1647. ETH-Bibliothek Zürich,
Rar 8932 q

PAGE 131
Robert Fludd, *Philosophia Moysaica. In qua sapientia & scientia
creationis & creaturarum Sacra veréque Christiana (ut pote
cujus basis sive Fundamentum est unicus ille Lapis Angularis Jesus
Christus) ad amussim & enucleaté explicatur.* [with:] *Responsum
ad Hoplocrisma-Spongum M. Fosteri Presbiteri, ab ipso,
ad unguenti armarii validitatem delendam ordinatum*, 1638
© Science History Institute

PAGE 132
Tomás Saraceno
W7029A15, p 16, 2018
From the series *Printed Matter*, printed with black carbon PM2.5
pollution, extracted from the air on 8-gram hand-made paper
Image from a special issue of NASA Cosmic Dust Catalogue,
April 1982, p. 16
Courtesy the artist; Andersen's, Copenhagen; Ruth Benzacar,
Buenos Aires; Tanya Bonakdar Gallery, New York/Los Angeles;
Pinksummer Contemporary Art, Genoa; Esther Schipper, Berlin
© Studio Tomás Saraceno, 2018

PAGE 133
Michael Maier, *Atalanta fugiens*, Oppenheim 1618

PAGE 134–35
Tomás Saraceno
Collage for *A Thermodynamic Imaginary*, 2019
Courtesy the artist

PAGE 138–39
Tomás Saraceno
A Thermodynamic Imaginary, 2018
Installation view at ON AIR, *carte blanche* exhibition
to Tomás Saraceno, Palais de Tokyo, Paris, 2018
Curated by Rebecca Lamarche-Vadel
Courtesy the artist; Andersen's, Copenhagen; Ruth Benzacar,
Buenos Aires; Tanya Bonakdar Gallery, New York/Los Angeles;
Pinksummer Contemporary Art, Genoa; Esther Schipper, Berlin
© Photography by Studio Tomás Saraceno, 2018

PAGE 140
Tomás Saraceno
A Thermodynamic Imaginary (detail), 2018
Installation view at ON AIR, *carte blanche* exhibition
to Tomás Saraceno, Palais de Tokyo, Paris, 2018
Curated by Rebecca Lamarche-Vadel
Courtesy the artist; Aerocene Foundation; Andersen's,
Copenhagen; Ruth Benzacar, Buenos Aires; Tanya Bonakdar
Gallery, New York/Los Angeles; Pinksummer Contemporary Art,
Genoa; Esther Schipper, Berlin
© Photography by Studio Tomás Saraceno, 2018

PAGE 142–43
Tomás Saraceno
A Thermodynamic Imaginary, 2018
Installation view at ON AIR, *carte blanche* exhibition
to Tomás Saraceno, Palais de Tokyo, Paris, 2018
Curated by Rebecca Lamarche-Vadel
Courtesy the artist; Andersen's, Copenhagen; Ruth Benzacar,
Buenos Aires; Tanya Bonakdar Gallery, New York/Los Angeles;
Pinksummer Contemporary Art, Genoa; Esther Schipper, Berlin
© Photography by Studio Tomás Saraceno, 2018

PAGE 145
Tomás Saraceno
SYM(BIO)POETICS
Card 3 out of a deck of 33 Arachnomancy Cards, 2019-ongoing
Card's drawings and reinterpretation based on Winifred Duncan
(1949), *Webs in the Wind, The Habits of Web-Weaving Spiders*.
New York, The Ronald Press Company
Courtesy the artist, with thanks to the Arachnophilia archives
Let your future be read by a spider/web and download the
Arachnomancy App, joining an exercise mapping against extinction
For more information visit Arachnophilia.net
© Studio Tomás Saraceno, 2019

PAGE 146
Studio Ghibli, screenshot from *Nausicaa of the Valley of
the Wind*, 1984. © Studio Ghibli

PAGE 147
Cornelii Giselberti Plempii, *Amsterodamum monogrammon*, 1616

PAGE 148
Tomás Saraceno
Spider/Web Pavilions, 2018
With thanks to Arachnophilia
Courtesy the artist
© Photography by Studio Tomás Saraceno, 2018

PAGE 151
Hyeronimus Bosch, *The Garden of Earthly Delights*, 1490–1500,
Museo del Prado, Madrid. © Bridgeman Images

PAGE 152–53
Tomás Saraceno
60SE Flying Garden-Air-Port-City, 2006
Installation view, Sudeley Castle, Gloucestershire, UK, 2006
Courtesy the artist; Andersen's, Copenhagen; Ruth Benzacar,
Buenos Aires; Tanya Bonakdar Gallery, New York/Los Angeles;
Pinksummer Contemporary Art, Genoa; Esther Schipper, Berlin
Photography © Studio Tomás Saraceno, 2006

PAGE 155
Tomás Saraceno
Flying Garden (detail), 2020
Courtesy the artist; Andersen's, Copenhagen; Ruth Benzacar,
Buenos Aires; Tanya Bonakdar Gallery, New York/Los Angeles;
Pinksummer Contemporary Art, Genoa; Esther Schipper, Berlin
© Photography by Studio Tomas Saraceno, 2019

PAGE 156
Tomás Saraceno
Flying Garden (detail), 2020
Courtesy the artist; Andersen's, Copenhagen; Ruth Benzacar,
Buenos Aires; Tanya Bonakdar Gallery, New York/Los Angeles;
Pinksummer Contemporary Art, Genoa; Esther Schipper, Berlin
© Photography by Studio Tomás Saraceno, 2019

PAGE 158–59
Tomás Saraceno
Flying Garden (detail), 2020
Courtesy the artist; Andersen's, Copenhagen; Ruth Benzacar,
Buenos Aires; Tanya Bonakdar Gallery, New York/Los Angeles;
Pinksummer Contemporary Art, Genoa; Esther Schipper, Berlin
© Photography by Studio Tomas Saraceno, 2019

PAGE 161
Tomás Saraceno
THE COSMIC WEB
Card 21 out of a deck of 33 Arachnomancy Cards, 2019-ongoing
Card's drawings and reinterpretation based on by Magda Weck
Gonzales, J.A Gonzales, and Harry Sparrowhawk (1988), *Native
American Tarot Deck*. U.S Games Systems Inc.
Courtesy the artist, with thanks to the Arachnophilia archives
Let your future be read by a spider/web and download the
Arachnomancy App, joining an exercise mapping against extinction
For more information visit Arachnophilia.net
© Studio Tomás Saraceno, 2019

PAGE 163
Henry Christopher McCook, *American Spiders and their Spinning
Work: A Natural History of the Orbweaving Spiders of the United
States, with Special Regard to Their Industry and Habits*, 1889,
vol. I, p. 249. © Cornell University Library

PAGE 164
Tryout for *A Thermodynamic Imaginary*, 2019
On the occasion of *Aria* solo exhibition of Tomás Saraceno
at Palazzo Strozzi, Florence, Italy, 2020.
Curated by Arturo Galansino
Courtesy the artist; Aerocene Foundation; Andersen's,
Copenhagen; Ruth Benzacar, Buenos Aires; Tanya Bonakdar
Gallery, New York/Los Angeles; Pinksummer Contemporary Art,
Genoa; Esther Schipper, Berlin
© Photography by Studio Tomás Saraceno, 2019

PAGE 167
AEROCENE TETHERED FLIGHT (AT)
A SIGNATURE FREE FROM BORDERS, FREE FROM FOSSIL FUELS
At I 023 I 46.9 I 51.2093° N, 3.2247° Ei 20.04.28 I 11:11 I 143 I 10.5 I 23.7 I
Signed with Erik Vogler, Gwilym Faulkner, Hannah Lee Turner
2018 print
Courtesy the artist

A huge cobweb covers the vegetation along the coast of Aitoliko,
about 250 km west of Athens, Greece, September 18, 2018
(issued 19 September 2019). EPA / Giannis Giannakopoulos

PAGE 168
Tomás Saraceno
Calendrier Lun-AIR (detail), 2018
Installation view at ON AIR, *carte blanche* exhibition
to Tomás Saraceno, Palais de Tokyo, Paris, 2018
Curated by Rebecca Lamarche-Vadel
Courtesy the artist; Andersen's, Copenhagen; Ruth Benzacar,
Buenos Aires; Tanya Bonakdar Gallery, New York/Los Angeles;
Pinksummer Contemporary Art, Genoa; Esther Schipper, Berlin
© Photography by Studio Tomás Saraceno, 2018

PAGE 172
Tomás Saraceno
Thermodynamic Suite (detail), 2018
Installation view at ON AIR, *carte blanche* exhibition
to Tomás Saraceno, Palais de Tokyo, Paris, 2018
Curated by Rebecca Lamarche-Vadel
Courtesy the artist; Andersen's, Copenhagen; Ruth Benzacar,
Buenos Aires; Tanya Bonakdar Gallery, New York/Los Angeles;
Pinksummer Contemporary Art, Genoa; Esther Schipper, Berlin
© Photography by Studio Tomás Saraceno, 2018

Tomás Saraceno
Thermodynamic Suite (detail), 2018
Installation view at ON AIR, *carte blanche* exhibition
to Tomás Saraceno, Palais de Tokyo, Paris, 2018
Curated by Rebecca Lamarche-Vadel
Courtesy the artist; Andersen's, Copenhagen; Ruth Benzacar,
Buenos Aires; Tanya Bonakdar Gallery, New York/Los Angeles;
Pinksummer Contemporary Art, Genoa; Esther Schipper, Berlin
© Photography by Studio Tomás Saraceno, 2018

PAGE 174–75
Tomás Saraceno
Resine Tree Connectome, 2020
Courtesy the artist; Andersen's, Copenhagen; Ruth Benzacar,
Buenos Aires; Tanya Bonakdar Gallery, New York/Los Angeles;
Pinksummer Contemporary Art, Genoa; Esther Schipper, Berlin
© Photography by Studio Tomas Saraceno, 2019

PAGE 176–77
Tomás Saraceno
Aerographies, 2018
Installation view at ON AIR, *carte blanche* exhibition
to Tomás Saraceno, Palais de Tokyo, Paris, 2018
Curated by Rebecca Lamarche-Vadel
Courtesy the artist; Andersen's, Copenhagen; Ruth Benzacar,
Buenos Aires; Tanya Bonakdar Gallery, New York/Los Angeles;
Pinksummer Contemporary Art, Genoa; Esther Schipper, Berlin
© Photography by Andrea Rossetti, 2018

PAGE 179
Tomás Saraceno
Around the world collage for *Aria*, 2020
Courtesy the artist.

PAGE 180–81
Museo Aero Solar, 2007–ongoing
At Prato, Italy, in 2009 with Alberto Pesavento, Tomás Saraceno,
Janis Elko, Till Hergenhahn, Giovanni Giaretta, Marco,
Alessandro, Manuel Scano, Michela Sacchetto, and Matteo
Mascheroni
Initiated by artist Tomás Saraceno in conversation with Alberto
Pesavento in 2007, Museo Aero Solar unfolds in the space formed
between human and non-human participants in the simple acts of
cooperation and reusing plastic bags, to collectively produce an
aerosolar sculpture. Fostered in more than 21 countries to date,
Museo Aero Solar embodies a vision of pollution-free futures
through the growth of self-assembling, geographically dispersed
participatory communities; in this way, the practice can be seen
as marking the beginning of the genealogy of Aerocene
Courtesy Museo Aero Solar and Aerocene Foundation
Photography by Janis Elko
Licensed under CC BY-SA 4.0

Museo Aero Solar, 2007–ongoing
At Aerocene Festival, Olympiaberg, Munich, Germany,
6–11 Sep 2019. with Tomás Saraceno, Susanne Witzgall,
Beate Engl, Denis Maksimov, Timo Tuominen, Erik Bordeleau,
Alice Lamperti, Roxanne Mackie, Erik Vogler, Gwilym Faulkner,
Camilla Berggren Lundell, Charles Gonzalez, Rebecca Schedler,
Jasper Humpert, Saverio Contini, Dario Lagana, Andrea Familari
Initiated by artist Tomás Saraceno in conversation with
Alberto Pesavento in 2007, *Museo Aero Solar* unfolds in
the space formed between human and nonhuman participants
in the simple acts of cooperation and reusing plastic bags,

to collectively produce an aerosolar sculpture. Fostered in more
than 21 countries to date, *Museo Aero Solar* embodies a vision
of pollution-free futures through the growth of self-assembling,
geographically dispersed participatory communities; in this way,
the practice can be seen as marking the beginning of the
genealogy of Aerocene
Courtesy *Museo Aero Solar* and Aerocene Foundation
Photography by Studio Tomás Saraceno, 2019
Licensed under CC BY-SA 4.0.

Aerocene Backpack (2016-ongoing)
Developed by the Aerocene community
The Aerocene Backpack is licensed under CC BY-SA 4.0
Courtesy the artist; Aerocene Foundation; Andersen's,
Copenhagen; Ruth Benzacar, Buenos Aires; Tanya Bonakdar
Gallery, New York/Los Angeles; Pinksummer Contemporary Art,
Genoa; Esther Schipper, Berlin
Photography by Studio Tomás Saraceno, 2018

PAGE 181
Stratosphere balloon driven beyond the Iron Curtain Mountains,
Aug. 08, 1960. Keystone Press / Alamy Stock Photo

PAGE 182–83
Aerocene Backpack launch. August 7, 2017
Salinas Grandes, Jujuy, Argentina
With the support of CCK Buenos Aires
Courtesy the Aerocene Foundation and CCK Agency
Photography by Studio Tomás Saraceno, 2017
Licensed under CC BY-SA 4.0 by Aerocene Foundation

AEROCENE TETHERED FLIGHT (AT)
A SIGNATURE FREE FROM BORDERS, FREE FROM FOSSIL FUELS
AT I 003 I 61.7 I 24.1858° S, 65.2995° WI 6.8.2017 I 08:55 I
203 I 26 I 229 I
Signed with Alicia De Arteaga, Maxi Bellman, Martin Bonadeo,
Joaouin Ezcurra, Agustina De Ganay, Guido Ignatti, Maximiliano
Laina, Pablo Lapadula, /Nes Leyba, Eduardo Marengo, Ana
Martinez Quijano, Tomas Saraceno, Sven Steudte, Pio Torroja,
Gabriela Urtiaga
2018 print
Courtesy the artist

Tomás Saraceno
Eclipse of the Aerocene Explorer, 2016
Performance in Salar de Uyuni, Bolivia, January 2016,
during Tomás Saraceno's artistic expedition
Courtesy the artist; Aerocene Foundation; Andersen's,
Copenhagen; Ruth Benzacar, Buenos Aires; Tanya Bonakdar
Gallery, New York/Los Angeles; Pinksummer Contemporary Art,
Genoa; Esther Schipper, Berlin
© Photography by Studio Tomás Saraceno, 2016

ARTIST'S ACKNOWLEDGEMENTS

Artist Tomás Saraceno would like to say a huge thank you, firstly to Arturo Galansino and the team of Palazzo Strozzi, for realizing such an amazing project together and for Arturo's thought provoking and insightful words in this publication. A special thanks also to Emanuele Coccia for weaving such inspiring thoughts into these pages and as well to Martina Mian for working together on such an exciting project as this beautiful book, made beautiful with care and sensitivity by Enrico Bardin, a huge thank you.

To the spider/webs, those living already in the Palazzo Strozzi, as well as *Nephila inaurata, Cyrtophora citricola, Larinioides sclopetarius, Agelena labyrinthica, Parasteatoda tepidariorum, Holocnemus pluchei*.

From my studio, with whom we never stop dreaming, an incredible thanks to the leading members, without whom, nothing would be possible; Lars Behrendt, Fabiola Bierhoff, Saverio Cantoni, Connie Chester, Manuela Mazure and Claudia Melendez. In particular for this project an additional huge thank you for their endless dedication; Sonia d'Agrain, Mateo Argerich, Stefan Brüning, Viola Cafuli, Tatiana Chaves, Sebastian Ducros, Andrea Familari, Alice Hall, Sarah Kisner, Dario Lagana, Alice Lamperti, Rosalie Laurin, Lucas Mateluna, Jillian Meyer, Jörg Niemann, Lea Nikou, Tania Patritti, Aysegul Seyhan, Hans-Martin Schlesier, Grace Sparapani, Desirée Valdes, Erik Vogler, Philipp Weber.
As well, for their enduring commitment to pushing our creative limits together, thank you to Ricardo Alarcón, Giulia Albarello, Giulia Ambrosini, Miriam Aller, Duncan Anderson, Scott Barnes, Xavier Barragan, Ally Bisshop, Timothy Blake, Francesca Boenzi, Irina Bogdan, Sascha Boldt, Elaine Bonavia, Stefan Brüning, Thomas Charil, Ben Clark, Filippo Corato, Carola Dietrich, Miriam Dreyer, Manie Du Plessis, Hugo Du Plessix, Sara Ferrer, Meike Fischer, Luca Girardini, Charles Gonzalez, Samantha Grob, Jan Grupp, Martin Heller, Marina Höxter, Adam Hudec, Eric Jones, Jennifer Jordan, Georgi Kazlachev, Sarah Kisner, Nemanja Kordic, Rosalie Laurin, Vicente Macellari, Roxanne Mackie, Sarah Martinus, Pepe Menéndez-Conde, Veronika Miskovicova, Olivia Moore, Roland Muehlethaler, Jaime Norambuena, Aurelia Nowak, Lugh O'Neill, Catarina Palma, Martina Pelacchi, Marco Pittaluga, Maria Soledad Pons, Diego Puerto, Alfredo Ramos, Matthew Raven, Patrick Reddy, Jekaterina Saveljeva, Gustavo Alonso Serafin, Jazmin Scherone, Anna Sophie Schmidt, Cordelia Soender, Sebastian Steinboeck, Judith Strassenberger, Ilka Tödt, Nicolas Val, Zaida Violan, Filippo Vogliazzo, Julius Weiland and Davide Zucco.

And, with the endless support and commitment of my galleries: Andersen's Contemporary (Copenhagen), Esther Schipper (Berlin), Pinksummer Contemporary Art (Genoa), Ruth Benzacar (Buenos Aires) & Tanya Bonakdar Gallery (New York/Los Angeles).

To all the Aerocene community, for dreaming on flying together to free the air. And also, the Arachnophilia community and archives, for the never ending journey of sensitivity, learning to live with our nonhuman neighbours.

AEROCENE

Thank you to the Center for Art, Science & Technology (CAST) at the Massachusetts Institute of Technology (MIT), CNES (French National Space Agency), CCK Argentina, Public Lab, The Goethe Institute, Radioamateur, Freifunk, IAK architecture-related Art Institute at Technische Universität Braunschweig, TBA21, the Earth, Atmospheric and Planetary Science Department – EAPS, Sembrando Juntos Community Center, ACIJ, Blog Proyecto Riachuelo, Universidad 3 de Febrero, the community TV channel Urbana Te Ve, Lighter Than Air GmbH, Global Western, European Commission for Transport, Art4Action, Balon Klub Zagreb, Palais de Tokyo, Artists4Paris Climate, Hopscotch and Public Systeme, Didier Saulnier, COP21, Potsdam Institute for Climate Impact Research, Red Cross Red Crescent, Astrovandalistas, Gravity by its Absence, the Rubin Centre for the Visual Arts, the Radiosondy Polska Community, Bollinger + Grohmann Ingenieure, and 350org,
People: Boris Groys, Bronislaw Szerszynski, Derek McCormack, Kiel Moe, Nicholas Shapiro, Oliver Morton, Olivier Michelon, Pierre Chabard, Sanford Kwinter, Sasha Engelmann, Jol Thomson, Leila Wheatley Kinney, Ludovica Illari, Glenn Flierl, Bill McKenna, Nigel Clark, Etienne Turpin, Juan Enriquez, Alice Lamperti, Gwilym Faulkner, Erik Vogler, Camilla Berggren Lundell, Sven Steudte, Daniel Schultz, Joaquin Ezcurra, Hannah Lee Turner, Lisa Lurati, Ignas Petronis, Adrian Krell, Anna Guðný Jónsdóttir Þór, Ali Anwar III, Irin Siriwattanagul, Vasily Sitnikov, Marco Ferrari, Elisa Pasqual, Luca Ferrario, Iacopo Leardini, Angelo Semeraro, Débora Swistun, Claudia Espínola, Rocío Luque, Ezequiel Viggiano, Gustavo Cañaveral, Maximiliano Laina, Gabriela Sorbi, Eduardo Marengo, Natalia Buceta, Jimena Rodriguez Berisso, Margarita Ezcurra, Veronica Fiorito, the residents of Inflamable, Abel Mamani, Agustina de Ganay, Alfio Demestre, Alicia de Arteaga, Ana Lia Laura Palavecino, Daniela Gutierrez, Eduardo Marengo, Erica Bohm, Froilán Colque, Guadalupe Pardo, Guido Ignatti, Guido Poloni, Hernán Soriano, Inés Leyba, Joaquin Ezcurra, Laura Daldin, Laura Nieves, Magdalena Molinari, Mariano Giraud, Martin Bonadeo, Mateo Amaral, Mauricio Corbalan, Mauricio Florentino, Maxi Bellman, Maximiliano Laina, Maximiliano Bellmann, Oliverio Duhalde, Pablo La Padula, Patricia Saragueta, Pio Torroja, Sabrina Martinez Zunni, Sofia Petit de Meurville, Sven Steudte, Yisell Sarasua, Nick Shapiro, Alexander Bouchner, Thomas Krahn Alexander Bouchner, Cara Cotner, Adrian Krell, Daniel Schulz, Irin Siriwattanagul, and Kotryna Šlapšinskaitė, Lars Behrendt, Daniel Dittmer, Ivanna Franke, Luca Girardini, Anna Holzapfel, Eleonora Pedretti, Nathaphon Phantounarakul, Adrian Porikys, Tomasz Stasiak, and Rirkrit Tiravanija, Larasati, Elinor Merkier, Minwoo Kim, Kristof van der Fluit, Andy, Florian Tiefenbach, Lok Chun, Fan, James Formby, Evelien van Bokhorst, Marco Ghilardi, Rachel Yalisove, Elena Falomo, Ahmed Asiliskender, Yilan Lu, Jing Sheng Pang, Audrey Gaulard, Kitty Liao, Sabine Weiss, and Raj Shah, Alice Lamperti, Sofia Lemos, Erik Vogler, Charlotte Jansen, Igor Miklocic, Gwilym Faulkner, Steef van Lent, Camilla Berggren Lundell, Felix van Boeam, Tom Miklousic, Barbara Bulc, Marco Ferrari, Eva Vasileska, Bostjan Perovsek, Grega Trcek, Erik Vogler, Sasha Engelmann, Camilla Berggren Lundell, Joaquin Ezcurra, Grace Pappas, Julieta Arancio, Francesco Cingolani, Romain Di Vozzo, Jean de Loisy, Rebecca Lamarche-Vadel, Claire Contamine, Myriam Ben Salah, Laurence Dreyfus, Caroline and Eric Freymond, Jean Marc

Charbonnier, Philippe Cocquerez, Arnaud Deramecourt, Jean Evrard, Alain Hauchecorne, Gerard Letrenne, Yasmil Raymond, Hans Ulrich Obrist, Daniel Birnbaum, Molly Nesbit, Udo Kittelmann, Marion Ackermann, Ute Meta Bauer, Joseph Grima, Andrea Lissoni, Luca Cerizza, Sara Arrhenius, Agnes Husslein-Arco and Mario Codognato, Marianne Torp, Rutger Wolfson, Elizabeth Thomas and Phyllis Wattis, Jacob Fabricius, Jean-Paul Felley and Olivier Kaeser, Nikola Dietrich, Ellie Buttrose, Florian Matzner, José Roca, Theo Tegelaers, Adrian Notz, Friedrich von Borries, Ralph Rugoff, Anna Tilroe, Gayatri Uppal, Sabrina van der Ley and Markus Richter, Mohammad Kazem, Eva Scharrer and Jonathan Watkins, Pierluigi and Natalina Remotti, Caroline Eggel and Christiane Rekade, Marco Biraghi, Maurizio Bortolotti, Bert Theis, Juan and Patricia Vergez, Anne Strauss, Meredith Malone, Yona Friedman, Nikolaus Hirsch, Peter Weibel, Filippo Garrone, Claudio Veckstein, Ciro Najle, Raqs Media Collective, Sofia Lemos, Barbara Bulc, EU Commissioner for Transport Violeta Bulc, Blaz Pongracic, Mark Lawrence, Stefan Schaffer, Alan Prohm, Bernd Schulz, Ilka Raupach, Ivana Franke, Sina Heffner, Michael Zwingmann, Natalija Miodragovic, Jol Thomson, Michael Braungart, Matthias Schuler, Walter Munk, Michael Kezirian, Iyad Rahwan, Jonathan Ledgard, Sara Dean, William Shubert, Pablo Suarez, Bruno Latour. Francesca von Habsburg, Markus Reymann, Juan Enriquez, Sam Campbell, Barney Broomfield, Rob La Frenais, Kerry Doyle, Karla Frausto, Michael Wyatt, Tom, Marija and Igor Miklousic, John Powell, Ewen Chardronnet, Nicola Triscott, Frederik Jacobi, Anthony Langdon, Tell Andersson, Saga Asgeirsdottir, Natasa Bandelj, Simo Barbagallo, Hoxha Besart, Benedikte Bjerre, Christoph Blum, Bob Sleighs, Juan Camilo, Maria Giulia Cantaluppi, Renaud Codron, Marc Colombaioni, Rolf Degel, Vivana Deluca, Pablito El-Drito, Janis Elko, Fabrizio, Fani, Mara Ferreri, James Flaten, Gaia Fugazza, Giovanni Giaretta, Simon Gillard, Till Hergenhahn, Andria Hickey, Juan Camillo Jaramillo, Rasmus Johannsen, Theresa Kampmeier, Kim, Daniel Kohl, Oliver Kral, Dominik Mader, Eduardo Ernesto Marengo, Persichina Matteo, Matteo Mascheroni, Natalija Miodragovic, Mohamed Nageh, Mustapha Nageh, Dragusha Njomza, Marco Orlando, Osmani, Sabine Pahl, Eduardo Perez, Alberto Pesavento, Alice Pintus, Cristian Raimondi, Yasmil Raymond, Christiana Rekada, Barrak Reiser, Jacob Remin Sikker, Hannah Rosales, Iuri Rottiers, Hoti Rinor, Tim Rottiers, Matteo Rubbi, Michela Sacchetto, Hugo Santamaria, Lahu Saranda, Manuel Scano, Tean, Saverio Tozzi, Ujjval, Emek Ulusay, Alejandro Uribe, Mauro Vignando, Lionel Wolberger, Marcin Pindor and Wlodek Tarnowski, Alice Lamperti, Anna Drewes, Aurelien Calpas, Aysegul Seyhan, Banu Çiçek Tülü, Camilla Berggren, Claudia Melendez, Dario Iannone, Denis Maksimov, Devrim Yasar, Erik Vogler, Esther Schipper, Gwilym Faulkner, Hannah Turner, Ilka Tödt, Joshua Depaiva, Kimberly Bradley, Leopold Schulenburg, Mariia Dubrovska, Martina Pelacchi, Matthias Böttger, Moonsung Cho, Roland Mühlethaler, Roxanne Mackie, Sara Ferrer, Sophie Rzepecky, Sven Steudte, Thomas Heidtmann, Timo Tuominen, Yelta Köm, Zaida Violan, Thomas Krahn, Yoon, Adam, Fiorella, Joaquín Ezcurra, Sofia Lemos, Dario J. Laganá, Saverio Cantoni, Marina Hoxter, Roxanne Mackie, Paola Antonelli, Willow Brugh, Chris McKay, Manfred Hermann, Katherine Higgins, Juan Herreros, Alexander Bormann, Andreas Kunze, Dominic Michaelis, Laurent Besset, Caroline Boettner, Martin Saraceno, Silke Neumann, Carlo Rizzo, Maximilian Laina, Victoire Guillonneau, Noura Elouardi, Alejandra Alonso de Noriega, Cara Cotner, Pedro Portellano, Laura Francia, Cesare Silvi, Renae Shadler, Maria Nurmela, Cedric Carlier, Christine Shaw, Alison Cooley, Students at Royal Holloway GeoHumanities 2018 and at Columbia University Engineering Class of 2019, Claus Andersen and Christian Just Linde, Alejandra Alonso de Noriega, Cara Cotner, Desirée Valdes, Pedro Portellano, Pio Torroja and Mauricio Corbalan, Don McCasland, Maximiliano Bellmann, Hannah Zindel, Marie Thébaud Sorger, Sam Hertz, Laura Francia, Stefania Itolli, Renae Shadler and Maria Nurmela, and Studio Tomás Saraceno.

ARACHNOPHILIA

Thank you to Frederique Ait-Touati, French National Centre for Scientific Research (Philosophy), Mitchell Akiyama, University of Toronto (Sound Theory), *Agelena labyrinthica* (Berlin), *Amaurobius erberi* (Venice), *Anelosimus studiosus* (USA, donated by Angela Chuang), *Araneus diadematus* (Berlin), *Araniella cucurbitina* (Berlin), *Argiope bruennich*i (Berlin), *Argiope lobata* (Croatia), *Argyroneta aquatica*, Sara Arrhenius, Royal Institute of Art Stockholm (Art History), Leticia Aviles, University of British Columbia (Arachnology), *Badumna longinqua* (Argentina, donated by Martin Ramirez, originally from Australia), Friedrich G. Barth, Department of Neurobiology, University of Vienna, *Bathyphantes gracilis* (Venice), Ute Meta Bauer, Centre for Contemporary Art, Nanyang Technical University (Singapore), Ilaria Bonacossa, Artissima, Turin (Art History), Markus J Buehler, Laboratory for Atomistic and Molecular Mechanics, MIT (Biomateriomics), *Centromerus sylvaticus* (Venice), Luca Cerizza, NABA (Art History), Moonsong Cho, Institute of Bioprocess Engineering, Technische Universität, Berlin (Aeronautical Engineering), Angela Chuang, University of Tennessee, Knoxville (Arachnology), Emanuele Coccia, Ecole des Hautes Etudes en Sciences Sociales Paris (Philosophy), Iain Couzin, Max Planck Institute Konstanz (Collective Behaviour), *Cyclosa conica* (Berlin), *Cyrtophora citricola* (Croatia/United States, some donated by Angela Chuang), *Cyrtophora* sp. (China, donated by Peter Jäger), Vinciane Despret, University of Liège (Ethology and Philosophy), *Diplocephalus connectens* (Venice), William Eberhard, Smithsonian Tropical Research Institute (Arachnology), Sasha Engelmann, Royal Holloway, University of London, *Enoplognatha ovata* (Berlin), *Eratigena atrica* (Berlin), *Erigone dentipalpis* (Venice), *Fecenia* sp. (China, donated by Peter Jäger), Lukas Feireiss, Berlin (Contemporary Art), *Frontinellina* sp., Gianni Garrera (Art Critic), Helena Granström, Sweden (Physics), Joseph Grima, Space Caviar, London (Architecture and Art), *Haplodrassus dalmatensis* (Venice), Bani Haykal, Singapore (Music), Stefan Helmreich, MIT (Anthropology), Peggy Hill, University of Tulsa, Texas (Biotremology), Hannelore Hoch, Natural History Museum, Berlin (Biotremology), *Holocnemus pluchei* (Paris/Croatia/Berlin), Marco Isaia, University of Turin (Arachnology), Peter Jäger, Senckenberg Research Institute and Natural History Museum (Arachnology), Caroline A Jones, Department of Architecture, MIT (Art & Science), Alex Jordan, Max Planck Institute for Ornithology, Konstanz (Group Animal Behaviour), Jeffrey Kastner, Cabinet Magazine (Contemporary Art), Stavros Katsanevas, National Center for Scientific Research (CNRS) Paris (Astrophysics), Leila Kinney, Centre for Art, Science and Technology, MIT (Art History),

Joyce Beetuan Koh, Singapore (Music), Joseph Koh, National
University of Singapore (Arachnology), *Kukulcania hibernalis*,
Larinioides sclopetarius (Berlin), Bruno Latour, Sciences Po, Paris
(Humanities and Social Sciences), *Latrodectus geometricus*
(Germany), *Latrodectus mactans*, *Lepthyphantes istrianus*
(Venice), *Lepthyphantes tenuis* (Venice), *Linyphia triangularis*
(Berlin), *Linyphiidae* spp. (Berlin/Croatia), Yael Lubin, Ben Gurion
University of the Negev (Arachnology), Alvin Lucier (Sound Art),
Mangora acalypha (Venice), Chus Martinez, Academy of Art
and Design Basel (Art History), Brian Massumi, University of
Montreal (Philosophy), Rosa Matteucci (Literature), *Mecopisthes
nicaeensis* (Venice), *Meioneta mollis* (Venice), *Meioneta
rurestris* (Venice), *Microctenonyx subitaneus* (Venice), Roland
Mühlethaler, Naturschutzbund Deutschland e.V. (Biotremology
and Entomology), *Nephila edulis* (Germany, originally from
Australia), *Nephila inaurata* (UK, originally from Africa),
Nephila senegalensis (Germany, donated by Jutta Schneider,
originally from Africa), *Neriene clathrata* (Berlin), *Neriene
peltata* (Berlin), Molly Nesbit, Vassar College (Art History),
Federico Nicolao, Paris (Aesthetics), Hans Ulrich Obrist,
Serpentine Galleries, London (Art Historian), Rolf Niedringhaus,
Carl von Ossietzky Universität Oldenburg (Biology), Brian
O'Reilly, Singapore (Music), *Pachygnatha degeeri* (Venice),
Joshua de Paiva, Musée de la Chasse et de la Nature Paris
(Philosophy), *Parasteatoda tepidariorum* (Berlin), *Parawixia
bistriata* (Argentina), Jussi Parikka, Winchester School of
Art, University of Southampton (Media Theory), *Pelecopsis
krausi* (Venice), Boštjan Perovšek, Slovenia (Bioacoustician),
Philoponella alata (China, donated by Peter Jäger), *Pholcus
phalangioides*, *Prinerigone vagans* (Venice), Elizabeth A Povinelli,
Columbia University (Anthropology, Critical Theory and Film),
Psechrus jaegeri (China, donated by Peter Jäger), Eliane Radigue,
Paris (Music), Federico Rahola, University of Genoa (Sociology),
Filipa Ramos, Kingston University and Central Saint Martins
(Experimental Film and Contemporary Art), Christine Rollard,
Paris National Museum of Natural History (Araneology),
David Rothenberg (Music), Jutta Schneider, University of
Hamburg (Arachnology), Helen Smith, Australian Museum,
Sydney (Arachnology), Volker Springel, Max-Planck-Institute
for Astrophysics, Munich (Astrophysics), *Steatoda grossa*
(Berlin), *Steatoda nobilis*, *Steatoda phalerata* (Venice), *Steatoda
triangulosa* (Berlin), Isabelle Su, Laboratory for Atomistic
and Molecular Mechanics, MIT (Biomateriomics), *Tegenaria
domestica* (Berlin), *Theridiidae* spp. (Berlin/China, some donated
by Peter Jäger), Jol Thomson, Doctoral candidate, University of
Westminster (Art and Science), *Tiso vagans*, David Toop (Music
Theory), *Trichopterna cito* (Venice), Etienne Turpin (Philosophy),
Gabriele Uhl, University of Greifswald (Arachnology),
Uloborus plumipes (Berlin), Andreas Wessel, Natural History
Museum, Berlin (Biotremology), Mark Wigley, Columbia
University (Architecture), Jonas Wolff, Macquarie University,
Sydney (Arachnology), David Zeitlyn, University of Oxford
(Anthropology), Evan Ziporyn, Centre for Art, Science and
Technology, MIT (Music), Samuel Zschokke, University of Basel
(Arachnology), *Zilla diodia* (Venice), *Zygiella x-notata* (Berlin).

BIBLIOGRAPHIC REFERENCES

Donald Barthelme, "The Balloon," in *Sixty Stories* (New York: G. P. Putnam's Sons, 1981): 53–8 © Donald Barthelme, 1981, 1982, used by permission of The Wylie Agency (UK) Limited.

James Bridle, *New Dark Age: Technology and the End of the Future* (London: Verso, 2018): 199–201. © Verso, 2018.

Italo Calvino, *Invisible Cities*, trans. William Weaver (San Diego: Harvest Books, 1974): 75. © 1972 by Giulio Einaudi editore, s.p.a. Torino. English translation copyright © 1983, 1984 by Houghton Mifflin Harcourt Publishing Company. Reprinted by permission of Houghton Mifflin Harcourt Publishing Company. All rights reserved.

Derek McCormack, "Stratospheric Envelopes: Notes for a Speculative Mode of Atmospheric Address", *GeoHumanities* 3, no. 2 (2017): 421.

Don DeLillo, *White Noise* (New York: Viking Press, 1985) © 1984, 1985 by Don DeLillo. Used by permission of Viking Books, an imprint of Penguin Publishing Group, a division of Penguin Random House LLC. All rights reserved.

Denis Diderot, *D'Alembert's Dream* (1769), in *Diderot, Interpreter of Nature*, 2nd ed., trans. Jean Stewart and Jonathan Kemp (New York: International Publishers, 1963): 80–91.

Annie Dillard, "Total Eclipse," in *Teaching a Stone to Talk: Expeditions and Encounters* (New York: Perennial Library, 1982): 89–93. © 2016 by Annie Dillard. Used by permission of HarperCollins Publishers.

Ralph Waldo Emerson, "Maiden Speech of the Aeolian Harp," in *The Complete Works of Ralph Waldo Emerson*, ed. Edward Waldo Emerson (New York and Boston: Houghton, Mifflin, 1904), https://www.bartleby.com/370/93.html.

Camilla Grudova "Notes from a Spider," in *The Doll's Alphabet* (London: Fitzcarraldo, 2017): 169–74. © Fitzcarraldo, 2017.

Ursula K. Le Guin, "Vaster than Empires and More Slow," in *The Wind's Twelve Quarters* (New York: Harper & Row, 1975): 207–13. © 1971 by Ursula K. Le Guin; First appeared in "New Dimension I" in 1971 published by HarperCollins in 1971. Reprinted by permission of Curtis Brown, Ltd.

Anna Lowenhaupt Tsing, *The Mushroom at the End of the World: On the Possibility of Life in Capitalist Ruins* (Princeton and Oxford: Princeton University Press, 2015): 27–32. © Princeton University Press, 2015.

Michael Marder, "A Shadow Sun," *Wallpaper* September 2018, 381–2.

China Miéville, "The Dusty Hat," in *Three Moments of an Explosion* (New York: Del Rey, 2016): 211–6. © Del Rey, 2016

Marijn Nieuwenhuis, "Breathing Materiality: Aerial Violence at a Time of Atmospheric Politics," *Critical Studies on Terrorism* 9, no. 3 (2015): 503–7.

Jussi Parikka, "Dust Matter," in *Depletion Design: A Glossary of Network Ecologies*, ed. Carolin Wiedemann and Soenke Zehle (Amsterdam: Institute of Network Cultures, 2012): 53–8. © 2012 by Jussi Parikka.

Hugh Raffles, "Air," in *Insectopedia* (New York: Pantheon, 2010): 10–2. © 2010 by Hugh Raffles.

Isabelle Stengers, "Reclaiming Animism," *e-flux Journal* 36 (July 2012): https://www.e-flux.com/journal/36/61245/reclaiming-animism/. Partly excerpted by permission of the author and the Generali Foundation from the first publication in: *Animismus. Moderne hinter den Spiegeln | Animism. Modernity through the Looking Glass*, Hg. von | ed. by Anselm Franke, Sabine Folie für | for Generali Foundation, Wien/Köln 2011.

University of Oxford, "How electricity helps spider webs snatch prey and pollutants," *ScienceDaily*, January 14, 2014, www.sciencedaily.com/releases/2014/01/140114113339.htm (accessed December 13, 2019).

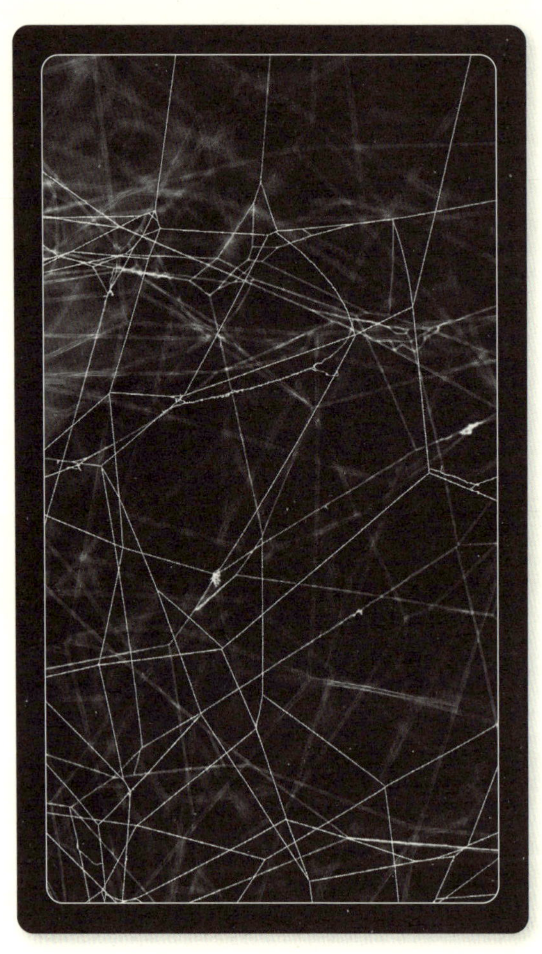